Beyond Borders

Beyond Borders

Cross-Culturalism and the Caribbean Canon

Edited by

Jennifer Rahim *with* Barbara Lalla

University of the West Indies Press
Jamaica • Barbados • Trinidad and Tobago

University of the West Indies Press
7A Gibraltar Hall Road   Mona
Kingston 7   Jamaica
www.uwipress.com

© 2009 by Jennifer Rahim and Barbara Lalla

All rights reserved. Published 2009

13 12 11 10 09   5 4 3 2 1

CATALOGUING IN PUBLICATION DATA

Beyond borders: cross-culturalism and the Caribbean canon / edited by Jennifer Rahim with Barbara Lalla.

p. cm.
"Selections of the presentations made at the cultural studies conference 'Cross-Culturalism and the Caribbean Canon' hosted by the Liberal Arts Department of the University of the West Indies, St Augustine, January, 2004." – Introd.

Includes bibliographical references.

ISBN: 978-976-640-216-7

1. Caribbean, English-speaking – Civilization. 2. Language and culture – Caribbean, English-speaking. 3. Caribbean, English-speaking – Intellectual life. 4. Postcolonialism – Caribbean, English-speaking. 5. Group identity – Caribbean, English-speaking – Cross-cultural studies. I. Rahim, Jennifer. II. Lalla, Barbara. III. Cross-Culturalism and the Caribbean Canon (2004: St Augustine, Trinidad and Tobago)

F2169.B 48 2004   972.9

Book and cover design by Robert Harris.
Set in Berkley 10/15 x 24
Printed in the United States of America.

Beyond Borders

Cross-Culturalism and the Caribbean Canon

Edited by

Jennifer Rahim *with* Barbara Lalla

University of the West Indies Press
Jamaica • Barbados • Trinidad and Tobago

University of the West Indies Press
7A Gibraltar Hall Road   Mona
Kingston 7   Jamaica
www.uwipress.com

© 2009 by Jennifer Rahim and Barbara Lalla

All rights reserved. Published 2009

13 12 11 10 09   5 4 3 2 1

CATALOGUING IN PUBLICATION DATA

Beyond borders: cross-culturalism and the Caribbean canon / edited by Jennifer Rahim with Barbara Lalla.

p. cm.
"Selections of the presentations made at the cultural studies conference 'Cross-Culturalism and the Caribbean Canon' hosted by the Liberal Arts Department of the University of the West Indies, St Augustine, January, 2004." – Introd.

Includes bibliographical references.

ISBN: 978-976-640-216-7

1. Caribbean, English-speaking – Civilization. 2. Language and culture – Caribbean, English-speaking. 3. Caribbean, English-speaking – Intellectual life. 4. Postcolonialism – Caribbean, English-speaking. 5. Group identity – Caribbean, English-speaking – Cross-cultural studies. I. Rahim, Jennifer. II. Lalla, Barbara. III. Cross-Culturalism and the Caribbean Canon (2004: St Augustine, Trinidad and Tobago)

F2169.B 48 2004   972.9

Book and cover design by Robert Harris.
Set in Berkley 10/15 x 24
Printed in the United States of America.

Contents

Acknowledgements / vii

Cross-Culturalism and the Caribbean Canon:
A Window to Future Possibilities / 1
Jennifer Rahim with *Barbara Lalla*

Part 1   Language and Cultural Evolution

1   Language and the Politics of Ethnicity / 17
    George Lamming

2   Gender and Genre: The Logic of Language and the
    Logistics of Identity / 34
    Patricia J. Saunders

3   More Than the Sum of Its Parts: Reflections on
    Caribbean Language in a Globalizing Age / 59
    Valerie Youssef

4   Caribbean Cross-Culturalism in the *Caribbean
    Multilingual Dictionary of Flora, Fauna and Foods* / 77
    Jeannette Allsopp

Part 2   Beyond Borders: Questioning the Canon

5   Borders, Boundaries and Frames: Cross-Culturalism
    and the Caribbean Canon / 99
    Sandra Pouchet Paquet

6   Mutual Ground: Post-Empire Canons of Art in Britain
    and the Caribbean / 116
    Leon Wainwright

Part 3   Negotiating Subjectivities, Finding Ease

7   Coping with the New Culture: The East Indian Advisory
    Board as Mediator, 1937–1945   /   **151**
    Brinsley Samaroo

8   Reflections on the Imaging of Africa in the Calypso of
    Trinidad and Tobago   /   **170**
    Louis Regis

9   Bordering on the Transgressive: (Re)constructing
    Cultural Identities in Indo-Caribbean Fictions   /   **192**
    Paula Morgan

Part 4   The Way Forward

10 Issues in Caribbean Cultural Studies: The Case of Jamaica   /   **217**
    Joseph Pereira

11 The School as a Forum for Cross-Culturalism:
    The Curriculum as an Intervention Strategy   /   **225**
    Sandra Ingrid Gift

12 Cultural Studies: The Way Forward   /   **256**
    Rex Nettleford

Contributors   /   **265**

Acknowledgements

This collection owes its greatest gratitude to the contributors, all of whom were patient and accommodating throughout the entire editing process. Appreciation for funding goes to the Campus Research and Publication Fund Committee of the University of the West Indies, St Augustine. Deep gratitude is also extended to the graduate students who worked along with the editors and the contributors. Thanks to Pincay Jughmohan, Vijay Maharaj, Amanda Macintyre and Karen Sanderson-Cole. A special word of thanks goes to Karen Mah-Chamberlin for the enthusiasm and efficiency with which she addressed the final preparation of all these essays. Thanks to Jacinta Mitchell for her technical expertise on the computer. These essays emanate originally from a cultural studies conference hosted by the Department of Liberal Arts, University of the West Indies, St Augustine, 8 to 10 January 2004. We thank all our colleagues in the Department of Liberal Arts for their support throughout the entire process.

JENNIFER RAHIM *with* BARBARA LALLA

Introduction

Cross-Culturalism and the Caribbean Canon
A Window to Future Possibilities

▶ JENNIFER RAHIM *WITH* BARBARA LALLA

Naming and defining Caribbean culture has always been a preoccupation of artists and scholars alike. The region's collective history as colonies of Europe meant that the initial "official" narratives of its cultural realities were recorded, described and often criticized according to the world view and civilizing agendas of those who held the reins of power. It is therefore understandable that the discourses attending the emergence of the Caribbean as a civilization have been informed by a long history of contestation with the various mutations of (neo)imperial cultural conditioning and systems of domination.

For many, the achievement of political independence symbolizes, and perhaps consolidates, this unrelenting opposition to cultural suppression and censorship. The ongoing project of reordering the colonial privilege of recognition implies nothing less than positioning the Caribbean as both subject and agent of its history and terms of representation. Yet even as independent Caribbean states take up their mandate to forge their own political, economic and cultural agendas, the world remains organized – more so in this era of globalization – to impede their quest for sovereignty at almost every level. However, as the region continues its journey into deeper engagement with the requirements of independence, new challenges arise, and with them the burden of responsibility to face up to the failings and betrayals that are of its own making. Simply pointing an accusatory finger at "history" or "the West" is no longer tenable, and in some cases the tactic is crass escapist politics. Maturity and responsibility are inseparable components, and when they are attached to the admittedly slippery issue of nationhood, they become even more complexly intertwined in today's interlocking world of relations.

The economic imperatives of Caribbean development remain critical concerns in a global market climate dominated by full-blown capitalism, with fiscal agendas at both the private and governmental levels that favour the economies of the so-called developed nations. In light of the emergence of culture as a key source of capital, developing nations need to take cognisance of the fact that economic power and cultural agency have been made more intimately interdependent. This nexus of control bears directly on the politics of representation. The production, marketing and dissemination of cultural knowledge and practice in the arenas of entertainment, research and pedagogy are major players in challenging and transforming alienating attitudes and images from outside, as well as within, regional and national borders.

Clearly the struggle for cultural confidence must be waged with even more vigilance and determination in a global environment that is characterized by, among other things, an aggressive North American culture industry that effectively uses modern media technologies to its advantage. The internationalization of American popular culture remains a real concern for many developing nations as they daily witness the gullibility with which their youth consume its attractive images and lifestyles. Indeed, no one can exist in a cultural bubble, remaining untouched by external influences. James Clifford reminds us that "cultural experience" is constitutive of the "specific dynamics of dwelling/travelling",[1] which underpin the contemporary attentiveness in academic methodologies and discourses to the inevitability of contact and exchange. Cultural insulation is therefore never an option. The sure sign of a society's maturity is its ability to negotiate its acceptance of the many streams, old and new, that converge to inform its continued becoming.

Nevertheless, the Caribbean's vulnerability to cultural estrangement and erosion by external forces is not to be underestimated. With accelerated mobility and information exchange, the region's openness to "foreign" cultural contact makes it increasingly futile to approach culture from either a preservationist or monolithic paradigm. The safeguarding of traditional cultural forms and expressions is necessary for their survival and can nurture a healthy nationalism and regionalism grounded in supportive ancestral moorings; however, a solely museological approach to culture is myopic and runs the risk of framing culture as a static rather than dynamic phenomenon. Indeed, the very cross-cultural nature of the Caribbean's genesis makes pure folly of such an approach.

An intensive meeting of peoples of African, Asian, Amerindian and European origin establishes the region as a prime example of what Stuart Hall calls a "diasporic aesthetic" that operates according to a "creolising or transcultural ethic".[2] In a world searching for ways to deal with the complex tensions and sometimes violent outcomes of poorly negotiated responses to difference, the Caribbean's multiethnic social orders and hybrid cultural expressions exist as original examples of the reformative possibilities of confluence. More importantly, they provide a necessary awakening from the tyrannical myopias inherent in purist and hierarchical myths of origin. Wilson Harris, for instance, believes that cross-cultural dynamics hold the possibility for humanizing sensibilities by bridging the divides in Manichean paradigms of cultural superiority to enable the "regeneration of the heart and mind".[3] The fact remains that cultural renewal is always dependent on exchanges, borrowings and fusions that emerge to give expression to the new conditions of life on the ground. Further, culture's tendency to consort with difference unveils the false and superficial barriers, such as race, ethnicity, class, age, nationality, gender and sexuality, that conspire to curtail the practice of more democratic habits of human relations.

Caribbean cultural studies engages directly with the issues of cultural survival and negotiation, bringing to the fore a history of domination, resistance and evolution that tells of the emergence of a civilization within and beyond the borders of this archipelago. Indeed, the intercultural and transcultural nature of the Caribbean offers a template for the future in a world that is fast becoming cosmopolitan, hybrid and increasingly borderless. There are enormous possibilities, as well as dangers to guard against, in such an environment of accelerated relations. This profile of culture as a confluence of differences is therefore not to be romanticized. Participants in the geopolitics of cultural exchange remain far from equal, and the power plays that attend individual, communal and global relations have not disappeared even as the globe has become more integrated.

Culture and cultural identification are without a doubt highly charged political Goliaths with both local and global ramifications. This is one of the reasons for the boom in global popularity that cultural studies has enjoyed over the past few decades, and the Caribbean is no exception. The international consensus seems to be that culture has emerged as a key stakeholder in world affairs that affects the policy decisions of both state and private institutions. Indeed, it is no longer possible to pass off culture as simply a matter of commonalities, interests and values as if politics and power were innocent of influencing what gets defined and circulated as valid culture.

The chapters in this collection represent a selection of the presentations made at the cultural studies conference "Cross-Culturalism and the Caribbean Canon", hosted by the Department of Liberal Arts of the University of the West Indies, St Augustine, in January 2004. They explore cross-cultural themes and issues across disciplines that include literature, language, education, history and popular culture. In providing a multidisciplinary forum for contemporary debate on Caribbean culture in this open-ended evolutionary journey, the collection makes an important contribution to the rapidly expanding discipline of Caribbean cultural studies, where there is a growing demand for information for both research and teaching purposes. If agency in the terrain of cultural knowledge and ownership of cultural representation are synonymous with forging a collective sense of belonging and understanding, then these essays serve that process well.

Part 1, Language Politics and Cultural Evolution, opens with George Lamming's essay, "Language and the Politics of Ethnicity", which was delivered as the conference's keynote address. With the breadth of his characteristic historical imagination and cogent reading of the political nuances of Caribbean cultural practice, Lamming locates language at the heart of the diaspora's cultural evolution, beginning with European colonization that set the stage for its multiethnic character and the entrenchment of debilitating hierarchies of human and cultural value. For Lamming, the politics of the "word" and its collusion with the politics of race and ethnicity are seminal to comprehending the workings of colonial subjugation and its aftermath in the Caribbean diaspora. Ironically, it is language's transculturation exchanges that subtly, even comically, undermine the very artificial ethnic divisions and social hierarchies instituted under colonialism. Further, as in the case of Indian-African relations, these continue to threaten the achievement of a truly civic nationalism in the era of independence.

Fully cognizant of the problems that visit the term *creole*, Lamming sees creolization's transcultural mechanics as a seminal force in the process of "deepening indigenization" which influences not only the creation of new languages but also the emergence of new diasporic ethnicities. These offer a possible corrective to the crippling disease of ethnocentric ideologies. In the context of post-independence power struggles, Lamming cautions against essentialist readings of race and ethnicity, as well as the error of misreading the role of race for that of power in contemporary contestations for the control of governance. The way forward seems to require a radical re-formation of epistemologies of knowledge about difference. In this regard, Lamming encourages development of a political discourse that will "embrace and re-creolize all ethnic types" towards the formation of more democratic nationalisms.

The symbiotic tie between language and identity (re)formation introduced by Lamming is picked up by Patricia Saunders in her chapter, "Gender and Genre: The Logic of Language and the Logistics of Identity", from the perspective of black female subjectivity. In the process of unlocking the layered poetics of M. NourbeSe Philip, Saunders makes a compelling case for remapping the terrain of black female sexuality in colonial and post-colonial Caribbean literature. This becomes necessary given the discursive continuities on issues of the silencing and stereotypical gendering of black women, first by imperial discourse and later by the masculinist narratives of nationhood. If language is a critical site where gender, genre, identity, body, geography and history converge, then the task for the women writers of the black diaspora is to escape its violent epistemologies by creating "alter/native" spaces of ideological and aesthetic possibility. As such, NourbeSe Philip's "polyvocular text" is elevated as a poetic, and therefore political, positioning that radically reconstitutes the very innards of the multilayered and multidisciplinary epistemologies of negation in the necessary work of voicing and remapping black female histories.

Valerie Youssef, in "More Than the Sum of Its Parts", continues the language debate from the vantage point of the region's Creole language culture. Noting that the Creole has been traditionally "most owned" as a sign of Caribbean cultural authenticity, she provocatively expands the debates on the Caribbean language situation by arguing for the validation of Caribbean Standard English forms. Youssef warns that to persist in seeing the standard as the property of others – Europe and the United States, for instance – is to court a kind of self-induced cultural schizophrenia that will deny the region the full range of its cultural power. Her case is grounded in careful research on a sub-variety of Caribbean Standard English she dubs Trinbagonian Standard English, and is further developed with reference to current globalization forces, where the internationalization of Standard English and collapsing national borders require greater communicability among peoples and across geographies. The Caribbean's need to be vigilant against contemporary forms of linguistic imperialism and to foster holistic cultural acceptance, as advanced in this chapter, are well worth heeding.

The dynamism of any culture is possibly equal to its language practices, both being interdependent, living forces nourished by their proclivity for exchange and interchange. Jeannette Allsopp's "Caribbean Cross-Culturalism in the *Caribbean Multilingual Dictionary of Flora, Fauna and Foods*" provides a fascinating cross-cultural tapestry of these three lexical categories in the languages of English, Spanish, French and French Creole Caribbean territories, including the surviving languages of First Nation peoples. The sometimes esoteric metaphors of *sea* and *rhizome* that lay claim to the Caribbean's "subterranean" unity of connections are demystified by Allsopp's concrete survey of the *Caribbean Multilingual Dictionary*. Indeed, the migration of items across territorial boundaries, regardless of either the official language or the Creole spoken, best demonstrates the inherent artificiality of the geographic, linguistic and national divides that separate the islands. Allsopp's examples of flora, fauna and food lexical items reconfirm most convincingly the region's creative linguistic cultural processes that not only thrive on diversity but revel in crossing borders.

Stuart Hall, with reference to the consistent movement of Caribbean peoples to various northern resettlement sites such as Britain, describes that cultural phenomenon as a "diaspora that re-diasporized itself",[4] thereby pointing to the continuities and inevitable reordering of identification practices in between spaces of belonging. The chapters in part 2, Beyond Borders: Questioning the Canon, merge cross-culturalism with debates about canon formation in the Caribbean and its diaspora in the United States and Britain, where these new environments enter into conversation with Caribbean identities simultaneously brought along and left behind. It opens with Sandra Pouchet Paquet's "Borders, Boundaries and Frames: Cross-Culturalism and the Caribbean Canon", which raises probing questions about the geopolitics of Caribbean canon formation and related pedagogical practices. Pouchet Paquet places herself squarely in the centre of the issues as a member of what she calls "the looming Caribbean diaspora in the United States". The configuration of "imaginary" canons and the designs of pedagogical programmes of study, she argues, directly interface with a host of variables, including ethnicity, geography, history, nationality and so on, that affect their formation and institutionalization.

Of interest in Paquet's argument is the new generation of transnational writers; they not only challenge the reconfiguration of the Caribbean canon to include their hyphenated identities but are also caught up in the changing politics around the inclusion of minorities in the American literary canon, in which the work of the Society for the Study of the Multi-Ethnic Literature of the United States is significant. Paquet notes that up to 2003, Caribbean-American literature remained a bastard category, while other American hyphenated identities and their literatures had been accommodated under the paternal umbrella of American literature. Even as efforts are in train to name what it means to be Caribbean and American, the complexities of such categorizations are enormous. While she notes the extreme difficulty of reaching consensus in approaching such a definition, given the plurality of the Caribbean presence, an item of serious concern is the oftentimes globalizing agenda of America's identity politics, which of course puts a contemporary spin on cultural imperialism. Nevertheless, Paquet ultimately redirects the debate towards the power of creative writers to force the reinvention of canons, beyond institutional categories represented by syllabi and reading lists.

Bridging the distance between home and abroad, Leon Wainwright's chapter, "Mutual Ground: Post-Empire Canons of Art in Britain and the Caribbean", takes on the "troubling presence" of canonicity and canonical exclusion with respect to the ethnic and aesthetic diversity of contemporary Caribbean and British visual art. His approach is to unsettle the oversimplified dynamic of these canon wars. What is most revealing in his analysis of the various fronts of resistance initiated by black minority artists, particularly in Britain, is the manner in which the mobilization of categories of difference can inadvertently serve to construct undemocratic "outsider" placements, both in the larger community and within the very groups they purport to represent. For instance, hypergeneralized paradigms such as "black art" and "ethnic art" can exacerbate the problems of social marginalization, given that the space relegated to these artists is normally "separate from mainstream commercial or prominent public galleries". Further, the rich and complex diversity of so-called minority groups is sacrificed on the altar of "arts activism", their "subtle differentiations lost". Crucial to his analysis is identification of several caveats in counter-canonical discourses and strategies mobilized in the British context. These, he argues, may be instructive to "alterNative" debates initiated by some contemporary Caribbean artists, such as Christopher Cozier, in response to dissatisfaction with exclusory, dated and insular discourses of nationalism, belonging and so on, as they relate to making art.

Certainly, the battle over control of intellectual resources in the assembly of canons remains a pertinent concern for the vulnerable nation-states of the developing world, and minority groups of whatever type or persuasion. The circulation of critical discourse bears directly upon institutional policies that affect funding, teaching, exhibitions and promotional language. Implicated in all of this is the contentious nexus of agency and representation. In a world that has become increasingly relational, though not necessarily equal in its relations, and in a diaspora of multiple and shifting identity spaces, Wainwright invites consideration of ways to develop a politics and language of criticism that stay clear of re-institutionalizing reductive and marginalizing norms, by overemphasizing textual codification of difference in resistance to hegemonic canons. He contends that the most enduring "mutual ground" of all art is its intrinsic complexity. The importance of keeping faith in the timeless power of art to influence social and perceptual change, without betraying its uncontainable nature, is the polemic with which this essay leaves the reader.

Earl Lovelace's definition of the nation – as a place where people can experience "a sense of belonging, a psychic ease, the valuing of [their] contributions"[5] – best orients the chapters in part 3, Negotiating Subjectivities, Finding Ease. Coming from the disciplines of history, literature and popular culture, these chapters examine the struggle of peoples of diaspora societies to rearticulate identity and claim the right of presence in their new homes. It is a struggle complicated by the alienating values and structures of colony, the powerful but at times ambivalent allegiances to natal traditions, the requirements of adaptation to newly adopted environments, and the challenge of accommodating a variety of ethnic traditions, narratives and ideologies that are competing for space. Together they reinforce the complementary roles of secular organizations, state authorities and the arts of the imagination in providing tangible policies, structures and imaginative landscapes by which notions of home and, by extension, articulation of identity can be interrogated and understood.

Brinsley Samaroo, in "Coping with the New Culture: The East Indian Advisory Board as Mediator, 1937–1945", performs the important task of historicizing the experience of East Indians in colonial Trinidad, as they sought to make space for themselves with the aid of the organizations and individuals that comprised the East Indian Advisory Board. Notable in this turbulent period of working-class unrest in the sugar and oil industries is the collaborative front of resistance maintained by the varied membership of the board as it worked towards improved living conditions for the group. Balancing the nervous surveillance of the colonial state with diplomatic agitation and skilful lobbying, the board was successful in winning cooperation on seminal issues, including the establishment of Hindu and Muslim schools, recognition of non-Christian marriages, and intervention in "factional disputes". The board was, as Samaroo argues, an influential transitional bridge in the process of East Indian adaptation to the New World. However, he courts healthy controversy with his persistence in using ideologically troublesome concepts such as *Orient* and *Occident*. Lamming, for instance, felt enough discomfort with Samaroo's application of *Orient* in another context to remark on it in his keynote address.

Whether or not Samaroo's usage signals appropriation, and therefore possible reinvention, of these imperialistic terms is open for debate. Nevertheless, the nagging ambivalence of association with their origins in colonial discourse provides an appropriate point of entry to Louis Regis's "Reflections on the Imaging of Africa in the Calypso of Trinidad and Tobago". His survey of presentations of Africa in calypso demonstrates the extreme difficulty of breaking free of hegemonic image-shaping influences, even in the very process of cultural reclamation and nation building. Regis notes that even though calypso artists participated in the aggressive decolonizing agendas of the 1960s and 1970s, in which Africa featured, the continent remained "an area of darkness". Many representations simply reproduced media-generated racialized and sexualized stereotypes as well as pastoral utopias that reinforced Africa's association with primitivism.

Ultimately, however, the impact of the art form on Afro-Trinidadian identity formation is multidimensional, as it stimulated positive reconstructions of blackness and boosted ancestral pride at the height of the nationalist movement, provoked healthy debate on cultural integration in an ethnically diverse society, and created stunningly imaginative bridges for compassionate reconnections, as in David Rudder's songs about South Africa. Of particular importance to calypso scholarship and pedagogy is the essay's delineation of a methodology for analysis, which elucidates the complex interactions of lyrical text with musicality, performance, audience response and socio-historical context. However, while calypso is affirmed as a valuable resource for reading cultural space and a prime re-educational tool, Regis points to the need for closing the gap between knowledge and imagination. He argues that continued intellectual ignorance of Africa's paradoxical realities will perpetuate a crisis of imaging that, together with the current invasion of foreign cable transmissions, can only foster a debilitating "marronage of spirit".

This challenge of negotiating new subjectivities by building enabling bridges between ancestral homes and new sites of dwelling is taken up by Paula Morgan with reference to the Indo-Trinidadian experience in "Bordering on the Transgressive: (Re)constructing Cultural Identities in Indo-Caribbean Fictions". Morgan interfaces the initial act of transgression – the crossing of the *kala pani* (black waters) – with the fictional constructions of post-exilic cultural identities by writers such as V.S. Naipaul, Lakshmi Persaud and Shani Mootoo. These represent imaginative attempts at cultural insertion and empowerment with and against strains of ancestral and (post)colonial epistemologies. Foregrounded in Morgan's analysis of the texts' "gendered ethnic (re)formations between indentureship and independence" is the essentially constructed nature of ethnicity, which is the foundation of its defiance of homogeneous and static frameworks of identification. The very nebulous question "What is Indianness?" emerges as the most probing locus of interrogation, as shared ethnic and geographical locations, as well as gender identifications, are not necessarily consistent with shared cultural and ideological space. The tensions between primordialism and ethnic renewal provide the recreative space wherein contestations for more authentic models of being and knowing are waged though the poetics of transgression.

The final section, Part 4, The Way Forward, brings together chapters that offer practical reflections on the tremendous academic wealth and social benefits to be derived from efforts to formalize the study of Caribbean culture under the discipline of cultural studies. They share sobriety and optimism in their consideration of the discipline's capacity to serve the region's quest to more systematically generate cultural knowledge in the interest of continued holistic development. Joseph Pereira, in "Issues in Caribbean Cultural Studies: The Case of Jamaica", unearths the subtle politics of exclusion concealed in regional cultural paradigms such as creolization and nationalist discourses, promoted in the cause of democratically representing diversity and fostering belonging. Deconstructing their myths of cohesion, he unmasks the internal contradictions and power plays that repeat old hierarchies of difference, suppress historically marginalized identities and advance elitist agendas. For Pereira, however, cultural space remains a site of intense ideological contestation with dominance, which makes the study of culture an invaluable asset for promoting more equitable social orders. He therefore identifies several examples from language, religion, music and sport that function as grassroots and working-class oppositional forces to various manifestations of hegemonic controls.

If Pereira identifies the primary goal of engaging with culture's complexities as "the fullest reclamation of the human self", then Sandra Gift offers practical insight into the way in which the school can be a non-threatening environment for nurturing understanding and respect for ethnic differences and cultural practices in "The School as a Forum for Cross-Culturalism: The Curriculum as an Intervention Strategy". As a microcosm of the plurality and cross-cultural dynamics that characterize Caribbean societies, the classroom therefore exists as an instructive laboratory. Gift's contribution advances the value of an organic approach to cultural analysis. She is guided by a rigorous empiricist methodology that indicates her choice to let the immediate environment yield its own truths rather than relying on the importation of prepackaged theoretical positions that can have reductive and misleading outcomes.

Further, there is confident investment in an informed and sensitive approach to curricula development to shape young minds and reform sensibilities towards the realization of what Lamming appropriately calls a "liberating civic nationalism". Gift demonstrates the value of maintaining a creative dialectic between the human realities of the classroom, curriculum design and teaching methods, and so reinforces in a different context Paquet's insight about the critical interface of the "pedagogical imperative with the geopolitical environment and institutional politics".

The collection ends with Rex Nettleford's closing address to the conference, titled "Cultural Studies: The Way Forward". He begins by demystifying the "belated legitimization" of Caribbean cultural studies, locating its practice in the earliest quests of Caribbean people like himself for relevance and "truth" grounded in their own realities. In short, the region has always been engaged in what today is fashionably called cultural studies. But, well aware of the limits of a developmental vision oftentimes too narrowly fixed on economic imperatives, he welcomes the discipline's formalization and the opportunity this offers for actively promoting a "culture-in-education" focus, in which the University of the West Indies can be a key facilitator. In affirming the role of the institution as a catalyst for generating original research, delineating analytical methodologies and devising pedagogical practices, he expands the connection that both Pereira and Gift advance in different ways between the school, cultural knowledge and development.

Critical of purist attitudes to academia, Nettleford offers a timely caution to researchers and academics against becoming entrapped in inherited and outdated categories of knowledge and practice. His vision seems to concur with post-modern dissatisfaction with separatist and hierarchical knowledge frames and methodologies. He therefore encourages "strategic alliances" across the many disciplines as a means of releasing revolutionary conversations, experiments and discoveries in the necessary work of laying down a knowledge base from which governments, educational institutions and the public at large can draw. His multidisciplinary and organic yet outward-reaching vision of the way forward consolidates the ideological thrust of all the chapters in this collection – that is, the essentially dialogic nature of culture and the immense value in its serious study for building a more humane world. In this regard, no other description seems to more appropriately capture the potential of a serious engagement with Caribbean cultural studies than Lamming's recommendations for developing a more authentic civic Caribbean nationalism to "educate feeling to respect the autonomy of the Other's difference, to negotiate the cultural spaces which are the legitimate claim of the Other, and to work toward an environment which could manage stability as a state of creative conflict".[6]

Notes

1. James Clifford, *Routes: Travel and Translation in the Late Twentieth Century* (Cambridge, MA: Harvard University Press, 1997), 24.
2. Stuart Hall, "Thinking the Diaspora: Home-Thoughts from Abroad", *Small Axe* 6 (September 1999): 6.
3. Wilson Harris, "Creoleness: The Crossroads of a Civilization?" in *Selected Essays of Wilson Harris: The Unfinished Genesis of the Imagination*, ed. Andrew Bundy (London: Routledge, 1999), 247.
4. Kuan-Hsing Chen, "The Formation of a Diasporic Intellectual: An Interview with Stuart Hall", in *Stuart Hall: Critical Dialogues in Cultural Studies*, ed. David Morley and Kuan-Hsing Chen (London: Routledge, 1996), 501.
5. Earl Lovelace, "Requiring of the World", in *Growing in the Dark (Selected Essays)*, ed. Funso Aiyejina (San Juan, Trinidad: Lexicon Trinidad, 2003), 230.
6. George Lamming, *The Sovereignty of Imagination* (Kingston: Arawak, 2004), 36.

Part 1

Language and Cultural Evolution

CHAPTER 1

Language and the Politics of Ethnicity

▸ GEORGE LAMMING

Principal and Pro Vice Chancellor and distinguished members of the Faculty of Humanities and Education, convenors of the conference, your excellencies, distinguished ladies and gentlemen, I would like to give a very special recognition and hello to my old colleague and collaborator Lloyd Best.

The title of these reflections, "Language and the Politics of Ethnicity", would be described in critical theory as a site of contention. I would like in a way to diffuse the potential for contention by beginning with two voices separated by generations, that is, voices which are in a way echoing the same kind of interior journey of discovery.

The first is a voice from Guyana – Mahadai Das, "If I Came to India":

> If I came to India
> shall I be on a broken pilgrimage
> to Mahatma?
>
> Resigned or rebellious
> at streetcorner hunger,
> shall I wear a penitence, a saffron
> robe, wooden beads of my days
> cast about my breast?
>
> Shall I be Methuselah
> in my tradition, a foreign vine
> grafted to the Deccan Peninsula?

> Shall I find
> the poet naked in the mountain?
> Shall I discover philosophy
> in mountain-caves where
> Everest reigns?
>
> Near the Tibetan border
> where monks levitate, is
> the secret of Being written
> on a parched leaf?
>
> If I come
> will I find my Self.[1]

And the second is "My Last Name", from the Cuban Nicolás Guillén:

> Have I not, then
> a grandfather who's Mandingo, Dahoman, Congolese?
> What is his name? Oh yes, give me his name!
> . . .
> Do you know my other last name, the one that comes
> to me from that enormous land, the captured
> bloody last name that came across the sea
> in chains, which came in chains across the sea?[2]

In any consideration of the role of language in the politics of ethnicity of diaspora cultures, it is always prudent to bear in mind the context or location from which you speak. It is context which gives meaning to every question you ask. "How many children do you have?" may appear to be a simple enough question. But it is context and location which will soon reveal its complexity. For an example of the importance of context, I must take you back to a visit I made to Kenya in the middle 1970s. I had spent a day in the village of Limuru, at the home of the very distinguished novelist Ngũgĩ Wa Thiong'o. There was a big family and much jubilation all around. In a very relaxed way I asked him, "How many children do you have?"

He asked me in turn whether I would like to have another drink. I said, "Yes, of course," accepted the drink and repeated my question: "How many children . . . ?" And he said, "As we were saying before . . . ." This abrupt detour made it clear there was not going to be an answer to my question. A day later I was talking to a mutual friend and reported this episode and was told, "Oh, but no, no, no, no, that question wouldn't be answered. Among the Kikuyu, you never count offspring; to do so is to invite calamity." And now, decades later, it makes me think how extraordinary are the multiple frontiers of behaviour we have to explore and negotiate, to find ways of entering with courtesy into each other's world.

Language is essentially a very political tool, and the term *political* is used here to define the dynamics of a people's cultural evolution, the way we organize our social lives together and the power relations which this involves. It is in the context of our political culture that we recognize the decisive authority of power in the creation of words and in the intentional construction of the sentence. I want to give you two examples to illustrate a certain historical continuity in two distinct geographical locations.

In the early 1970s I was giving some lectures to what was then the Extramural Department of the University of the West Indies. It was on the afternoon of my arrival in Antigua that my host and I ran into the minister of education, whom I was meeting for the first time. When he heard that I was going to speak on the evolution of Caribbean literature, his response was immediate and uncompromising: "Doh bring no broken English in my school, please," he said, completed the handshake and continued on his business. The university representative appeared embarrassed, but it was for me a very fruitful example of the contradictions at work in the consciousness of this honourable citizen. His reproach was itself a fine example of breaking up the English language which he had asked to be left unimpaired.

In 1976 an even more complex situation arose in the island of St Lucia, where English is the official language of instruction. However, the island's long experience of French rule has bestowed on St Lucia the gift of another tongue: the entire population, irrespective of social background, is born into an oral tradition of French Creole, which has the pervasive character of a national language. Everybody speaks it but it is not accorded the authority of English, which is the language of government and official exchange required by state institutions.

The situation I am referring to here involved an elected member of the local parliament, who rose and gave the speaker warning that he was going to address the parliament in Creole. The speaker said he could not, because the existing constitution did not allow it. When the member persisted, the speaker threatened him with expulsion from the chamber. The threat was made in Creole, purely as a matter of emphasis and intention.

The contradiction is not, strictly speaking, about language – it is about power; it is about the politics of cultural subjugation and the transitional period of resistance to that hierarchical authority which makes a clear distinction between the language of negotiation (that is, government, school, church and so on) and language in action (the language of the marketplace, the school yard, the playing field) – between, let us say, state language and street or people's language. The minister of education may have had good reason to be worried, for the orthodoxies of language he represented were being transformed into bridges through the subversive intervention of our novelists and poets, who had narrowed the distance between what was called Standard English and the variety of non-standard forms which are now the occasion of much critical academic scrutiny.

Language was a major instrument in the creation of Empire. There is remarkable evidence from some nineteenth-century diaries that *Empire* has also been a metaphor of racial diversity and cultural miscegenation which challenges the imagination to discover its true location. The Antigua Ministry of Education would have found a sympathetic missionary witness in Lady Maria Nugent, whose journal was written between 1801 and 1805, and with the authority and privilege of the wife of the governor of Jamaica. She has a very fine sense of the relation of language to power, and laments the influence of the black tongue on the English ladies around her. She writes:

> The Creole language is not confined to the negroes. Many of the ladies, who have not been educated in England, speak a sort of broken English, with an indolent drawling out of their words, that is very tiresome if not disgusting. I stood next to a lady one night, near a window, and, by way of saying something, remarked that the air was much cooler than usual; to which she answered, "Yes, ma-am, *him rail-ly too fra-ish.*"[3]

But if it is the sound, the indolent and tedious drawling which disturbed Lady Nugent, the Reverend William Jones, who was in that island during the same period, is struck by a more dangerous tendency: the way language may be experienced as a mode of thinking, of receiving and articulating experience. He writes: "I have heard it observed as a fault of the white inhabitants, that instead of correcting the crude speech of the Negroes and better informing them, they descend so low as to join in their gibberish and by insensible degrees almost acquire the same habit of thinking and speaking."[4]

We must ask, "Is this mockery or is it the initial stages in the process of transculturation?" Journeys of conquest, initiated by an interior thirst for expansion, order and settlement, give way to involuntary migration and the conflicting claims of different groups to equal partnership in new homelands. Our context and location, which is the Caribbean, is perhaps a unique enclosure for identifying these histories of dominance and transculturation. The narratives recur of Europe imposing its will on the pastoral landscapes of aboriginal peoples, whose world collapses and fragments, then dissolves before new waves of Africans in bondage and rebellion. Subsequently came the arrival of East Indians indentured to sugar plantations, whose lives alternated between jail and hospital, strike and sickouts, and who were architects of resistance, as were their African predecessors.

In order to prepare ourselves for conflict (and conflict must be accepted as a norm and not a distortion), we must remind ourselves of the unique character of this movement of peoples into this archipelago, and remember that in this struggle of finding self through language and discovering language through self, we have a situation in which many contestants are making rival claims on our attention. There is not only an African diaspora, there is also an Indian and a wider Asian diaspora, and this confluence generates a tense creative challenge in the demands for democratic claims on the landscape. It is from this turmoil of diverse human encounters that Lady Nugent's term, *creole*, acquires a very special resonance, and a resonance for us which would have been beyond her imagination. For it is a word I know which subverts traditional orthodoxies of inheritance and at the same time offers itself as a stabilizing constraint on the fragmenting tendencies inherent in a plural society.

To avoid too great a conflict about the different applications of the term *creole*, I am going to settle for a single derivation in the Spanish *criar*, which means in the Caribbean context to nourish, to nurse, to bring forth, to be the evolving product of and to indigenize. We choose that route/root because it opens the possibility of an authentic civic nationalism which would embrace every self-defined ethnic type. Time and the political economy of the landscape in the form of the plantation allowed no one to be exempt from the inexorable process of creolization. There are those who claim European ancestry but who were made, shaped and seeded by the cultural forces of the archipelago, and whose interaction with others has made them a distinct breed from the stock from whom they descended. Fernando Ortiz and the discovery of Cubanidad is a fine example.

Moreover, the relations of intimacy, voluntary or otherwise, which characterized plantation society in the Caribbean did not allow for any reliable claim to any form of ancestral purity. *Creole* is the name of their anatomy. The sons and daughters of Indian indentured labourers arriving in the third decade of the nineteenth century may argue a stronger case for ancestral heritage than their African predecessors, but this proximity in time to the ancestral homeland does not erase or obscure their sense of belonging to the creolized world of Trinidad or Guyana.

The Indian discomfort with the term *creole* (and it is a word which arouses a certain antagonism) cannot be a denial of the process of creolization, although it may be a correct rejection of the cultural dominance which power conferred on one particular ethnic group. In his essay "Asian Identity and Culture in the Caribbean", Brinsley Samaroo raises the very vexatious question: "When therefore the Indo-Caribbean person is being constantly told that he must subscribe to the larger ill-defined something that is Creole culture, we must ask the more relevant question, namely, what is there in that culture that is superior to what orientalism offers?"[5]

Orientalism is a European concept unacceptable to the Indo-Caribbean and therefore an awkward alternative with which to challenge. But it is this use of Orientalism that brings us close to the heart of the question. It was the European dominant mode of thought which gave a decisive shape and content to the entire colonial experience, and the African's longer and more intimate association with this mode of thought made creolization appear to be a more natural and affirming inheritance than his Indian equivalent could accept. But creolization is not a static condition; it is an open-ended process of collective self-definition and deepening indigenization. It cannot be thought of as the final and irreversible project.

It was the African scholar Ali Mazrui who reminded us how Europe turned what was its own local experience into a universal imperative, inventing a vocabulary which would determine our ways of thinking about the planet: "This little continent called Europe invented the names for everything we encountered, so that we dared not think in any other terms than those they bequeathed to us." Against all reason we go on using terms like *Far East* and *Near East* without wondering, far from where? near where? – because we know the answer is Europe. And it is the consequence of this Eurocentric triumph which much of the world, including the Caribbean, is engaged in resisting and (wherever possible) neutralizing. Globalization is not new. It is an old European adventure which has evolved with miraculous virulence into a Euro-American nightmare for the poor, small and powerless.

But it may also be helpful to remind ourselves that we distort reality if we encourage thinking about Africans and Indians in uniform and monolithic terms. Controversy about self-definition prevails not only between different groups but also between different layers of the same group. There is a relevant and very touching autobiographic passage from Cheddi Jagan's *The West on Trial* (1966). He is discussing the emotional shock experienced during his transition from rural to urban living as a schoolboy of about twelve and a boarder in Georgetown:

> To compensate for the small amount of money my father paid for my board and lodging, I had to do many chores such as washing the elder's car, carrying his lunch on my bicycle, going to market, and cutting grass for his goats. I particularly resented the latter. Cutting and fetching grass in the country was one thing, but doing so in Georgetown as a Queen's College student was quite another. Georgetown middle class snobbery had so influenced me that I soon found some pretext to persuade my father to find me other lodgings.[6]

Dr Jagan escaped from the indignities of cutting and fetching grass under the glare of Georgetown, but something no less painful was to follow. He continues:

> The new family with whom I stayed belonged to the Kshatriya caste. One of the daughters had married a Brahmin and had three sons and one daughter . . . . Two things particularly irked me about my position in this household: firstly, I was singled out to go occasionally to the market; secondly, I had to sleep on the floor, although there was an empty room with a vacant bed. Apparently this was for reasons of status, based on caste – my family caste was Kurmi, lower in status than a Kshatriya or a Brahmin. Until then, I had heard my mother occasionally mention caste. I had never really encountered it . . . .[7]

Caribbean literature will provide us with the most vivid description of the school as an institution whose most critical function – or dysfunction – was to initiate and make permanent the existing layers of social stratification. Deschooling the mind from this early catastrophe is an agonizing task. C.L.R. James spent much of a long life negotiating a complete divorce from Queen's Royal College, and he was to say, "It was only long years after that I understood the limitation on spirit, vision and self-respect which was imposed upon us."[8]

This phenomenon of social distance, of class, is common to all ethnic categories and is a very decisive influence in the process of cultural formation. A large Indian agricultural proletariat in Trinidad or Guyana would not be unaware of the difference in the material interests which distance them from the modernizing consumerist lifestyle of their own professional and entrepreneurial elites. Nor is the African creole working class any less aware of this divide among Afro-Trinidadians. But individuals responding to the imagined threat of group pressure are very vulnerable to the most vulgar and opportunistic appeals which warn them about probable destruction by the Other. And when the political goal is about not just securing minority civil rights but actually acquiring the instruments of power for the regulation of the total society, racial and ethnic demagogy on either side makes sure of its advantages even when the fundamental issue is objectively not Race, but Power.

In her novel *Sastra*, Lakshmi Persaud engages the character Dr Capildeo in a discourse on this organic connection between the construct of race and the exercise of power. After a disastrous fire, thought to be arson by Afro-Trinidad rivals, Dr Capildeo offers this explanation:

> We must come to terms with the fact that whichever group is in power, once it has a majority, it will keep power and stay there until the resurrection, because, no matter how corrupt they are, what a mess they make of things, year in year out, all the time, at the back of their minds, they know they have a trump card – the strong, tribal card – primeval, instinctive. They only have to play it on that deep gut prejudice, that preference for ourselves when under threat.[9]

There are numerous examples in our literature of hostility between individuals which derives from these toxic sources of power that manipulate the original neutral difference between characters – the innocent malice, for example, of Mazie that is directed at Philomen in James's *Minty Alley*, or the censoring of Pariag's inclusion and participation in the activities of the yard in Lovelace's *The Dragon Can't Dance*. The strategy of ensuring allegiance by dramatizing the menace of the Indian was most effectively used by the old colonial power, and it has often been called into service by both African and Indian political leadership in the new independent countries. It has been a major obstacle to the realization of an *authentic, civic nationalism* that will embrace and recreolize all ethnic types in Caribbean society.

It was really my first experience of Guyana when I discovered the theme for the novel *Of Age and Innocence* (1958). In this novel I tried to explore a reflection of – and the inherent possibilities that existed in – what was then the People's Progressive Party in Guyana. Something quite extraordinary happened there in the early 1950s. What was new, and I think without precedent, was the forging of two separate armies of labour – African and Indian – into a single political force, and the creation of a consciousness born of that collaboration which led these armies of labour to understand that they were the foundation on which the social order rested. It was no doubt this newly forged consciousness combined with their numerical superiority and the morality of their purpose that equipped them to challenge, and ultimately seek to dismantle, the colonial authority's structure of rule in what was then British Guiana.

In the early 1950s, the People's Progressive Party in Guyana created an environment and a sense of possibilities and expectations which affected in one way or another every section of the society. It set the agenda of intellectual discourse that influenced the mood and themes of creative expression. This was the soil from which the early and strongest poems of the Guyanese Martin Carter would blossom. This was the soil that nourished Gordon Rohlehr and Walter Rodney, and neither of them succumbed to the virus of ethnocentricity. But Carter's dream suffered a traumatic collapse from which, in my view, the peoples of Guyana have never quite recovered.

I am aware of the external forces which were hostile to this dream, the manipulative power of forces able to intervene and erode what was in the making. However, I do not think we can settle for this as a sole explanation of the collapse of that radical movement. A fundamental part of the weakness of that historical moment resulted from the party leadership's assuming a human solidarity which had not yet been consolidated. This attribute of human solidarity is not a given; this attribute of human solidarity does not arise by chance or miracle. It has to be learned; it has to be nurtured; it has to be cultivated. This requires a kind of educational work, a kind of indoctrination, a reciprocal sharing of cultural histories which has never been at the centre of our political agendas in the Caribbean.

Perhaps there was not time enough; perhaps it was a misfortune that the People's Progressive Party came to power when it did in 1953. Perhaps a period of opposition without consuming their energies in the emergencies of administration might have allowed for that fundamental groundwork in political education and cultural dialogue. This recent consciousness of possibilities among the ranks of labour would have given a new dimension and a most substantial content. But tolerance was the adjustment they made in the struggle, and tolerance is a fragile bond. When the leadership broke, the armies turned with a tribal and atavistic fury on each other. We ourselves had fertilized the ground for the enemy to plant further mischief. I think it is a profound illusion and a tragic error to transfer this act of self-mutilation to a foreign conscience we call imperialist. There are certain defeats for which we must be prepared to take full responsibility.

In Barbados, the concept of race was articulated most effectively through the division of labour (agricultural labour was very exclusively black, and bank clerks exclusively white). We've witnessed the reversal of roles in the administration of the country. Now the executive branches of the state – that is, the government, the judiciary and the upper layers of the civil service – are almost entirely black. There is no traditional anxiety about an Indian threat. But the loss or conceding of political power by white Barbados has alerted us to a novel and challenging grievance, articulated by the literate voices of that social entity. In the *Trinidad and Tobago Review* publication *Enterprise of the Indies*, the journalist Robert Goddard, who is a member of a very powerful white Barbadian merchant family, makes a charge of Afrocentrism and its debilitating effect on the prospect of regional coherence:

> Black nationalism in the region is predicated on the idea that the West Indies is culturally black, and by inescapable implication, racially black as well. To be black is to be authentically Caribbean. To be non-black is to be an intruder. . . . Many white West Indians can relate to situations where they have disappointed non–West

Indians by appearing in the flesh wearing a white skin, as it were, after their accent had led their listeners to assume they must be black on the telephone.[10]

I offer this as an example of the truth we are very reluctant to accept: that race and ethnicity are socially constructed categories. Mr Goddard's voice on the telephone is ethnic black. In appearance his skin reveals him to be, racially, white. He wears both categories – same citizen, two ways of being located in the civic frame of reference. We have given these categories the power to generate antagonisms that affect our sectional and communal interests at the expense and even the sacrifice of a *liberating civic nationalism*.

The question arises, where is home and when does it begin? In this same publication, *Enterprise of the Indies* (which I must say should be compulsory reading – I don't think there is a literate student on this campus who should not be assigned a copy), the Indo-Trinidadian historian Kusha Haraksingh, in a remarkable contribution, draws attention to the predicament of the first generation of Indian indentured labourers, whose contract carried the option of return to India after five years. A choice had to be made, and it is Haraksingh's contention that this choice to stay carried a symbolic significance which was deliberately ignored or lost on those who were not Indian:

> The decision to stay was often coupled with a residential move away from plantations to "free" villages, which itself often involved the acquisition of title to property. This served as a major platform for belonging, an urge that soon became more evident in efforts to redesign the landscape. Thus, the trees which were planted around emergent homesteads, including religious vegetation, constituted a statement about belonging; so too did the temples and mosques which began to dot the landscape. And the rearing of animals which could not be abandoned; and the construction of ponds and tanks; and the diversion of watercourses; and the clearing of lands. When all this is put together, it is hard to resist the conclusion that Indians had begun to think of Trinidad as their home long before general opinion in the country had awakened to that possibility.[11]

There is abundant evidence in many of our narratives of that perception of the Indian as alien and Other, a problem to be contained after the departure of imperial power. This has been a major part of the thought and feeling of many citizens of African descent and a particularly stubborn conviction among the black middle classes of Trinidad and Guyana. Indian achievement in politics or business has been regarded as an example of an Indian strategy for conquest, and even where such achievement did not exist, there could still be heard the satirical assault on those Indians who appeared to identify too readily with a creolizing process. Gordon Rohlehr has been very helpful here in his inventory of calypsos; if you check the calypsos between 1946 and the 1960s, these are authentic examples of what we're saying:

> What's wrong with these Indian people?
> As though their intention is for trouble.
> Long ago you'd meet an Indian boy by the road
> With his capra waiting to take people load
> But I notice there is no Indian again
> Since the women and them taking Creole name
> Long ago was Sumintra, Ramnalawia,
> Bullbasia and Oosankilia
> But now is Emily, Jean and Dinah
> And Doris and Dorothy.[12]

And the mischievous mocking of Ramjohn's struggle for literacy:

> Ramjohn taking classes daily
> From a high school up in Laventille
> The first day's lesson was dictation
> and a little punctuation
> After class he come home hungry to death
> His wife aint cook Ramjohn start to fret
> Whole day you sit down on big fat comma
> You aint cook nothing up
> But ah go a hyphen in your semi colon
> And bus your fullstop and stop.[13]

If there is something blasphemous or heretical in this kind of representation, it becomes less so when this drama is seen from a different perspective.

The significance of Indians making a home may now be weighed against the African's rebellious feeling that a home has been stolen. In his very remarkable novel *Salt* (1996), Lovelace traces through four or five generations the history of this feeling, which the character Jojo records. He has been a rebel and a runaway who has lost an ear as punishment. But with rumours of emancipation, he sends petitions to Her Majesty through her secretary of state for colonial development, and his argument runs like this: "As a result of the circumstances of our enslavement Your Memorialists have no other option now but to make this island their home since it is the place that many of them have been born into and it is the place that their labour has gone to build."[14]

The appeal is ignored and we witness the bewilderment when he encounters for the first time a presence he had vaguely heard of:

> One morning JoJo was out in the yard, just about to go to the estate, when he heard the sound of cutlassing from the land nearby. . . .
>
> "You know," he told Faustin, "they give these Indian people contract and land to work on these estates."
>
> "It not their fault," Faustin tell him. "You should have squat on a piece of land yourself."
>
> But JoJo did not agree. It was clear to him that the Colony's treatment of the Indians had given him an even greater claim to reparation, but what was worrying, was his feeling that he had made an enemy of Feroze and the rest of the Indian people.[15]

It is this fracture which would remain unhealed, but which would also alert the imagination to the possibility of a novel kind of generosity. It is this possibility which Walcott is referring to in his 1992 Nobel speech:

> Break a vase, and the love that reassembles the fragments is stronger than that love which took its symmetry for granted when it was whole. The glue that fits the pieces is the sealing of its original shape. It is such a love that reassembles our African and Asiatic fragments, the cracked heirlooms whose restoration shows its white scars. This gathering of broken pieces is the care and pain of the Antilles, and if the pieces are disparate, ill-fitting, they contain more pain than the original sculpture, those icons and sacred vessels taken for granted in their ancestral places. Antillean art is this restoration of our shattered histories, our shards of vocabulary, our archipelago becoming a synonym for pieces broken off from the original continent.[16]

If language was the major instrument of Empire, it is the very flexible and varying ranges of language, the subtle and exquisite manipulations of native rhythms of speech which have won our writers a very special attention. If the metropole directed what is standard and required by the cultural establishment, it is at the periphery of colony or neo-colony that the imagination resists, destabilzes and transforms the status of the word in action. This is a mark of cultural sovereignty, the free definition and articulation of the collective self, whatever the rigour of external constraints.

I believe that labour and the relations experienced in the process of labour constitute the foundation of all culture. It is through work that men and women make nature a part of their own history. The way we see, the way we hear, our nurtured sense of touch and smell – the whole complex of feelings which we call sensibility – are influenced by the particular features of the landscape which has been humanized by our work. And so there can be no history of Trinidad or Guyana that is not also the history of the humanization of those landscapes by African and Indian forces of labour.

This is at once the identity and the conflict of interests which engage the deepest feeling of those indentured workers inscribing their signatures on a landscape that would be converted into home, and also the bitter taste of loss, which the emancipated African JoJo experiences as he sees land become a symbol of his dispossession. How to reconcile these contradictions was really the engagement of creative artists for its resolution. But the past was for us in these circumstances not just an exercise in memory and the retrieval of some ration of consolation for our labour; the past became a weapon with ethnicity summoned as evidence of group solidarity. Politics would become an expression of ethnic grievance made rational and just by any evidence which the past could sanction. We were given warning of this sentiment when JoJo, in spite of the undeserved card which emancipation had played him, experiences a worry he would never have wished on anyone: "What was worrying him was his feeling that he had made an enemy of Feroze and the rest of the Indian people."[17]

The colonization of the female by an arbitrary division of labour would in time give rise to a crusade of sexual politics which has become a major challenge to all established orthodoxy in the contemporary Caribbean. The patriarchal character of Caribbean literature has been immensely enriched by the range and quality of women's writing. It was almost a certainty that one of the most fertile areas of its expansion would be occupied by what previously and by traditional stereotype was the most dormant of all voices: the voice of the Indo-Caribbean woman. After less than half a century of access to the school and with swift migration from barrack room and cane patch to the professional citadels of the nation's workplace, these voices have now broken through forever that curtain of silence and submission behind which we were made to believe was their chosen location. In the *Trinidad Guardian*'s Indian Arrival Supplement of 1992, Sita Bridgemohan offers this poignant statement of her claims on the Trinidad landscape: "My forefathers came from India to work in the cane fields. They were Hindu. With sweat, tears, hard work and courage, they created a life in a different land, a land in which I was born. By right of birth I have a place in this land and don't have to fight for it."[18] If African labour and the cultural dimensions of that labour constitute the first floor on which this Caribbean house was built, then the second floor and central pillar on which its creative survival depends is the total democratic participation of the Indo-Caribbean presence.

The concepts of Race, Nation and Ethnicity constitute a family of constructs of largely European origin which served to influence the attitudes we adopt in any encounter with difference. European racism was a form of ethnic nationalism that invested the colour line with a power of definition which neither the Asian nor African colonized could have escaped. Difference in religion, difference in modes of cultural affirmation require a new agenda of perspectives, a wholly new way of looking at the concept of nation, of finding a way to immunize sense and sensibility against the virus of ethnic nationalism (for the culture of an ethnic group is no more than the set of rules into which parents belonging to that ethnic group are pressured to socialize their children). And this new perspective is needed in order to educate feeling to respect the autonomy of the Other's difference, to negotiate the cultural spaces which are the legitimate claim of the Other, and to work towards an environment which could manage stability as a state of creative conflict. The challenge of diversity and the peculiar nature of our own diasporic adventure could be made a fertilizing soil and the crusading theme of political party discourse. Indeed, this diversity has been an abundant blessing for cultural workers in all the arts in the Caribbean: the novel, the visual arts, the syncretic splendour of our festivals. Creative conflict is the dynamic which drives the Caribbean imagination.

I have never been able to separate the creative imagination from the political culture in which it functions. And so I will close with an extract from American sociologist C. Wright-Mills:

> The independent artist and intellectual are among the few remaining personalities equipped to resist and to fight the stereotyping and consequent death of genuinely living things. Fresh perception now involves the capacity to continually unmask and smash the stereotypes of vision and intellect with which modern communications [that is, modern systems of representations now] swamp us. These worlds of mass art and mass thought are increasingly geared to the demands of market politics.

That is why it is in politics that intellectual solidarity and effort must be centered. If the thinker does not relate himself [or herself] to the value of truth in political struggle, he [or she] cannot responsibly cope with the whole of lived experience.[19]

And this has been the singular privilege and burden of my entire adult life: to help to create a civil environment that would teach the love and nurturing of genuine living things.

Notes

1. Mahadai Das, "If I Came to India", in *Enterprise of the Indies*, ed. George Lamming (Port of Spain: Trinidad and Tobago Institute of the West Indies, 1999), 37.
2. Nicolás Guillén, "My Last Name", in *Man-Making Words*, trans. Robert Márquez and David Arthur McMurray (Havana: Editorial de Arte y Literatura, 1973), 75.
3. Maria Nugent, *Lady Nugent's Journal*, ed. Phillip Wright (Jamaica: University of the West Indies Press, 2002), 98.
4. William Jones, *The Diary of the Reverend William Jones*, ed. O.F. Christie (London: Brentano's, 1929), 16.
5. Brinsely Samaroo, "Asian Identity and Culture in the Caribbean", in *Enterprise of the Indies*, ed. George Lamming (Port of Spain: Trinidad and Tobago Institute of the West Indies, 1999), 45.
6. Cheddi Jagan, *The West on Trial* (Berlin: Seven Seas Books, 1966), 22.
7. Ibid.
8. C.L.R. James, *Beyond a Boundary* (London: Hutchinson, 1963), 38.
9. Lakshmi Persaud, *Sastra* (Leeds: Peepal Tree Books, 1993), 84.
10. Robert Goddard, "Last to Bat", in *Enterprise of the Indies*, ed. George Lamming (Port of Spain: Trinidad and Tobago Institute of the West Indies, 1999), 32–33.
11. Kusha Haraksingh, "Indenture and Self Emancipation", in *Enterprise of the Indies*, ed. George Lamming (Port of Spain: Trinidad and Tobago Institute of the West Indies, 1999), 40.
12. Mighty Killer [Cephus Alexander], "Indian People with Creole Name" (1952), quoted by Gordon Rohlehr, in *Calypso and Society in Pre-Independence Trinidad* (Port of Spain: Lexicon, 1990), 498.
13. Mighty Skipper [Robert Stafford], "Punctuation", *Calypso Exposed* (Cook LP COOK01189), 1961.
14. Earl Lovelace, *Salt* (London: Faber and Faber, 1996), 181–82.
15. Ibid., 185–87.

16. Derek Walcott, *The Antilles: Fragments of Epic Memory* (New York: Farrar, Straus and Giroux, 1993), 8–9.
17. Lovelace, *Salt*, 187.
18. Sita Bridgemohan, "Growing Up Against a Background of Hinduism", *Trinidad Guardian*, Indian Arrival/Aagaman Supplement (Port of Spain: Trinidad Publishing, 1992), 41.
19. C. Wright Mills, *Power, Politics, and People: The Collected Essays of C. Wright Mills* (London: Oxford University Press, 1967), 299.

CHAPTER 2

Gender and Genre
The Logic of Language and the Logistics of Identity

▶ PATRICIA SAUNDERS

Finding a Language for the Experience of S/Place

M. NourbeSe Philip describes a phenomenon that sits at the crux of contemporary debates about Caribbean literature and identity:

> Speech, voice, language, and word – all are ways of being in the world, and the artist working with the i-mage and giving voice to it is being in the world. The only way the African artist could be in this world, that is the New World, was to give voice to this split i-mage of voiced silence. Ways to transcend that contradiction had to and still have to be developed, for that silence continues to shroud the experience, the i-mage and so the word.[1]

> Does the inner space exist whole in any language? Other than "threat" and "fear"? What is the language of the inner space? To read the text that lies "missing" in the silence of the inner space, we needing a new language – the language of jamettes, possessing their inner and outer space. The be-coming and coming-to-be of a jamette poet.[2]

Trapped in a discourse that simultaneously denied their humanity while emphasizing their presence as a form of alterity, colonial subjects could only imagine and represent their selves in a language of contradiction which made them what they in fact were not. In an effort to transcend these contradictions,

Caribbean writers revised the categories/institutions of history and identity in order to create a space that could accommodate their lived experiences and their expressions of them. These spaces, though reconstructed, still depend largely on the authority endowed upon them by imperialist discourses and hierarchies. Appropriations of various traditions and tropes have been deployed effectively to recentre black female subjectivity as a normative part of colonial and post-colonial Caribbean literature. Narrative representations of the nation are overtly gendered (female) and specifically sexualized. The mapping of nationalist agendas onto women's bodies raises immediate questions about the possibility of transcending these contradictions without engaging the constructed silence of black women's histories, genealogies and experiences in colonial and post-colonial Caribbean literature. Contemporary texts by critics and writers alike have argued that the logic of language and the logistics of identity have developed along an axis of masculinist discourses which police and appropriate black female sexualities in the service of black nationalist movements.[3]

Literary representations of the lived realities of women remain locked in traditional notions of genre, identity, language and gender, despite the ironic shift that saw women become a prominent part of the social landscape of Caribbean literature during the Trinidad Renaissance of the 1930s. The "discursive unities" between colonialist narratives and post-independence narratives presented reading audiences with a discursive terrain endowed with canonical authority and political force that constructed women as present, yet silent, historical subjects. This tradition was reproduced and disseminated in the new political and cultural landscape of the modern Caribbean nation-state. Writing a generation later, Caribbean women experiencing the pains (not pleasures) of exile needed to craft a political and cultural landscape that was conducive to their own sense of logic, language, history and identity. Erna Brodber's novels are examples of the form and critical scope these efforts might take. However, there is still much to be written about remapping the terrain of black female sexuality in colonial and post-colonial Caribbean literature.

Despite the similarities in the geographic trajectories between contemporary Caribbean women writers and their male counterparts during the 1950s and 1960s, the cultural and political circumstances surrounding these waves of migration are worlds apart. Migration for women writers of the 1980s and 1990s was not hailed with the same sense of national pride as the previous exodus of the "sons of the nation". Moreover, the institutional assurances (island scholarships, jobs with the BBC, teaching posts, freelance reporting and so on) available to young colonials like C.L.R. James, Eric Williams and others were not available for women migrating a generation later. The absence of these benefits, as well as a changing relationship between the metropoles and "foreigners", was an indication of the shift in racial politics in North America, Britain and Canada. Britain, for example, no longer the benevolent provider, shifted its cultural perspectives to taking care of its "own" and preserving its sense of Britishness.[4]

My interest in examining the relatedness of the phenomenon of second-wave migration by women writers and discourses of identity is twofold. First, I want to suggest that for contemporary Caribbean women writers, the political geography of their migration meant coming to terms with their experiences of alienation, oppression and dispossession, both in their Caribbean homelands and now in their new homelands in the black diaspora. Second, I want to examine the extent to which women writers employ a gendered critique of genre through implicating "form" as well as discourses of identity that shape women's (physical, linguistic, geographic and existential) spaces and places. The deconstruction of narrative form, which, I argue, is becoming characteristic of Caribbean women's contemporary literature,[5] complicates traditional relationships between language and identity. My engagement with NourbeSe Philip's writing examines her exploration of the inextricable links among traditional constructions of gender, sexuality and identity. NourbeSe Philip's writing is distinct from Brodber's in its critical and artistic interpretation of history and identity. The former's explicit linking of language, sexuality and history in her poetry highlights the hegemony exercised and experienced through colonialist discourses. However, their work shares a critical focus on colonialist discourse and the construction of history in the processes of be(com)ing for black subjects.

NourbeSe Philip emphasizes the psychological damage to black slaves caused by language and (H)istory, but more specifically she stresses the use of language as a tool of violence which represses the imagination while oppressing the physical body. The questions posed by NourbeSe Philip threaten the boundaries of our understanding of language and representation. She asks, "Does the inner space exist whole in any language? Other than 'threat' and 'fear'?" To begin to formulate a response to this question, we need to reconceptualize the relationship between language and the environments language inhabits. Implicit in this question is a critique of how space is defined and controlled, as well as the centrality of power in how it is represented and experienced. In her prose/diary/play/poem/letter "Dis Place – The Space Between", NourbeSe Philip recentres a critique of power through her engagement with historical constructions of women, their lives and their bodies in discursive "fields of play". These fields of play and production include colonial legal documents, historical records, scientific studies, personal letters and colonial traditions.

NourbeSe Philip's disregard for unity of genre is part of her attempt to highlight the discursive and political dispersion of language that has disciplined women's bodies while also distancing them from language in which to express their realities. This "voiced silence" is produced among discourses that operate in the "spaces between" disciplines, genres, histories, identities and personal accounts. An awareness of these spaces, according to NourbeSe Philip, creates an environment where the "polyvocular text" can be engaged as an articulation of alter/native models for representing Caribbean history and identity.

NourbeSe Philip's "Dis Place – The Space Between" therefore represents the "polyvocularity" of Caribbean discourses on identity, discourses that extend beyond traditional boundaries which separate disciplines, genres and linguistic and national communities, as well as historical periods. This community of voices includes personal letters from the author and from Ferdinand, King of Spain; court records (presented as a play) from the trial of notorious *jamettes* in Port of Spain, Trinidad; calypso songs and quotes from musicians and dancers such as Rex Nettleford and Miles Davis; critiques by intellectuals such as Michel Foucault, Gayatri Spivak, C.L.R. James and Lucille Mathurin Mair; and commentary on cricket and carnival.

But what is this "s/place" to which NourbeSe Philip refers, and how does it affect how black subjects, particularly female subjects, experience their selves? Can this s/place provide what Belinda Edmondson succinctly describes as a "theory of Caribbean female writing that identifies an 'essential' Caribbean female subject"?[6] According to NourbeSe Philip this s/place represents the postmodern realities of black women across the world.[7] This space, in between, is the physical experience of external space and how this experience is configured internally through the mind and body. From the early exploits of Columbus to the Trinidad Renaissance to the brain drain migration of the 1960s and 1970s, the terrain of Caribbean literature has been defined through these spaces "in between". This space represents the sexualized landscape of national identity and the gendered discourses that instituted Caribbean literary traditions. Once more, traversing geographies to gain the advantage of critical distance is one of the privileges of Caribbean (male) intellectuals, one that has borne itself out in the language used to describe Caribbean historical and cultural landscapes.

There can be no separation of these two constructions, sexuality and national identity, because female sexuality has long been the context out of which the "nation" emerges in all its contradictions. Women's relationships to the physical landscape of their own bodies is mediated (to put it mildly) by the threat and fear of violation, which has long been a staple in nationalist narratives of resistance and rebellion. In patriarchal societies (the only societies we have known), the female body always presents a subversive threat. By far the most efficient tool for managing women is the possibility of uninvited and forceful invasion of the space between the legs – rape.[8]

This possibility is a constant. A threat to *the* space – the inner space between the legs. Even if never carried out, this threat continually and persistently inflects how the female reads the external language of place, or public space – the outer space. One woman raped is sufficient to vocalize and reify the threat of outer space, and the need to protect this inner space means that the female always reads the outer space from a dichotomous position: safe/unsafe, prohibited/unprohibited. How the female poet interacts with the land, the countryside, or the urban landscape – with the outer space in all its variety, or place in its most physical sense – is, therefore, entirely affected by gender. She must read place – the outer space – in a gendered language. Is the choice, therefore, either to accept the restrictions on physical behaviour and available space that the threat of rape brings, to limit one's activities to the daytime and to specific places ... or what? The female poet's understanding of place in its most physical sense will be different from and necessarily more restricted than that of the male poets.[9]

The language of colonialism, in its earliest literary representations, was a language of oppression and violation, particularly sexual violation. The journals of great "explorers" make (in)famous the illusions of conquering "virgin territories" and "penetrating" deep into the "heart of darkness". Both the discourse and practice of rape as a tool of efficient management of women is fictionalized as a trope in colonialist narratives of discovery and the lived reality of black women in the New World. The accounts of rape chronicled in the journals and diaries of travellers to the New World, as well as colonial legislation that granted slave owners power over black women's bodies, are a testimony to the historical connections between women's bodies and the landscape under siege in the New World. Resolutions from the Council of War of 1665 are appropriated to express the historical power of the letter of the (L)aw to govern black women's bodies.

It Is Our Royal Will and Pleasure

The Articles of War legislation enacts the "efficient management" of rebellious blacks through the forceful invasion of women and children, who are singled out as the recipients of any treatment that is the "pleasure and will" (as implied in the use of the term *shall*) of those exercising the law: "If any number of persons shall find out the Pallenque of the said Negroes, they shall have and enjoy to their uses all the Women and Children and all the plunder they can find there for their reward."[10]

The invasion of the inner spaces of the New World enabled and empowered disciplinary discourses grounded in the language of conquering, penetration and pillage in the name of "taming" the landscape, the savage and the darkness "in between". In so doing, it also produced the framework for nineteenth-century Victorian ideals of sexuality and womanhood that would be used to exclude and distance black female subjects from their identity as women. Black women writing slave narratives in North America (like Harriet Jacobs) had to revise their modes of expression in order to write out of the double bind of their race and gender.[11] In twentieth-century writing from the Caribbean we see a similar formulation of bind, this time articulated through Caribbean nationalism and nationalist politics. The nationalist landscapes mapped out in early constructions of West Indianness, brilliantly expressed through the barrack-yard fiction of the 1930s, follow a trajectory of representations in which women's bodies are tropes for embattled conceptualizations of Caribbean national identity. Apart from demonstrating the integral connectedness of race and gender, the allegorical nature of the barrack yard and storefront narratives gave a face and a voice to the exploitation of the working poor.

But it is not simply the appropriation of women's bodies that is of significance here. These appropriations became a means of disciplining the discourse of black female identity in subsequent Caribbean writing. The inner spaces of the barrack yard and the women who resided there were defined in, and indeed through, the outer spaces of colonial patriarchal society in Trinidad. The financial dependence on their "keepers" highlights the extent to which outer spaces determine the shape of power systems in the yard, if not its values. However, the power struggles in early barrack-yard narratives also provide the first glimpses of the discursive disciplining that emerges in the second wave of Caribbean literature written in exile. The women who people the stories of the *Beacon* represent a wayward wilfulness that tramples over every social institution of Victorian colonial society in the interests of self-preservation. This radical positioning of women in relation to the nation-state is swiftly revised in order to make way for a more socially responsible and politically astute nation on the march towards independence.

The embracing of women's bodies as a trope for representing West Indian realities by writers of the Trinidadian Renaissance was replaced by a backlash of nationalist politics that required men to have access to mobility and the ability to exercise control over their social surroundings. While on the surface this mobility offered an equal opportunity for both men and women, the dis/placement of women during this period of Caribbean writing would have a lasting effect on how women would occupy nationalist landscapes. The experience of displacement meant something significantly different for men than it did for women. For men, this displacement was an opportunity to sharpen their insights. George Lamming's *The Pleasures of Exile* (1960) and *Water with Berries* (1971) both characterize displacement as a necessary stage of development for Caribbean artists. As exile emerged as a mode of representation in the second wave of Caribbean writing, there was a corresponding systematic marginalization and/or erasure of black women in these narratives of exile. For women, the experience of displacement amounted to the absent presence of women in the literature and landscape of the period. Edmondson offers a convincing argument for reading the critical vantage point of outer spaces as a hegemonic space that can be accessed only through masculinist discourses on sexuality and national identity.

Edmondson delineates the specific implications of migration and exile for Caribbean women writers during the first wave of intellectual migration.

Caribbean women were, and still are, predominantly economic migrants who have dis/placed themselves in the interests of gaining economic stability for their families. In contrast, the experience of their male counterparts, then as now, is represented as a necessary step that will enhance their "*power* to invoke authority".[12] The power of "elsewhere" has historically endowed Caribbean male writers with (canonical, political and cultural) authority to speak on behalf of the nation and its citizens, despite their distance from both. According to Edmondson,

> If exile . . . is predicated on the banishment of the writer by patriarchal authority, the place "he" is banished *from*, the native land, the "*matria*", is maternalized. Similarly, Freud equates exile from one's native land with exile from the mother: the nostalgia for the home country is in actuality a nostalgia for the mother's body.[13] The land as mother plays the "object" to the exile's "subject" status. A return of the exile to the "motherland" is then a reappropriation of it. The *matria* is the "internal exclusion" of *patria*, "the other by and through which patria is defined. Its exclusion or "exile" therefore is the very condition of patriarchy's existence since "*matria* is always ex*patriated*".[14]

This formulation of the gendered implications of exile is a productive point of entry into my primary consideration in this chapter: How can we begin to situate women's writing "in between" the paradigms and problematics expressed by Edmondson and NourbeSe Philip? If ex/patri/ation is necessary for Caribbean men to ensure their presence as subjects on the national stage of history, what does this mean for Caribbean women writers attempting to construct a black female subjectivity not predicated on this formulation? How do women writers represent the female body, which has been distanced from its self (through sexuality) and its surroundings? How do they begin to formulate a discourse to express their experiences of s/place? Can this language provide a means for revising the traditions that have disciplined both their bodies and their discourses into silence?

NourbeSe Philip advances a complex critical response to these questions through her engagement with the "logic of language" in post-colonial discourses. Her collection *She Tries Her Tongue, Her Silence Softly Breaks* yokes discourses of sexuality, language and oppression into immediate visual, spatial and historical proximity to one another on the page. In so doing, she translates narrative form into a vehicle for (dis)forming, or exposing the cracks and complicity across various discursive communities and traditions. This approach pays particular attention to the configuration of human science and its construction of the female body through image and language.

Imag(in)ing the Word/World Through "Voiced Silence"

The intimate connections between sexual and physical space (or what NourbeSe Philip refers to as "scapes") inform the processes through which bodies of language and, indeed, bodies are disciplined into discourses that reflect the restrictions, genealogies and conventions of the s/places from which they emerge. Moreover, the (psychological, physical and emotional) distance between the subject and the s/place in Caribbean literature has historically been mediated by the "privilege" of exile. As I suggested earlier, migration provided the first generation of Caribbean male writers with the critical distance necessary to reflect on their condition as colonial subjects. However, if we consider the problematic described by NourbeSe Philip regarding the physical and psychic limitations imposed on and through the inner spaces of women's bodies, the freedom of movement across geographic, linguistic and cultural boundaries necessarily takes on more significance for women writers.

NourbeSe Philip's *She Tries Her Tongue, Her Silence Softly Breaks* challenges the structure and dispersion of discourses, the instituted boundaries erected between poetry, prose and personal narrative, as well as the human and social sciences. In her opening essay, "The Absence of Writing or How I Almost Became a Spy", as in many of the narratives that follow, NourbeSe Philip challenges her reading audience to confront the historical and cultural interconnectedness between the body and the word – more specifically, the female subject's body and the (W)ord. This relationship is one that is repeated throughout the entire body of NourbeSe Philip's writing, as it represents an effort to re-historicize and de-legitimize discourses that have subsumed and, indeed, disrupted the processes of be(com)ing for Africans in the New World. If, as NourbeSe Philip asserts, "speech, voice, language and word – all are ways of being in the world",[15] then in order to begin to represent the experiences of Africans in the New World, the writer would have to forge a different relationship to the language which has historically constructed black subjectivity and identity.

Through the image of voiced silence, NourbeSe Philip captures the nature of the contradiction at work within discourses of identity that locked black subjects out of the processes of making meaning in their own language. The intimate connection between language and labour in the New World ensured that the primary function of language was not to express but to oppress and repress the experiences of Africans. The possibility of a language capable of expressing what they were experiencing, therefore, was never available to Africans in the New World. As NourbeSe Philip asserts,

> The African in the Caribbean could move away from the experience of slavery in time; she could even acquire some perspective on it, but the experience, having never been reclaimed and integrated metaphorically through language and so within the psyche, could never be transcended. To reclaim and integrate the experience required autonomous i-mage makers and therefore a language with the emotional, linguistic, and historical resources capable of giving voice to the particular i-mages arising out of the experience . . . . I would argue further that it is impossible for any language which denies the humanity of any group or people to be truly capable of giving voice to the i-mages of experiences of that group without tremendous fundamental changes within the language itself.[16]

In such a situation, slaves learned a language (English) that served to keep them silenced and reduced both language and the body to a unit of production. The "voice" created out of this relationship, therefore, spoke nothing of (or to) the lived experiences of Africans in the New World, creating the "voiced silence" to which NourbeSe Philip refers.

How then would the writer, particularly the woman writer, begin to construct for herself an "i-mage" out of these layered contradictions? If Africans in the New World had (and still have) only English (or French, Spanish or Dutch, depending on the colonizers' tongue) to express themselves, were they, as many Caribbean writers have suggested, doomed to Prospero's prison-house of language? Or was there another alternative, one that could bend the medium to meet the needs of Africans in the New World? Far from asserting the creation of a new language or resorting to a romanticized notion that African languages could be made to serve the needs of generations of African-Caribbean peoples for whom Africa was only a distant memory, NourbeSe Philip asserts that "English, in its broadest spectrum must be made to do the job". In other words, somewhere between what we refer to as "Standard" English and Caribbean

English would emerge a "demotic variant of English", representative of both the "havoc that Africans wreaked on the English language" and the "metaphorical equivalent of the havoc that coming to the New World represented for the African".[17]

The problematic of language for the Caribbean writer has been well documented, and the debates on both sides of the English/Caribbean English divide have continued for centuries.[18] As NourbeSe Philip suggests, the African-Caribbean experience cannot be expressed solely in one or the other of these languages without both of them being adversely affected. Therefore the challenge for Caribbean writers is to exploit this aspect of the language and further subvert it in order to make the language truly belong to Caribbean peoples. These processes of subversion are instrumental if Caribbean subjects are to begin to endow their language with a meaning of their own, to create their own i-mages.

However, NourbeSe Philip does not leave her critique at the level of language and words. She also subverts the forms used to disseminate words and the communities in which they circulate. Exploring the structure of literary traditions within the Western canonical tradition, African mythology and the Caribbean demotic provides the Caribbean writer with an opportunity to formulate new patterns, systems and modalities to represent African-Caribbean realities:

> The continuing challenge for me as a writer/poet is to find some deeper patterning – a deep structure, as Chomsky puts it – of my language, the Caribbean demotic. As James Baldwin has written, "Negro speech is not a question of dropping s's or n's or g's but a question of the beat." At present the greatest strength of the Caribbean demotic lies in its oratorical energies which do not necessarily translate to the page easily.... To keep the deep structure, the movement, the kinetic energy, the tone and pitch, the slides and glissandos of the demotic within a tradition that is primarily page bound – that is the challenge.[19]

As NourbeSe Philip suggests, the contradictory forces so characteristic of Caribbean culture also trouble any attempt to find a neat conclusion. In this case, the greatest tool available for the Caribbean writer is also the difficulty faced in any attempt at finding a solution. The response, however, has not been one of utter distress at the obstacles facing Caribbean writers. Quite the contrary, NourbeSe Philip herself comments that the problems and issues discussed in the opening essay of *She Tries Her Tongue* have served as "something of a blueprint" for her poetic engagement with the Caribbean demotic. NourbeSe Philip successfully situates her critique of language, power and identity within these contradictions, drawing both on her colonial heritage – her mother and father tongues – and the other wisdoms from African cultures that have so infiltrated New World Caribbean traditions.

The "deep structure" to which NourbeSe Philip refers should be read in all its complexities, which include both the "form" of language as well as the modalities through which language and meaning are constructed, disseminated and interpreted. She also reminds us of the questions raised earlier about the black female body in its relationship to language, by way of explicitly linking the loss of control of language to that of black women's loss of control over their physical spaces and places. Disruptions of language inevitably affected the ability of the black female subject to express her experiences, and thus her relationship to her histories, myths, i-mages and identities. In the opening poem, NourbeSe Philip evokes an embodied language by reconfiguring the economies at work in myths such as Ovid's treatment of Proserpine and Ceres. The section "And Over Every Land and Sea" includes a series of poems that repossess the language of mother–daughter relationships in Western literary traditions. The frantic search by a mother, Ceres, for her abducted daughter is rewritten, using lines from Ovid's *Metamorphoses* as captions for each section. The landscape of the narrative is reclaimed to reflect the embodied realities of black mothers seeing their children being bought and sold on the slave market. The search in Ovid's tale is made all the more impossible if we read it through the experience and ruptures that occured in the Middle Passage. NourbeSe Philip's rereading of this myth reveals the privilege of Western feminist constructions of women's bodies, mothering, and the notion of community. By repossessing the historical landscape, the text is embodied through black women's experiences, forcing the same language of the tale to take on a very different meaning.

When Ceres discovers Proserpine's girdle, her worst fears are confirmed, and she laments the rape and loss of her daughter. Read in relationship to the sexual economy of colonial slave plantations, the romanticism of the mother–daughter relationship is starkly contrasted with the violation and exploitation of black women's bodies for profit and for the "will and pleasure" of slave masters. This contrast highlights the assumptions of Western feminism and its efforts to reclaim the female body without dealing with the historical specificities of black women's histories. In her rereading and rewriting of this myth, NourbeSe Philip undoes the uniformity of the sign "woman" by articulating the experiences of black women, experiences that have historically been subsumed beneath women's histories and disciplined into romances or total silence. In this instance, Ceres' search is juxtaposed with the experience of a black woman whose child has been sold away: generations dispersed, the lineage disrupted, scattered in space and time – irrecoverable.

NourbeSe Philip engages this same "deep structure" in her textual representations of the ruptures in English language(s) and its limitations as a mode of expression for black subjects. These limitations, however, leave room for creative reimaginings of language, i-maginings that provide for the possibility of speaking in tongues – "mother tongues" and "father tongues". Once more, the problem is precisely the key to the solution, as the "trying" (difficult) tongue of English also opens room for "trying" (experimenting) to de-centre English as we know it. NourbeSe Philip's "Discourse on the Logic of Language" is a performative representation of the processes involved in the act of de-centring or deconstructing language. Despite what NourbeSe Philip describes as "the anguish of English", her poetry explores the possibility of black subjects in the New World speaking, as it were, in tongues. "Father tongues" have historically served as a means of alienating black subjects from their selves and, more particularly, have been part of a history of violence and oppression. Therefore, in "Discourse on the Logic of Language", language, sexuality and identity are intimately connected through a rather intricate cartography of language acquisition, dissemination and interpretation. The first page of the poem poses an interesting dilemma for its readers because of the unusual positioning of the written word on the page:

English
is my mother tongue.
A mother tongue is not
not a foreign lan lan lang
language
l/anguish
anguish – a foreign anguish.

EDICT 1

English is
my father tongue

*Every owner of slaves
shall, whenever possible* . . .[20]

The polyvocularity of the text, which plays with *mother tongue, mammy tongue, mammy tongue, modder tongue,* and *ma tongue,* is created both through sight and sound, producing an effect of fragmented images that are constantly being disrupted by the other narratives that share the page, as well as the same historical s/place. NourbeSe Philip's miscegenation of form disrupts the seemingly natural order of things which the reader and listener try to absorb. The difficulty of engaging the content, along with the multiple forms of (re)presentation, forces audiences to question the relationship between the form and the discursive terrain which informs how we produce meaning and, therefore, knowledge. NourbeSe Philip's engagement with form, then, asks us to consider the ways in which each of these narratives always already contains traces of the other, whether verbally articulated or not.

In an essay entitled "To 'Heal the Word Wounded': Agency and the Materiality of Language and Form in M. NourbeSe Philip's *She Tries Her Tongue, Her Silence Softly Breaks*", Brenda Carr asserts: "In *She Tries Her Tongue*, miscegenation of form runs a kind of textual interference, incites a collision of discourses, that reveals language to be anything but indeterminate in its material effects. This text activates engagement with the mutual implication of discourses and bodies."[21] The bodies of people, knowledge and geography that inform "Discourse on the Logic of Language" assert historical and cultural links between language, sexuality and oppressions that manifest themselves in a variety of physical and disciplinary discourses. The piece of writing, which flows down the left-hand margin of the page, constructs an-Other narrative, presumably fictive, that expresses the care administered by a mother to her child and the importance of the tongue as used to remove the afterbirth from her newborn daughter. Though the piece is presented as a fiction narrated by an omniscient narrator, its relationship to the other texts on the page is significant; it is positioned in an authoritative relationship to the other discourses at work in the poem. Far from situating itself as fact or truth, the narrative is offered as a text that leans on the other discourses for its authority, depending on the reader's ability and willingness to connect it to the other representations on the page.

Through her engagement with form, NourbeSe Philip deconstructs the "sensible" terms of social-historical institutions through a closer examination of the processes by which this "sense" is produced and disseminated through coercion, through terror and through legal and cultural practices and discourses. The capitalized text that occupies the margins of the page where "Discourse on the Logic of Language" and "EDICT 1" appear is a reconstruction of the locale of power and language in shaping identity. The story tells of a child/being that, upon birth, is cleansed of what is presumably the afterbirth. Here the mother (tongue) is the progenitor of language and a source of protection.[22]

The multiplicity of meaning inherent in this narrative is part of the dialectic created among the other texts on the page. As such, the different genres and discursive representations of the edict and the poem make two primary readings possible. One reading suggests that NourbeSe Philip's spatial arrangement of texts on the page provides a visual and discursive juxtaposing of the possible meanings between the texts, forcing us to imagine the relationship of each text to the other. *Tonguing*, in this instance, becomes a verb in the sense of "giving words". However, as we will see later, this same act of tonguing takes on a different meaning if we consider the imposition of a "father tongue"; the edicts alert us to violence, where the word *lick* becomes a form of brutality which disciplines the subject into silence. The British use of *lick* (to hit or slap) changes what appears to be an act of nurturing into an act of aggression against the physical and discursive body of the subject.

In her essay "En/Gendering Spaces: The Poetry of Marlene Nourbese Philip and Pamela Mordecai", Elaine Savory asserts that "the text which runs along the page vertically is entirely in capital letters and describes a mother's tongue licking a newborn child clean of the white substance which covers its body. As she does this, the child falls quiet. Within these two different scripts and meanings, lies the poem, which takes the idea of the mother tongue and father tongue and plays them against each other . . . ."[23] The mother tongue, in this instance, is the same organ described in the multiple-choice exam as an organ similar to the penis, both a "tapering, blunt tipped, muscular, soft and fleshy organ".[24] The implicit critique of the father tongue, the nation(al) language which is said to be the voice of the larger community, is not only challenged but (dis)formed through NourbeSe Philip's engagement with the multiplicity of meanings and language forms in this poem. Once more the scientific discourse, which appears on a page by itself, offers another complication in how we are to interpret this act of "giving words". Distinguishing between the functions of Wernicke's and Broca's areas of the brain, NourbeSe Philip highlights the separateness of recognizing the spoken word and the act of actually speaking the word, while the "motor cortex", she tells us, "controls the muscles of speech".[25]

Though the mother's agency gives words to her daughter, it does not guarantee the context or conditions through which the daughter's utterances will be received, or the field of play into which they will enter. This s/place is a point where negotiations of power can, and have, dis/placed the female subject from her modes of expression. The edicts, therefore, play an important role in enforcing the historical terror that produced a father tongue. The question, then, of how women begin to articulate words, or try their tongues (which have been disciplined into submission), comes to the fore forcefully in NourbeSe Philip's collection. The engagement with the discursive terrain of colonialist discourses effectively asserts another aspect of the "trying" nature of language and the politics of "trying tongues" which resist at every turn when their authority is put under a critical lens. Her critical examination of the phrase *mother tongue* pushes the construction of the mother as progenitor of language. The question she raises – What do we call a language that is a foreign language (a foreign tongue)? – recognizes the role of power in circumventing that intimate act of tonguing and giving language.

Moreover, NourbeSe Philip's engagement with scientific discourse brings our attention to the complicity between science, sexism and racism. The poem's opening statement is meant to draw our attention to the "authority" of science and scientific discourse to shape how we think about language and identity.[26] The positioning of this passage in the centre of the page is significant for a number of reasons. First, it disrupts the tri-genre poetic in the first page of the poem without introduction, heading or any indication that it is related to the edict, fiction or poetry on the first page. Second, NourbeSe Philip's appropriation of this piece of scientific prose is an explicit commentary on the thematic of language and where it comes into being in the human brain. Last, and most important, is NourbeSe Philip's engagement with the findings of the learned doctors.

The Broca's and Wernicke's areas of the brain are responsible for different aspects of language and speech. Broca's area is named after Pierre-Paul Broca, a French surgeon and anthropologist, while Wernicke's area is named after the German neurologist Carl Wernicke. For the purposes of this essay, the significance of these parts of the brain lies not so much in how they function as in what happens when they do not function. When a patient suffers a trauma to the brain, in the form of either a blow or a stroke, these particular parts of the brain are extremely susceptible to what, in neurological parlance, is called aphasia. *Aphasia* refers to a group of language disorders that can occur when the language-dominant hemisphere of the brain is damaged.[27] If we return to the first page of NourbeSe Philip's poem, we can see a perfect example of this kind of language pattern:

> English
> is my mother tongue.
> A mother tongue is not
> not a foreign lan lan lang
> language
> l/anguish
> anguish
> – a foreign anguish. . . .
>
> I have no mother
> tongue
> no mother to tongue
> no tongue to mother
> to mother
> me[28]

This pattern, when read out loud, sounds similar to the speech of a patient who presents with symptoms of aphasia. The repetition in particular duplicates the series of words that, though seemingly related to one another, are not sequenced in a sensible order, like what neurologists would call meaningless neologisms. Neologisms, or newly coined words, have an interesting etymology: "all neologisms begin as slang, except in those branches of terminology where there is an established tradition of word coinage and redefinition".[29] If we look up the most notable references to these kinds of neologisms, we find examples that include broken English, lingua franca, confusion of tongues, dialect, idiom, accent and patois. In light of NourbeSe Philip's earlier assertions about the challenge she faces as a writer, the characterization by the good doctors Wernicke and Broca of aphasia as a form of illness complicates the relationship of the black subject to language and expression: it becomes defined through medical and social discourses.

If we consider the trauma and terror expressed through the edicts and enacted on the bodies of slaves, particularly female slaves, what are we to make of the Caribbean demotic in the face of several hundred years of scientific inquiry that has disciplined certain voices and expressions into the realm of psychosis? Aphasia in this instance can also be produced through sexual, linguistic and physical violence. We are asked, then, to consider the impact of being separated from your linguistic community and the impact it has on the "muscles of speech" or the tongue. Certainly there must be extensive damage to the language-dominant hemisphere of the brain. NourbeSe Philip notes, "for the African in the New World, our revelation to ourselves in the New World was simultaneous with a negative re-presentation of ourselves to ourselves, by a hostile imperialistic power, and articulated in a language endemically and etymologically hostile to our very existence". She says, therefore, that the Caribbean writer, rather than writing about kinky hair and flat noses, "should be writing about the language that kinked the hair and flattened the noses".[30]

By placing the scientific definitions in the same context as historical and social discourses, NourbeSe Philip closes the constructed gaps between the discourses of science as fact and as truth, creating a space for conceptualizing scientific discourses as both informed and produced by other social and cultural agendas. In so doing, she attempts to bridge the disciplines of history, sociology, anthropology, and medicine. Later, she appropriates Broca's and Wernicke's findings on differences in brain size (in a short scientific treatise on the left and right brain) as "proof" of the superiority of white males in comparison to "women, Blacks, and other peoples of colour", opening the sacred space of science and exposing it as overtly shaped by racist ideologies of the nineteenth century. The second edict appears later, one that considers a "cure" for any breach in the proclamation made earlier, that is, removal of the slave's tongue, "the offending organ", which is to be "hung on high in / a central place", as an example.[31] The discursive terror represented across these genres is pushed further when we consider the history of colonialism that constructed communities in order to prevent any means of communicating, while at the same time implementing a language used to define labour and oppression. Here, the father tongue needs to be read through the visual placement of the edict on the page. Its position as well as its visual appearance – in italics with its own heading – is meant to signify the authority of the *patria* ("law of the father") to dis/place the subject from its self-expression. The "space in between" also becomes a space of dismemberment, (dis)empowerment and disembodiment.

The examination format for investigating the function of the tongue[32] is particularly effective in the context of NourbeSe Philip's critique of language, science and racism, as it suggests that the practice of exercising choice presumes a certain relationship between power and authority in the knowledge of the subject matter. Each of the questions is skilfully crafted in order to highlight the similarities in the answers, depending on the perspective and vantage point of the reader. The inherent contradiction present in each selection highlights how the knowledge produced in various discourses and disciplines depends largely upon the agendas at work in the dissemination of this knowledge. The final selection in the multiple-choice exam draws all the choices in this question together to stress that the selections could be as equally true as false, depending on the agenda, perspective and position of authority from which these decisions are made. "Freedom" of choice in the poem therefore becomes a precarious issue, because the readers, like the colonized speaker of English, can only work out of their knowledge of a language that is at once their inheritance and their anguish. In this context, freedom can be read only through the implicit privileges upon which these discourses depend, much in the same manner that the freedom to search for a lost child presupposes a mother's right of possession of her body and her children. All choices are filtered through the authority of discursive communities, laws and landscapes that impose limits on freedom for black female subjects. The tongue, as an organ of taste, speech and expression is at the same time a part of the anatomy of oppression and exploitation. In the plantation economy, both linguistic oppression and sexual exploitation (en)act the language of violence and the law on the body of black female slaves, since black mothers equal black children, and black children are property. The tongue and the penis are one and the same in this act of rape – both violate the spaces "in between".

Contemporary Caribbean women's writing is concerned with de-centring the language and authority of the law of the land/nation/patria/father. Where previous debates about language and identity were based on a telos of being constructed through imperialist discourses, NourbeSe Philip and other women writers recast these debates in order to emphasize the relationship between language, expression and the process of be(com)ing. The emphasis on the continuity of movement, negotiations and articulations between subjects and their surroundings suggests that this motion is not aimed as an end but takes place in the interest of preserving the possibility of be(com)ing for black subjects. The shape and form of expression become more accessible and more flexible through the relational nature of exchange between mother tongues and father tongues. Rather than attempting to escape the prison house of colonialist discourses, NourbeSe Philip's poem subverts the logic of language to allow for multiple voiced expressions of identity, authority and power – speaking in tongues, as it were.

The emphasis on knowledge and language in contemporary Caribbean women's writing reflects the significance of addressing the law of the land/nation, which NourbeSe Philip describes as "nine-tenths possession, and one-tenth legitimization".[33] This is a significant refusal of institutionalized paradigms such as the Calibanesque tradition, in that it departs from the historical prison house of language approach to colonial discourse. Hence, the issue of liberatory capacity lies in the subject's ability to possess language through manipulating and negotiating the systems of dispersion. This refusal, however, is not meant to suggest that NourbeSe Philip's narratives are not engaged with these instituting systems. In fact, her engagement with "hard" science ensures a firm footing in one of the most authoritative institutions in the history of humankind. The links between "hard" science, anthropology and sociology become clearer, less attributable to occurrences based on a predetermined system of signs.

NourbeSe Philip identifies the task of the writer in relation to the processes of representation at work in various communities and contexts. This is a notable shift away from the notion of consolidated identities which reside and emerge within a particular set of historical or social circumstances (slavery, emancipation, post-colonialism). These processes, she argues, range across diverse landscapes of experiences:

> If we accept that living language continually encapsulates, reflects and refines the entire experiential life and world view of the tribe, the race, and consequently of society at large; and if we accept that the poet, the story-teller, the singer or balladeer (through their words), express this *process* in their work then we must accept that this process becomes one way in which the society continually accepts, integrates and transcends its experiences positive or negative. [emphasis added][34]

This genealogy of "living language" and the creative process of self-expression link the subject and her surroundings to processes that make translating her experiences through language possible. In so doing, the subject is able to transcend these experiences as part of the processes of be(com)ing. It is through these negotiations that these processes are legitimated, brought to bear on the lives of these historical subjects. Where previous debates about language and identity in Caribbean literature were based on a telos of being, NourbeSe Philip recasts this debate as one that requires us to consider the relationship between language, expression and the process of be(com)ing. The emphasis for NourbeSe Philip is on the continuity of movement, negotiations and articulations between the subject and her surroundings, not simply a process progressing towards an end. Her emphasis, therefore, is on the movement between discursive spaces and the possibilities which emerge as a result of engagement with the productive capacities of the imagination that make expression more accessible, more flexible through exchanges between mother tongues and father tongues.

Rather than conceptualizing the discourses of identity through what words "mean", NourbeSe Philip's texts argue for a relationship to language which permits subjects to "speak in tongues" that have emerged as a result of generations of "trying tongues" and have become the key to breaking silences. This process, however, cannot occur without re/membering stories, myths and figures and continually reintegrating experiences that have been disciplined out of our histories and landscapes. These discourses, according to NourbeSe Philip, are part of the "grammar of dissent" for unvoiced generations of blacks in the New World. Though unvoiced for generations, they are part of the performative aspects of language which emerge in the *kinopoesis* of the written word on the page.[35] Capturing this movement in written language can be achieved only by pressing back the boundaries that restrain genre, structure, form and, indeed, voice in literature.

Discussing the processes and objectives involved in the production of *She Tries Her Tongue; Her Silence Softly Breaks*, NourbeSe Philip asserts that her aim was to subvert the lyrical voice in order to make the text more "polyvocular". She recalls,

> Long after the completion of *She Tries Her Tongue: Her Silence Softly Breaks*, the question of how I would "read" these poems plagued me. The traditional poetry "reading" entails one person, most often the poet, standing before a group – most often the audience – and reading his or her words.

> What does a poet do when the work to be read requires several voices? Nothing. Except read those poems that are most conducive to being read in the traditional sense. Until one day a young student asks:
> "Would you read Universal Grammar for me?"
> "*I will if you will read it with me.*"
> Suddenly it all falls into place: I *had* been successful in subverting the lyric voice. I had so disrupted the lyric voice by interruptions, eruptions, digressions, and a variety of other techniques, that the text had now become a polyvocular text, requiring more than one voice to give voice to it.[36]

By subverting the lyrical voice in a textual context, NourbeSe Philip develops a model which disrupts what Édouard Glissant refers to as a "forced poetics" that is obsessed with silencing the "din" of discourse.[37] As a noun, *din* is a loud, annoying noise. As a verb, the word *din* is the act of forcing information into a person by continually repeating it. NourbeSe Philip preserves this *din* in its entire complexity of meanings by manipulating the visual layout of her text so that it reproduces the multiplicity of voices being heard at once. Once more her emphasis on the rhythm and movement of these sounds reflects the systematic production of meaning in the Caribbean demotic. Each reading, hearing, voicing of her text therefore represents a new experience between speakers and audiences.

For Caribbean women writers, this mode of expression creates another continuum of representation for Caribbean subjects. However, in the face of history, one is left with a similar problematic in Caribbean literature. If representing the i-mages and experiences of blacks in the New World requires a form such as a demotic, can Caribbean histories be written out of such a model? If language is a reflection of the environments that subjects inhabit, is there a model for writing a history that can accommodate the rapid movements which have shaped Caribbean reality? If, as NourbeSe Philip argues, the voice that speaks the subject and its experiences is best expressed through this polyvocular narrative form, what are the implications for how we write the histories of black subjects in the diaspora? Can history be written with a similar subversive, creative voice and still maintain its disciplinary, social and cultural authority? Or do such narratives leave the realm of history and migrate towards fiction because it is not rooted in "facts" which can be substantiated by others in the same voice? If this polyvocular voice is the modality for expressing the realities of black subjects, how does this performativity manifest itself in the processes of be(com)ing in the world?

Notes

1. M. NourbeSe Philip, "The Absence of Writing or How I Almost Became a Spy", in *She Tries Her Tongue, Her Silence Softly Breaks* (Charlottetown, PE: Ragweed, 1989), 16.
2. M. NourbeSe Philip, "Dis Place – The Space Between", in *A Genealogy of Resistance and Other Essays* (Toronto: Mercury Press, 1997), 101.
3. See, for example, the works of Paule Marshall, Elizabeth Nunez, Dionne Brand and Sylvia Wynter.
4. For example, in her collection of poetry *Rotten Pomerack* (London: Virago, 1992), Merle Collins writes a poem titled "No Dialects Please" in response to a call for submissions to a poetry contest. The advertisement, according to Collins, ends by stating that submissions in "dialects" would not be considered because "after all we are British". The implicit assertion that those who might speak or write in dialects – English dialects – were first and foremost not British, and not a part of the British landscape, would become a major obstacle facing Caribbean writers (particularly women) in the 1990s.
5. Particularly in the case of Erna Brodber, *Louisiana* (London: New Beacon, 1994); NourbeSe Philip, *She Tries Her Tongue*; Maryse Condé, *Crossing the Mangrove*, trans. Richard Philcox (New York: Anchor-Doubleday, 1995); and Merle Collins, *Angel* (Seattle: Seal, 1988).
6. Belinda Edmondson, *Making Men: Gender, Literary Authority and Women's Writing in Caribbean Narrative* (Durham, NC: Duke University Press, 1999), 83.
7. NourbeSe Philip, "Dis Place", 77.
8. NourbeSe Philip provides the following endnote to "Dis Place" (ibid., 110): "Anthony Giddens in *The Transformation of Intimacy* writes that in 'pre-modern development of Europe rape flourished mainly on the margins, at the margins, at the frontiers, in colonies, in states of nature amongst marauding invading armies.' Allegations of mass rape of Bosnian Muslim women in 1992 by Serbian forces, as a way of spreading terror and asserting control, suggest that these practices defy a simple linkage to 'pre-modern' times. In a *Ms.* editorial, March/April 1993, on the issue of rape of Bosnian women, Robin Morgan asks: 'If rape in war is a weapon, what is it in peace time?' "
9. Ibid., 75–76.
10. NourbeSe Philip provides the following endnote to "Dis Place" (ibid., 111): "Resolutions from the Council of War. Article of War by Governor, Sir Thomas Modyford and Council, August 15, 1665, occasioned by 'the Rebellion of the Carmahaly Negroes and Other Outlying Negroes'."
11. Harriet Jacobs, *Incidents in the Life of a Slave Girl* (New York: Dover, 2001). Jacobs's narrative includes numerous references to her sexual abuse and exploitation at the

hands of her master. Writing to an audience of white women, Jacobs has to maintain the ideals of the "cult of true womanhood", which denied the sexuality of all women and held black slave women to a standard of respectability which was impossible to achieve, given their conditions as slaves. Jacobs is forced to finesse the explicit details of her abuse to gain the trust and empathy of her reading audience.

12. Edmondson, *Making Men,* 142.
13. Edmondson provides the following endnote to *Making Men* (ibid., 200): "See Sigmund Freud, 'The Uncanny' ('Das Unheimliche'), in *Standard Edition of the Complete Psychological Works of Sigmund Freud,* trans. and ed. James Strachey (London: Hogarth Press, 1955), quoted in Samantha Heigh, 'The Return of Africa's Daughters: Negritude and the Gendering of Exile' (paper presented at the African Literature Association Conference, Guadeloupe, 1993), 13. I am indebted to Samantha Heigh's reading of Irigaray, Benstock, and Freud in my teasing out the meanings of exile and 'motherland' here."
14. Edmondson cites the following source in her footnote: Shari Benstock, "Expatriate Modernism", in *Women's Writing and Exile,* ed. Mary Lynn Broe and Angela Ingrham (Chapel Hill: University of North Carolina Press, 1989), 25.
15. NourbeSe Philip, "Absence of Writing", 16.
16. The term *i-mage* instead of *image* is used by NourbeSe Philip both to represent the deconstructive elements of her engagement with language and to stress the "Rastafarian practice of privileging the 'I' in many words. This unconventional use of orthography enables her to represent the processes of giving meaning through the experience of the 'I' which possesses the language and, therefore, the ability to engage in i-magining or i-magination" (ibid., 15–16).
17. Ibid., 18.
18. See Sandra Pouchet Paquet, *The Novels of George Lamming* (Kingston: Heinemann, 1982); Ngũgĩ Wa Thiong'o, *Decolonizing the Mind: The Politics of Language in African Literature* (London: Heinemann, 1986); Patrick Taylor, *The Narrative of Liberation: Perspectives on Afro-Caribbean Literature, Popular Culture, and Politics* (Ithaca, NY: Cornell University Press, 1989); and Margaret Paul Joseph, *Caliban in Exile: The Outsider in Caribbean Fiction* (New York: Greenwood Press, 1992).
19. NourbeSe Philip, "Absence of Writing", 23.
20. NourbeSe Philip provides the following endnote in "Absence of Writing", 28: Fred L. Stanley and Louis Pratt, eds., *Conversations with James Baldwin* (University Press of Mississippi, 1989).
21. Brenda Carr, "To 'Heal the Word Wounded': Agency and the Materiality of Language and Form in M. NourbeSe Philip's *She Tries Her Tongue, Her Silence Softly Breaks*", *Studies in Caribbean Literature* 19, no. 1 (1994): 72–94.
22. NourbeSe Philip, "Discourse on the Logic of Language", in *She Tries Her Tongue,* 56.

23. Elaine Savory, "En/Gendering Spaces: The Poetry of Marlene Nourbese Philip and Pamela Mordecai", in *Framing the Word: Gender and Genre in Caribbean Women's Writing*, ed. Joan Anim-Addo (London: Whiting and Birch, 1996), 18.
24. NourbeSe Philip, "Discourse", 59.
25. Ibid., 57.
26. Ibid.
27. D. Joanne Lynn, Herbert B. Newton and Alexander D. Rae-Grant, *The 5-Minute Neurology Consult* (Philadelphia: Lippincott, Williams and Wilkins, 2003), 2.
28. NourbeSe Philip, "Discourse", 56.
29. Benjamin J. Sadock and Virginia A. Sadock, *Kaplan and Sadock's Concise Textbook of Clinical Psychiatry*, 9th ed. (Philadelphia: Lippincott, Williams and Wilkins, 2002), 250.
30. NourbeSe Philip, "Absence of Writing", 20.
31. NourbeSe Philip, "Discourse", 58.
32. Ibid., 59.
33. NourbeSe Philip, "Absence of Writing", 21.
34. Ibid., 14.
35. NourbeSe Philip, "African Roots and Continuities: Race, Space and the Poetics of Moving", in *Genealogy of Resistance*, 231. NourbeSe Philip coins this term in relation to Ezra Pound's systematization of languages according to their varying qualities. She notes that Pound, in his work *The ABC of Writing*, defined languages in this manner: "phanopoesis: beautiful to look at (Chinese); melopoesis: beautiful sounding (Greek); and logopoeisis: logical (English)". To this system of classification, NourbeSe Philip adds her term *kinopoesis*: dynamic and quick-moving (African languages and their demotics).
36. NourbeSe Philip, "Notes on the Completion of Potentiality", in *Genealogy of Resistance*, 126.
37. Édouard Glissant, *Caribbean Discourse: Selected Essays*, trans. J. Michael Dash (Charlottesville: Virginia University Press, 1989), 123. Glissant uses this term in his discussion of the manner in which syntax, as well as language, was imposed during communication between master and slave. Glissant argues that for Caribbean people the word takes on its meaning from sound or the pitch of a word as well as a continuous stream of language, which to white slave masters resonated as "unstructured" use of language. NourbeSe Philip has commented about this quality in Trinidadian English, describing it as a "language that moves, like the Carnival band, through space rhythmed by time" ("African Roots and Continuities", 203).

CHAPTER 3

More Than the Sum of Its Parts
Reflections on Caribbean Language in a Globalizing Age

▸ VALERIE YOUSSEF

Introduction

Language conveys the culture of a people. It represents them. It establishes their identity. It conveys their heritage. Yet often it escapes the net of attention within cultural studies, which focuses more readily on literature and the arts than on language. From the first half of the twentieth century, anthropologists such as Edward Sapir and Benjamin Lee Whorf were pointing out to us the inseparability of culture from the language which represents that culture. We have recognized since then that, where cultures differ and one language represents them, language becomes adapted to suit the particular needs of each people it represents. For these reasons it is critical that we all have an absolute sense of each of the languages which are our inheritance and of the particular ways in which they convey Caribbean cultures.

This chapter focuses, perhaps surprisingly, on Caribbean Standard English (CSE), more particularly its sub-variety Trinbagonian Standard English (TSE), simply because it is a variety of which we vigorously deny ownership. When we examine Caribbean language, we talk exclusively about the Creole, we describe only the Creole and we totally resist regarding the standard variety as our own. We hold that it belongs to the American, to the Australian, to the Englishman; in the very act of speaking a local variety of Standard English (SE), we ask one another, "If there is a local Standard, what is it?"

Clearly we need to adjust this perception. As much as we need our own language variety – the Creole – in an exclusive sense, we equally need our own variety in an inclusive sense. SE, which stands as the twenty-first century's international preference and the majority language of Internet communication, fills that role. As barriers between nations tumble down as a result of an ever-encroaching globalization trend, we cannot continue to regard SE merely as the language of the Other, but must embrace it as our own and have a clear recognition of its integrity as a sub-variety of International Standard English. To embrace positively the increased connectivity among societies – which in the broadest sense is what globalization and its transculturation effects are about – we need an absolute sense of nationhood, represented linguistically by both Creole and Standard.

Background

It was when describing the spectrum of language varieties spoken in Tobago[1] that this reality first hit me. The language, elicited from persons in a variety of walks of life and recorded the length and breadth of Tobago for the University of the West Indies Tobago Language Project (1990–98), included in many cases a flawless SE. Yes, there were some who spoke only the basilectal Creole, but most commanded mesolectal Creole, and many the acrolect, a local variety of SE with its own distinctive phonology, some minor distinctive features of grammar and some distinctive vocabulary. When I tried informally to convince others of this Trinbagonian variety, however, they failed to recognize it. I was obliged to make a recording of a subset of my own third-year students, randomly selected and including both Trinidadians and Tobagonians, speaking in a seminar class session. This discourse was transcribed to provide further evidence of our Standard variety.

But if we have to be convinced of our Standard, what of the global giants beyond the territory, whose new imperialism – one of the negative threats of globalization – demands recognition and counter-thrust at every level, including the linguistic? In an age when English has become the global language, we cannot continue to regard it as the property of the United Kingdom or the United States of America, or any other single territory: *It is the language of all those who use it at an official level, of all those who acquire it as a major discourse mode.*

There is a real linguistic imperialism which needs to be vigorously countered. Each semester, University of the West Indies staff members are beset with requests from new graduates to comment on their level of English competence as part of their applications to enter universities in the metropole. Despite written confirmation by university staff, the students are then required to take the Test of English as a Foreign Language or some other English language test to demonstrate their competence – in a variety they command as well as any US citizen. As evidenced further by an initiative by then US president George W. Bush to bring literacy to the Caribbean, US officialdom in every sphere has no sense of the linguistic range and proficiency of Caribbean peoples. They assume that so-called Third World peoples are ignorant of "their" language; they act, without even realizing they do, as the "superpower", bestowing their patrimony on the world at large. In face of this, we need to have a clear view of ourselves.

The Politics of Language: Standard English and Co-varieties in Perspective

Language Ownership

Where does English stand today, and why do we refuse to claim it as our own? It is a fact that "traditionally, most people have regarded languages as ethnic and communicative monoliths, regardless of any regional or other differences between them . . . . By and large we tend to think 'to each nation its language'."[2] This partially explains our mindset. We regard the Creole as ours and we regard the Standard as the property of the colonizers, old and new. Though it was mainly non-standard varieties which came to the Caribbean,[3] the notion of rulership affects our minds particularly strongly. So we see ourselves with a history of SE as the dominant language, the language of the oppressor, and reject ownership of it ourselves for these very connotations. Out of an early position of enforced inferiority and oppression, Caribbean societies have worked actively and consistently to establish their Creoles as independent varieties, not just because of their real linguistic qualities but also because of the psychological burden that is lifted by so doing. In establishing our own language, we become an independent people speaking an independent language. However, we deny a part of the reality that we have evolved our own variety of Standard that is ours just as much as the Creole.

We need to move in step with present-day reality and to recognize that, in a globalizing age, there can be no ownership of English beyond its being the property of all those who command it. Modern communications have evolved to a level such that we need a language of maximum communicability; experiments with languages such as Esperanto failed because English was already halfway to fulfilling that global function when the need arose for creation of a global language. Spread first through colonialism, it was ultimately retained in the majority of newly independent countries because it militated against the subnational nationalisms represented by different language groups within vast nation-states. In Nigeria, as well as in India, inter-language struggling could be resolved by the retention of neutral, external English as an official variety. English today has a special status as the official (or unstated official) language in more than seventy countries. With the vast increase in travel worldwide, with the establishment of a whole range of international political institutions like the UN-related bodies, with the establishment of a world media and the Internet, there was a need for a lingua franca. The language ready for usage was English, a language which an estimated 300 million people speak as a native language but which has an estimated total of between 1.2 and 1.5 billion speakers worldwide today – more even than Chinese, with an estimated 1.1 billion speakers.[4]

It is at this point that we recognize the need to change our perceptions. In the words of our own former University of the West Indies chancellor Sir Shridath Ramphal, "It is not the language of imperialism; it is the language we have seen that has evolved out of a history . . . whose legacies we must use to good effect . . . there is no retreat from English as the world language, no retreat from an English-speaking world."[5] SE is a real part of the linguistic repertoire of anglophone Caribbean people, who have the absolute right to embrace it as their own, since it is shared and used as one of its native varieties.

A Minority Variety

As in other English-speaking territories, SE is a minority variety, spoken largely by the educated, but this is the reality in all SE-speaking territories,[6] and we must recognize this instead of persistently downgrading ourselves. David Crystal has argued that most English-speakers are bidialectal in a local variety and the Standard, and that there is the capacity for developing a World Standard Spoken English, which we would use for international communication alongside the other two identified.[7] This identification of at least three varieties as being peculiar to each English-speaking state fits the Caribbean situation exactly.

Let us examine a single example. While the Gaelic of the Highlands of Scotland and Ireland is widely recognized as a separate language from English, there are also varieties such as Scots – the vernacular variety of the Lowlands of Scotland – which are worth comparing to Creole varieties in the extent of their diversity from SE. Scots has its own grammar, as well as pronunciation and vocabulary, and can trace a separate historical development from its origins in the Anglian kingdom of Northumbria. It has dialects of its own and has been recognized as a language in its own right by the European Union of Lesser-Used Languages. Finally, its less educated speakers are uncertain about the cut-off points between Scots and English, and the midway variety has a nebulous status. Tom MacArthur makes direct comparisons between Scots and African American, Jamaican and Tok Pisin, noting that "these varieties have a comparable vigour and uneasy and unstable continua that shade into internationally accepted usage. *They also have the same sense of an insider speech which those outside cannot easily follow*" (emphasis added).[8] It is almost as if he were describing the Caribbean language experience, but the majority of Caribbean speakers are unaware of the diversity of UK varieties and thus do not begin to compare that situation to their own.

In relation to these varieties, SE no longer receives homage as a superior entity; diversity among different standards, at least at the level of pronunciation, is recognized and accepted. All native varieties of SE are accepted as equally valid, and non-native varieties, such as Indian English and numerous African forms, are gaining increasing credibility as international varieties. To quote Anthony Hughes in his *Online English Grammar*:

> There no longer is, if there ever was, a standard English to which all speakers should pay homage. Now we recognize as legitimate variations American English, Australian English, British English, Indian English, there is even a variety called Singlish from Singapore.... For the first time a natural language has attained the status of an international (Universal) language, essentially for cross-cultural communication ... this new role of English puts a burden on its speakers which demands *attitudinal readjustments*.[9] [emphasis added]

In the Caribbean, then, we can identify a CSE, which Richard Allsopp, in his *Dictionary of Caribbean English Usage*, describes as follows: "The literate English of educated nationals of Caribbean territories and their spoken English such as is natural in formal social contexts.... the total body of regional lexicon and usage bound to a common core of syntax and morphology shared with Internationally Accepted English, but aurally distinguished as a discrete type by certain phonological features."[10] Manfred Görlach diagrammatically constructs a circular model of English usage worldwide, with regional Standard Englishes occurring as an inner circle; CSE is represented as part of this inner circle.[11] CSE is then a subset of internationally accepted English, and Trinbagonian English is a subset of this variety; at another level again, we might want to distinguish Trinidadian from Tobagonian Standard. The outer circle in the diagram includes the individual Creole varieties and local non-standards. For the most part, however, as indicated by Allsopp's statement above, the differences at these sub-levels would be applicable to pronunciation.

The Linguistic Reality and Range of Trinidad and Tobago

Today the normative community is more open-ended than in the past. Systems of relationship within the community are multiplex: we interact within different circles of people in each part of our lives. Where formerly people lived among the people they worked with and extended familial relations characterized many living communities, today many persons encounter distinctly separate groups as they move from home to work and to recreation. Inevitably dialect divergence is the norm. Moreover, non-discrete register variation is normative.

Our expectation would be that a speaker balancing language appropriately would shift to incorporation of some Creole speech when moving towards a consultative register for semiformal conversation on serious topics, and more so when moving towards casual speech. But if the speaker were in the company of mono-varietal Standard speakers unfamiliar with the Creole, the shift would be unlikely. In all but formal spoken language, people actually mix varieties, including some Creole with the Standard, but the mixing is systematic, producing a blended variety which captures the right level of formality and freshness, calling on the symbolic values of both codes in producing the complete utterance. To use only one code would be to diminish the communicative range of the speaker's capacity.

Hereunder I include spoken extracts from a young Tobagonian woman educated at Bishop's High School, Tobago's most prestigious secondary school. Not only does her language exhibit the full range of Trinbagonian varieties, her analysis of the language situation and her own experience within it provides a picture of the current language scene and the language attitudes which support it. She tells of the lack of exposure many people have to the full language range of the community, making for less code-switching than she is capable of producing. She speaks of the partial knowledge of SE of some children in school, as well as their teachers, and of an external world value system which causes Tobagonians outside Tobago to lose their distinctive speech. All in all, she recognizes the need to shift one's speech in different situations, not because of a lack of pride in the Creole but rather because of the existence of appropriacy norms which determine what is applicable in any given situation.

1. I feel that, in a situation where it becomes necessary, you should be able to shift without too much problems, so there are times when you would say, "Well, that is not how it is done." But not because you despise what you grew up with . . . . A lot of the young people you would find dropped out of high school or finished at fifteen, and they feel that they have to impress. Maybe I did drop out along the line (*laughs*). I did drop out, but I have lived in Trinidad for a while and I have been out of Trinidad and Tobago once or twice as well, but I have seen things that indicate to me that it is not necessary. Because when you **bounce up** on a Jamaican **is a Jamaican is a Jamaican**.

She recognizes language attitude as a significant factor which for her was not so developed as a child.

2. As a child **growin** up you **doesn** really be so aware. I could remember a time when I was goin to high school – I **get took**. The teacher **call** on me to say something – English class in full swing – an when me start **fu rattle** away the story, she come, "Phyllis, you are in English class." So **me ha: to come change** the whole story, put **am** in English **fu she**.

[*As a child growing up you aren't really aware. I could remember a time when I was going to high school – I got taken. The teacher called on me to say something –the English class was in full swing – and when I started to rattle off the story, she came to say, "Phyllis, you are in English class." So I had to change the whole story and put it in English for her.*]

As she speaks of having to tell a story in class, she shows how she adopted the Creole to illustrate how well that variety suits an oral narrative. This creates ambivalence in the child as to which variety to use: the code demanded of the setting and situation, which does not entail immediacy, or the one of narrative discourse within the community. This kind of dilemma still creates problems for Trinbagonian students today.[12]

The speaker's wide range of production is indicated by the following narrative extract:

3. **Me dere in dem** [photos], I look. Then **me start** to write a little letter. Me hear somebody a call. "Marnin, Good marnin." **Me want fu know** who come disturb me this hour in the morning. And then the **house not sweep**. So people **a come**. They **a come** see this **nasty ouse**. You can beat that? So me **gæn** out now. So you **hafto try fu play nice** an say, "Well, okay." **You kyan shame again, eh?** You **hafto** put on King's English: "Have a seat" – you know, this kinda way. **I try fu write** a little love letter. **Mi nah write, eh? Me a try fu mamaguy** somebody, **tief dey head** to see if they **go send** a little ticket **fu me**.

[*I was there in them. Then I started to write a little letter. I heard somebody calling, "Morning, good morning." I wanted to know who was coming to disturb me at this hour in the morning. And the house is not even swept. So people are coming. They are coming to see this nasty house. Can you beat that? So I went out now. So you have to try to play nice and say, "Well, okay."' You can't be shamed again, can you? You have to put on the King's English. "Have a seat" – you know, this kind of way. I tried to write a little love letter. Normally, I don't* write, eh? I'm trying to flatter someone, to "steal his head" to see if he is going to send a little ticket for me.]

This is the longest Creole extract the speaker produces. She selects it for a very personal stream-of-consciousness narrative, indicating that this language variety is her choice for matters of a personal and emotional nature.

Notwithstanding the above, however, there are contexts where SE alone may be used and called upon, just as there are those for exclusive use of one or another Creole variety. What distinguishes a member of a speech community is recognition of which variety (or varieties) is appropriate to which situation, regardless of whether the speaker can actually produce them or not. The reality, however, is that Trinbagonians more often produce the Standard than they themselves acknowledge. I give three short extracts below:

4. **Teacher**: I don't want to be offensive to anybody – we must think twice before we speak once. I think what is responsible for that is the inexperience of some teachers on the staff . . . number one, and secondly, the commitment you had some years ago. I'm not quite sure that commitment is still present in some teachers: commitment to their work and their pupils.
    Researcher: What about the calibre of the students?
    Teacher: Well, I said before the standard has fallen . . . . One of the reasons, I think, a teacher should be an exemplar, a person setting an example, somebody you should look up to, and in many instances I don't think . . . in few instances would they find persons who are exemplary in their conduct.

In the above extract, a retired headmaster is talking in his own home with two researchers from the University of the West Indies, one a foreigner.

5. **Lawyer**: Dr Williams brought in a new era there in education. He came to the reach of the poor man, you know. It's like education was there but it was just for **who could have afforded it**, but now it came down and everybody who – most people who would not have had that same opportunity before . . . now it was not only for the middle class and so on; it came down to any and everybody once you had the ability.

Here, a lawyer in his early sixties is commenting on the shift to education for all. He is speaking to the foreign researcher in his office. In bold type are paralectal features close to the acrolect: the use of *who* as a subject pronoun without the necessity for demonstrative *those*; the use of *could have* for *could*.

6. Well, **dat** was still to come. For the past twenty years the administration who are presently in power have neglected the people of Bethel in terms of laying the necessary infrastructure, improving roads, community centre and these kinds of hard-core facilities . . . And the candidate who is here won, she is here and she **have been** working with the community for a great number of years and people are seeing that she **have de** potential for change and thus, you know, they have elected that person.

In the above extract, a sixth-form youth is discussing the elections; in bold are two "errors" of agreement and the use of *de* for *the*, a stereotypical feature of local phonology. It is arguable that the speaker is here shifting from SE to upper-mesolectal Creole and that the features identified are evidence of mixing varieties, not the production of erroneous Standard.

What surprised me more was a discourse recorded in a University of the West Indies (St Augustine) classroom, in which eight third-year female students spoke briefly on the tragedy of 9/11 and then disputed aspects of the political scenario among themselves. In a thirty-minute interaction encompassing heated discussion as well as monologic speech, the only diversions from SE were to be found in five irrealis "errors", three errors of agreement and a single omission of auxiliary *is*, a casual mesolectal variant of present continuous speech which I argue later may be accepted as local Standard. Only parts of this discourse are set out below, since it is too long to include in its entirety:

7. But I think somebody from Afghanistan or any one of these nations would argue, "Why didn't America do that in the beginning? Why didn't America do that in the first place?" Why is it that Americans always use military might? And don't believe that because we are not bombarded by what America does that they don't do it. They do it continuously. I think what Tricia was also speaking about is the situation that exists between the Muslims and the Jews in Palestine – that whole Palestinian issue. America has always used military might; they've always been supplying Israel with weapons, and nobody talks about that. Why should the Afghans use talk now, when the Americans have always used military might? If Bin Laden was an American, he'd be a hero . . .

8. I have been living with an American-based world power because that's what I've been born into, and that's what I've grown up into and that's what I've been socialized into, so I can accept it. Certainly if I were born with an Islamic power being a world power, that's the same way I'd feel about it.

Even at the phonological level, there were only eight tokens of -*in* for -*ing*, and minimal usage of non-standard vowel variants. One student, who has lived her whole life in a small village in South Trinidad and whose speech is more consistently Creole than the rest, retained almost totally consistent Standard grammar. As a university community, we commonly speak as if in despair over our students' command of SE. An extract like this, however, recorded quite arbitrarily, shows clearly that the Standard is alive and well among a subset of tertiary-level young people. If we deny this, we deny a part of the Trinbagonian's range of linguistic competence, which is as critically Caribbean as the Creole.

Comparisons Across Standards, with a Focus on Trinidad and Tobago

There is a similar level of variation between British (BSE) and American (ASE) Standards as between Caribbean Standard varieties and the metropolitan models.[13] What is clear is that, even within Standards, a modicum of variation is realistically accepted. A few examples of the kind of grammatical alternation often exhibited, and in common with those found in ASE and BSE, are listed below.

Perfect and SE'ed Alternation

It is noted by Peter Trudgill and Jean Hannah that ASE makes greater use of past tenses in contexts where BSE would use present perfect.[14] They cite in particular the recent past and perfect of persistent situation; for example, *He hasn't eaten his dinner yet* in BSE might be rendered *He didn't eat his dinner yet* in AE. The same form is found in TSE. Don Winford has shown the way in which different subcategories of present perfect have been absorbed differentially into speaker competence in Trinidad, such that resultative contexts (and modals) attract perfect marking the most, while the persistent situation and experiential past attract other SE forms.[15] Since the perfect is representative of a cluster of meanings rather than just one core meaning,[16] it is to be expected that the range of subcategorial meanings will interact differently across the range of Englishes according to how they correspond and relate to other dialectal varieties within each territory.[17]

Differential Usage of Would for Past Habitual

Trudgill and Hannah also indicate that *would* is more common for the habitual past in American than in British English, where *used to* takes precedence.[18] It is unclear whether this is a statistically supported observation. Certainly there is variation in the use of these two forms for past habituality in Trinidad and Tobago, and specific differences have been observed in Tobago between older (over sixty-five) and younger (under twenty-five) speakers, with the former using *would* and the younger using *used to* almost exclusively.[19] Both are accepted as Standard, but *would* is clearly more formal and more readily observed in classical literature and writing generally.

Prepositional Reference

Another area of grammar which displays variation is that of prepositional reference. Trudgill and Hannah compare ASE *in back of* with BSE *behind* or *at the back of*, ASE *quarter of* and BSE *quarter to*.[20] Peter Louwenberg reports *agreeing* without the preposition *with* for BSE, but *approximate to* for BSE and with no preposition following in ASE.[21] Verbal particle variation in TSE includes *to go by* as a most salient form when one visits a person's home: for example, *I am going by Jo-Anne tonight*. In a similar context we may compare ASE *visit with* to BSE *visit*. It is also common to speak of *living on* a hall of residence in TSE rather than *living in*.

Collectives and Non-count Nouns

Alternation in the range of collective and non-countable nouns is found wherever they occur; collective nouns within ASE regularly take singular verbs and pronouns, whereas Trudgill and Hannah note that they take the plural in BSE: for example, *Your team are doing well this year, aren't they?*[22] Louwenberg has made the point that worldwide there is a tendency for the class of collectives as well as count versus non-count nouns to vary, and that the tendency of "new Englishes" such as Nigerian and Indian to embrace such forms as *furnitures* is not limited to non-native varieties but also occurs within native ones; specifically he quotes an American usage of *a digital equipment*.[23] Trudgill and Hannah also report for ASE *Good accommodations are hard to find*.[24] This way of carving up semantic space differently is clearly common worldwide; in Trinidad and Tobago, commonly heard forms include *equipments* and *furnitures*.

Unmarked Adverbials

Adverbial alternation exists in ASE, with a casual non-*ly* form being used quite frequently as well as in the Caribbean. The same is true of TSE: for example, *He's driving real fast*.

Uninverted Questions

Like both BSE and ASE, TSE accommodates uninverted questions in more casual speech, for example, *You went to the cinema?* Casual speech worldwide is characterized by an economy which leads us to mark functions once rather than twice or more in cases where more formal usage of the language demands more. The intonation pattern which distinguishes a question allows it to be quite distinctive without inversion. There are, additionally, some few specifically Caribbean additional adaptations.

The Range of Present Continuous

The use of present continuous for perceptions results in, for example, *I'm hearing you*. CSEs, including TSE, are characterized by a slightly different subdivision of verbs with regard to progressivity. Temporary states, perceptions and conditions are marked by present progressive, allowing forms like *Where are you living?* rather than *Where do you live?* and *Are you hearing me?* as opposed to *Can you hear me?* If we examine the semantics of these verb types closely, we recognize that this division actually gives consistency to the marking of non-permanent conditions by the progressive.

Use of Had in Remote-Past Contexts

The use of superficially past perfect forms as calques on Creole structures – for example, *I had set you the assignment last week* – is quite common. This kind of usage could be termed a paralectal feature of Caribbean varieties of SE. It is used by many speakers in contexts which demand Standard, even when the speaker also uses *had* fluently on the past perfect pattern. It emanates from the remote past range of meaning associated with *bin* and *did* in the Creole but now operates at the Standard level, not just through erroneous usage of *had* but also through the filling of a semantic gap for speakers who shift between varieties and are faced with non-equivalence of categories in the tense-aspect system when so doing.

Hypothetical Reference

Trudgill and Hannah report differences in hypothetical usage between British and American: ASE allows forms like *I wish I would have done it* where BSE uses *I wish I had done it*.[25] *Would* is more widely used for the future in TSE than in ASE and BSE; and it is common to say, for example, *The meeting would be held at ten o' clock*. There is clear influence from the Creole here, since that variety has an irrealis system which does not distinguish between definite and hypothetical future, making the distinction a little problematic for Creole speakers. It is possible to see such a form as a semantic extension, however, which exhibits no more deviation from the norm than does the ASE form *I wish I would have done it*. Moreover, it is worth observing that more "polite" forms of English tend to exaggerate and overuse *would* and *should*.

"Misuse" of Tenses in a Sequence of Tenses

These last relate to confusion as to the use of *will* and *would* and *can* and *could*, since in the Creole *would* and *could* have a much wider range of applicability, as noted above, in a unified irrealis form. Like the previous feature, they may be regarded as paralectal. An example is found in the following: *They tended to assume that the lecturer will not understand Jamaican Creole.*

There are, as with all varieties of language, vocabulary innovations in TSE which emanate from its history. Amerindian, African, Indic and other cultures have all contributed to Trinidad and Tobago's chequered history, and innovations were also created when the Creole language came into being. In many cases, items have passed through more than one language, for example, *arepa* – originally Amerindian, then Spanish and today a part of TSE. It has been possible to codify the features of the Caribbean Standard lexicon in Allsopp's *Dictionary of Caribbean Usage*, which is an authoritative and welcome guide to Caribbean varieties and is available worldwide. Although speakers of TSE differ widely in their estimation of the terms which may be considered Standard, contexts of usage ultimately settle these issues. Terms of the type listed would be included in conversation up to the most formal level because of their national recognition and unique referential meaning; they would need to be explained to a "foreigner", although not necessarily to another Caribbean person.

As for phonology, the major difference in consonants at the Standard level is the reduction of consonant clusters, particularly, for example, *walkin* for *walking* and *correk* for *correct*. In addition there is the very salient use of /t/ for /θ/ and /d/ for /ð/. At the Standard spoken level, these are very commonly heard today.

Among the vowel sounds, there is homophony between the vowels in such words as *beer* and *bear*; both are rendered as /'ɛ:/. There is a lack of length distinction between /æ/ and /a:/. This is eliminated not just in words where there is a clear orthographic difference, as in *pack* and *park*, but also more generally. Similarly /I/ is often rendered as /i:/ initially. These variations in no way affect understanding, although speakers have sensitivity to the stereotypical /t/ and /d/ and tend to "correct" them in "foreign" company.

Conclusions

Overall we recognize a complex communicative competence in the Caribbean, with young children learning to mix varieties appropriately from age two. Speakers may acquire two or three codes fully, but it is likely that they may acquire at least one only partially. Many contexts will demand mixed usage but a few will demand the use of one variety. With all this, there is a need to recognize not only Caribbean creoles but also Caribbean Standard varieties, as well as the unique modes of interaction which balance among them. We have to acknowledge incomplete mastery in some cases and the presence of paralectal features in Standard contexts in others, but these are inevitable results of intense language contact and should not detract from the fact that there is a valid SE variety.

As noted earlier, there is a strong tendency among Caribbean people to resist recognition of a local Standard, out of an inherent propensity for downgrading what is their own and upgrading the metropolitan model. In order to take its rightful place on the global stage, however, the region must have an accurate view of its own range of competence. Examination of the range within the Standard variety in use reveals that it is no more "different" than American Standard is from British, and that the real difference lies in perceptions rather than in the language itself.

A difference in the local situation is the intense mixing of Creole with Standard which occurs at all except the most formal levels, but this mixing in itself is not random but rule-governed. Because the Creole serves important functions within society, systematic code-mixing goes on constantly between the two varieties; individuals seek a balance of varieties which will mesh with the precise stylistic appropriacy demands of the given situation. The selective use of Creole in high places should not be derided as lack of knowledge of the Standard but rather as part of the effective balancing which is the essence of true communicative competence. Ultimately, the language competence which serves the Trinidad and Tobago community best entails fluency in both SE and the Creole, and the capacity to mix between them. With such competence individuals can function effectively in any local as well as international setting, and this should be their aim in a rapidly globalizing world.

Notes

1. Winford James and Valerie Youssef, *The Languages of Tobago: Genesis, Structure and Perspectives* (St Augustine: School of Continuing Studies, University of the West Indies, 2002).
2. Tom MacArthur, *The English Languages* (Cambridge: Cambridge University Press, 1998), 32.
3. Barbara Lalla and Jean D'Costa, *Language in Exile: Three Hundred Years of Jamaican Creole* (Tuscaloosa: Alabama University Press, 1990).
4. Milton A. Turner, "The World's Most Widely Spoken Languages" (Cleveland, OH: St Ignatius High School, 2006), http://www2.ignatius.edu/faculty/turner/languages.htm, using data from Raymond G. Gordon, ed., *Ethnologue: Languages of the World,* 15th ed. (Dallas, TX: SIL International, 2005), http://www.ethnologue.com.
5. Shridath Ramphal, "World Language: Opportunities, Challenges, Responsibilities" (speech to the English-Speaking Union, 1996), 16.
6. David Crystal, *The Cambridge Encyclopedia of the English Language* (Cambridge: Cambridge University Press, 1995), 110.
7. David Crystal, *English as a Global Language* (Cambridge: Cambridge University Press, 1997), 136–37.
8. MacArthur, *English Languages*, 149.
9. Anthony Hughes, *The Online English Grammar* (PDF Version 1.1) (New York: prax-Matrix, 2005), http://education4today.com.
10. Richard Allsopp, *Dictionary of Caribbean English Usage* (Oxford: Oxford University Press, 1996), lvi.
11. Cited in MacArthur, *English Languages*, 101.
12. Cf. James and Youssef, *Languages of Tobago*.
13. Peter Trudgill and Jean Hannah, *International English: A Guide to Varieties of Standard English* (London: Edward Arnold, 1985).
14. Trudgill and Hannah, *International English*, 66.
15. Don Winford, "Variation in the Use of Perfect *Have* in Trinidadian English: A Problem of Categorial and Semantic Mismatch", *Language Variation and Change* 5 (1993): 177.
16. Cf. Lloyd B. Anderson, "The 'Perfect' as a Universal and Language-Specific Category", in *Tense-Aspect: Between Semantics and Pragmatics*, ed. Paul J. Hopper (Amsterdam: John Benjamins, 1982), 227–64.
17. See also John Harris for Hiberno-English, "Syntactic Variation and Dialect Divergence", *Journal of Linguistics* 20, no. 2 (1984): 303–27.
18. Trudgill and Hannah, *International English*, 49.

19. Valerie Youssef, "Age-Grading in the Anglophone Creole of Tobago", *World Englishes* 20, no. 1 (2001): 29–46.
20. Trudgill and Hannah, *International English*, 67–68.
21. Peter Louwenberg, "Non-Native Varieties and the Socio-Politics of English Proficiency Assessment", in *The Sociopolitics of English Language Teaching*, ed. Joan Kelly Hall and William G. Eggington (Clevedon, UK: Multilingual Matters, 2000), 67–82.
22. Trudgill and Hannah, *International English*, 61.
23. Louwenberg, "Non-Native Varieties", 72.
24. Trudgill and Hannah, *International English*, 61.
25. Ibid., 49.

CHAPTER 4

Caribbean Cross-Culturalism in *The Caribbean Multilingual Dictionary of Flora, Fauna and Foods*

▸ JEANNETTE ALLSOPP

Cross-culturalism is based on the notion of *culture*, which in its broadest sense denotes speech, customs, traditions, morals, laws – in fact, every aspect of activity engaged in by members of human societies. It also involves the process of getting to know and understand, as well as relate to and benefit from, the social systems that contribute to the ongoing development of society. In fact, the term *culturalism* indicates the flexibility of the self to be involved in the communication and interpretation of verbal and non-verbal signals and to correctly and appropriately respond in similar fashion. The idea of *cross* combined with *culturalism* denotes the confluence of zones or barriers, moving from one construct to another, and consequently to an expansion of boundaries.[1] The multicultural and multilingual diversity of the Caribbean has resulted in a constant "crossing" of values, ideas and lexical items among the various territories, and this has led to what may be called cross-culturalism. It is this cross-cultural nature of the Caribbean region that the *Caribbean Multilingual Dictionary of Flora, Fauna and Foods* (*CMD*),[2] written in English, French, French Creole and Spanish, seeks to capture. The entries contained in the *CMD* therefore cross the major language barriers of the Caribbean by chronicling creole cultures in English-official, French-official and Spanish-official territories. By so doing, the

CMD also crosses cultures, as each language reflects the cultural outlook of its speakers.

With regard to the territories of the Caribbean, the similarities among the three major cultures under consideration in this chapter bear witness to the overall experience of European colonization and settlement, which included the vitally important transatlantic slave trade. The latter had a pervasive and lasting impact on the language and culture of all Caribbean territories. The contact between the hundreds of West African languages brought by the slaves and the European languages of the colonizers produced creolized varieties of language (or languages) whose structure, idiom and morphosyntax reflect a distinctly African worldview. Similarities among these varieties, whether English, French or (to a lesser extent) Spanish, are reflected in the languages of the region in the way in which products of the environment are labelled, as well as in the folk usage of items of Caribbean flora, fauna and foods across the cultures.

The *CMD* explores the lexicon of the creolized languages of the Caribbean, including French Creole. It gives definitions of each lexical item in English, along with encyclopedic information on the items. It supplies cross-references in all the languages used, as well as notes on usage and, in as many cases as possible, etymological information.

The present constitution of the Caribbean region is the result of the merging of many cultures. Historical migrations of peoples brought with them their languages, religions, folk practices and lifestyles, which were merged with already present indigenous ones. From the time that Columbus made his so-called discovery of the New World, the region experienced the dominance of European culture through the Spanish, the French, the Dutch and the British. Unfortunately for the region, the indigenous element was largely eliminated by the Spanish on their arrival, but it has endured, if not in linguistic structure, in the lexicon of all the languages of the Caribbean in areas that include art, craft and foods. Territories with significant retention of indigenous peoples, such as Guyana, Trinidad, Belize, Dominica and St Vincent, also manifest linguistic survivals, and in some cases the survival of actual languages. In Guyana there are Arawakan languages, two of which survive, namely Arawak (Lokono) and Wapishana. There are also Cariban languages, six of which survive, namely Akawaio, Arekuna, Makushi, Patamuna, Carib, Wai-Wai and one surviving

Warrau language. Similarly, in Belize, words from the three Mayan languages – Kekchi, Mopan and Yucatecan – survive, as well as from the Miskito Indian languages and from Garifuna, which originated in St Vincent as the result of contact between Island Carib and African languages. There are also other survivals from Taino and Tupi and other retentions of Carib and Arawak languages in other Caribbean islands, apart from the ones named above.[3]

Also worthy of mention when considering the lexicon of Guyanese and Trinidadian English is the fact that, in the post-emancipation era, both of those territories were recipients of a significant number of East Indian immigrants imported to work as indentured labourers on the sugar plantations. Those immigrants brought with them a cousin dialect of Hindi, Bhojpuri, which has had a major impact on the creolized varieties of English spoken in those territories, in particular adding hundreds of lexical items, notably in the areas of foods, dress, music, dance, religion and festivals. However, the greatest linguistic contribution made to the Caribbean, together with the European input, is that of the numerous languages of sub-Saharan Africa brought to the region by millions of slaves through the triangular slave trade.

As a result of so many linguistic and cultural influences, Caribbean languages are a rich mix of a number of lexical items culled from indigenous languages, sub-Saharan African languages, European languages and Indic ones. The second set is the most productive in terms of Caribbean idiom and proverbs, and its influence is clearly seen right across the major languages of the region. Lexical items also show the linguistic and cultural influences referred to above, particularly in the area of labelling items of flora, fauna and foods. This is seen in the folk usage of a number of items of flora and fauna and, quite significantly, in the similarities between many Caribbean dishes across Caribbean languages and cultures.

This chapter will give samples of representative items of flora, fauna and foods, as well as folk usage of specific items. It will show that the process of creolization that resulted from the contact of European languages with the numerous languages of sub-Saharan Africa, in addition to contact of the languages of the latter group with each other, is fully reflected in the naming of items found in the Caribbean environment. The following lists of items within the three lexical categories treated in the *CMD* will exemplify the constant crossing of territorial borders within the Caribbean, regardless of which major official language is used, and including the Creole and non-standard varieties spoken in the various territories of the region.

Indigenous Languages

Flora

Item	French Equivalent	Spanish Equivalent
anato (anglophone Caribbean)	**roucou** *m.* (French Caribbean)	**achote** *m.* (Costa Rica, Venezuela) **achiote** *m.* (Puerto Rico, Santo Domingo) **bija** *f.* (Cuba, Puerto Rico, Santo Domingo, Venezuela) **bija cimarrona** *f.* (Santo Domingo) **onoto** *m.* (Venezuela)

The word *anato* originates from Cariban languages, Akawaio *amondö* and the Arekuna *anontö*, meaning "fruit used to make red dye with which Amerindians paint themselves".[4] It is to be noted that all the French Creole–speaking or French Creole–influenced territories of the anglophone Caribbean – Dominica, Grenada, St Lucia and Trinidad – use the French equivalent *roucou*. Guyana also has this word as another name for anato. The item is used as a dye in cooking and also for cosmetic purposes.

Item	French Equivalent	Spanish Equivalent
awara (Guyana)	**aovara, tucum** *m.* (French Caribbean)	**awara** *f.* (Spanish Caribbean) **tucum** *m.* (Costa Rica)

Awara is an Arawak word meaning "spiny palm . . . bearing red, edible fruit".[5] This is a fruit not generally known in the Caribbean but found in Guyana and French Guiana. It is usually much eaten by children in those countries.

Item	French Equivalent	Spanish Equivalent
cassava (anglophone Caribbean)	manioc *m.*, manioc amer *m.*, manioc doux *m.*, camanioc *m.* (French Caribbean)	yuca *f.*, yuca dulce *f.*, yuca agria *f.*, yuca amarga *f.* (Spanish Caribbean)
	mannyòk (Guadeloupe, Haiti)	

The word *cassava* probably originated from Arawakan/Taino through Spanish, in which are found the variants *casaba* and *cazaba*. Compare the French *cassave*. The French equivalent *manioc* is from Guaraní *mandio*, "mandioca plant and root".[6] The Spanish equivalent *yuca* is also of Amerindian origin, and is the name of the plant. The vegetable is also known as manioc in the Eastern Caribbean. It is used across the Caribbean as a vegetable and to make cassava bread and cassava flour. In Guyana the juice of the bitter variety of cassava is boiled into a thick, dark brown liquid called casareep; it is used to make pepperpot, the national dish of Guyana, in which various kinds of regular or wild meat, pepper and other herbs are boiled together in the casareep.

Item	French Equivalent	Spanish Equivalent
guinep (anglophone Caribbean)	quénette *f.* (French Guiana, Guadeloupe, Martinique)	quenepa *f.* (Puerto Rico, Santo Domingo)
	quénèpe *m.* (Haiti)	
	French Creole tjénèt (Guadeloupe, Martinique) tjennèt (Dominica, St Lucia, Trinidad)	

Guinep comes originally from the Arawakan *genipa* through the Spanish *quenepa* (the fruit) and *quenepo* (the tree).[7] There are other Spanish equivalents, such as *mamón* (Venezuela), *mamoncillo* (Cuba) and *limoncillo* (Santo Domingo). The fruit is widely eaten throughout the Caribbean.

Item	French Equivalent	Spanish Equivalent
sapodilla (anglophone Caribbean)	sapotille *f.* (French Caribbean) <u>French Creole</u> chapoti (French Caribbean)	zapotillo *m.* (Costa Rica) sapote *m.* (Cuba)

Originally from the Aztec *tzapotl*, *zapote* yields the Anglicized form *sapodilla*.[8] This item has several variants in Creole English, for example, *dilly* in the Bahamas and the Turks and Caicos Islands, *mesple* in the Virgin Islands, *sapadili* in Belize, *sapidilla* in Bermuda and *sapotie* and *shapotie* in Dominica and St Lucia. The sapodilla is widely used as a fruit, and the trunk of the tree yields a milky latex which forms the base for chicle gum.

Fauna

Item	French Equivalent	Spanish Equivalent
abouya (Guyana)	pakira *m.*, patira *m.*, pécari à collier *m.* (French Guiana)	báquiro de collar *m.* (Venezuela)

Abouya comes originally from the Arawak *abuya*, "peccary" (the smaller kind). The word has also been influenced by folk etymology, and an aphetic form with an epenthetic [n] inserted gives Guyanese Creole the item *bunya*, found in the phrase "stink as a bunya", which means having a strong and unpleasant body odour. The abouya is usually hunted for its meat.

Item	French Equivalent	Spanish Equivalent
accoushi-ant(s) (Guyana)	fourmi(s) champignonniste(s) *f.(pl.)* fourmi(s) manioc(s) *f.(pl.)* fourmi parasol *f.* (Guadeloupe)	hormiga *f.* (Spanish Caribbean)

Accoushi-ants comes from the Arawak *khose*, "ants, the type known as parasol ants which are fond of eating the leaves of garden plants".⁹ There are other names for this insect in the non-standard or Creole varieties in other Caribbean territories, for example, *umbrella-ants* (Belize, Guyana), *tactac-ant(s)* (Dominica), *coushi-ants*, *cush-cush* (*cuss-cuss*) *ant(s)*, *drogher-ant(s)*, *kooshi* or *kushy-ant(s)* (Guyana), and *bachac* or *parasol-ant(s)* (Trinidad).

Item	French Equivalent	Spanish Equivalent
haimara (Guyana)	aïmara *m.* (French Guiana)	aimara *f.* (Venezuela)

The *haimara* is a large, edible freshwater fish which is usually found in creeks and pools of waterfalls and is much prized for its flesh. The name is originally from the Arekuna *aimara* – "name of this fish" – plus prosthetic *h*.¹⁰

Item	French Equivalent	Spanish Equivalent
hassar (Guyana)	cascadura *m.* (French Caribbean)	curito *m.* (Venezuela)

From the Arawak *asa* – "a small, highly prized, edible fish" – plus prosthetic *h*. In Trinidadian non-standard English this item is known as *cascadu* (also spelt *cascadoo*). It is usually considered a delicacy in the territories where it is found.

Item	French Equivalent	Spanish Equivalent
manatee (Antigua, Belize, Guyana, Jamaica)	lamantin *m.* (French Caribbean)	manatí *m.* (Spanish Caribbean)

Manatee is originally from the Carib *manattouii* through Spanish *manatí* and then to the English form.¹¹ This aquatic mammal is also known as *water-cow* (Guyana) or *sea-cow* (Jamaica).

Foods

Item	French Equivalent	Spanish Equivalent
cassava bread (anglophone Caribbean)	cassave *f.* (French Caribbean)	casabe *m.* (Cuba, Puerto Rico, Venezuela)
	French Creole kassav (French Caribbean)	pan de yuca *m.* (Costa Rica, Santo Domingo)

Cassava bread has other names in the Creole English varieties of Jamaica, such as *bammy*. In Bajan dialect the word *cassava-bake* becomes a compound, similar to the original word for the item in Caribbean English. In the non-standard English of the US Virgin Islands it is called *bang-bang*; in the non-standard English of Anguilla, *choky banjo*; and in the non-standard English of Carriacou, Grenada and St Vincent, *bam-bam*. It is a staple food throughout the Caribbean.

Item	French Equivalent	Spanish Equivalent
pepperpot (anglophone Caribbean)	pepperpot *m.* (French Caribbean)	pepperpot *m.* (Spanish Caribbean)

In its first sense, *pepperpot* is the Guyanese dish of meat boiled with casareep, pepper and herbs to make a dark brown stew which can last indefinitely because of the preservative properties of the casareep. In its second sense, it is a thick soup made of *calalu*, which is discussed under West African languages. Calalu is the national dish of Trinidad and Tobago.

Item	French Equivalent	Spanish Equivalent
farine (Anguilla, Dominica, Grenada, Guyana, St Lucia, St Vincent, Tobago)	farine *f.* farine de manioc *f.* (French Caribbean)	harina de yuca *f.* (Spanish Caribbean)

Farine comes originally from the French *farine*, "flour", or (especially in Guyana) the Portuguese *farinha*, "flour" or "meal", from Amerindian contact with Brazil. Note also the Standard English *farina*, "flour or meal of cereal, nuts or starchy roots". Other names are *coco* (British Virgin Islands, St Kitts), *cassava farine* (Dominica) and *manioc-farine* (St Lucia). Farine is a coarse-grained meal made by stirring the grated remains of bitter cassava, after squeezing out the juice, in a large open iron pot over the fire. It is used all over the Caribbean in many ways: as a cereal, to thicken gravy, to make dumplings, and so on.

From the spread of territories across which they are found, the above samples of words of indigenous origin in the lexical categories of flora, fauna and foods show us that the indigenous legacy extends beyond the borders of the territories of the Caribbean. Lexical items filter across language barriers and into Caribbean creoles and non-standard dialects, as well as into the Standard varieties. It is to be noted that some words – whether of Arawakan origin like *guinep*, Arawakan/Taino like *cassava*, or Cariban like *manatee* – came into Caribbean English via Caribbean Spanish, which was the first European language to enter the Caribbean with the advent of Christopher Columbus.

Probably the most significant linguistic contribution is that made by the huge numbers of slaves from sub-Saharan African, who were forcibly brought to the Caribbean through the triangular slave trade. The resulting contact which occurred not only created new languages in the region but also forged a new culture that made Caribbean languages unique for at least two reasons: the linguistic economy found in Caribbean creoles and the nature of Caribbean idioms and proverbs, regardless of which European language was dominant.

West African Languages

The West African languages that had such an influence on Caribbean languages as they exist today were numerous, but the most significant ones were Yoruba, Igbo, Twi, Hausa, Gã-Adangme, Wolof, Mende, Fante, Asante, Mandinga and the Bantu languages. The following is a sample of the African contribution which includes not only the linguistic influences but also the folk usage to which these items are put.

Flora

Item	French Equivalent	Spanish Equivalent
belly-ache bush (anglophone Caribbean)	herbe à mal de ventre *f.* (French Guiana) médicinier bâtard *m.* (Guadeloupe, Martinique) médicinier barachin *m.*, petit médicinier *m.* (Haiti)	tua-tua/túa-túa *f.* (Cuba, Puerto Rico, Venezuela)

This item is used across the territories of the Caribbean in exactly the same way. An oil is made from the seeds and administered orally, and a decoction is made from the leaves and either applied locally or taken orally. The name is therefore entirely applicable to the plant, given its folk usage, and illustrates a view of the world that is African as opposed to European.

Item	French Equivalent	Spanish Equivalent
duppy-basil (Barbados)	grand basilic *m* petit frambasin *m.* (French Guiana, Guadeloupe, Martinique) frambasin *m.* (Haiti)	albahaca de clavo *f.* (Cuba) albahaca cimarrona *f.* (Puerto Rico, Santo Domingo) albahaca clavo *f.*, albahaquita *f.*, albahaca de vaca *f.*, atiyayo *m.* (Santo Domingo)

The word *duppy* has two possible origins in African languages and is associated with a creature that instils fear in people. The first is from the Fante *adɔpe*, "a species of ape said to be so fierce as to kill twenty men at once". The second is from the Kikongo *ndoki*, "a sorcerer, bewitcher who takes a person's life by witchcraft".[12] The Caribbean English rendering, whether Standard or non-standard, is *duppy*, which is supposed to be a harmful invisible supernatural being that has been raised from the dead, or an evil spirit. The association of such a being with a plant usually means that the plant has negative properties; it may be poisonous or cause discomfort of some kind. However, in this case the plant is widely used in all the cultures of the major official Caribbean languages for colds and stomach disorders, and the leaves are applied externally for the relief of rheumatic pains.

Item	French Equivalent	Spanish Equivalent
monkey-tambran/ tamarind (Bahamas)	pois-gratter *m.* pois à gratter *m.* (French Caribbean) <u>French Creole</u> pwa gwaté (Dominica, Grenada, St Lucia)	pica-pica *m.* (Spanish Caribbean)

The name by which this plant is commonly known in the rest of the anglophone Caribbean is *cowitch*, probably because of the itching caused by contact with the hairs on the pod. Note that the prefix *monkey-* in Bahamian non-standard English denotes something idiotic or silly in the folk mind, and emanates from West African influence. However, the vine on which the fruit grows is used by some Caribbean folk to treat worms in children. Similarly, the French, Spanish and French Creole equivalents also refer to scratching or biting.

Fauna

Item	French Equivalent	Spanish Equivalent
cock-lizard (Barbados)	anoli *m.*, lézard *m* (French Caribbean) <u>French Creole</u> zandoli (French Caribbean)	lagartija *f.* (Costa Rica, Cuba, Santo Domingo) lagarto *m.* (Puerto Rico) saca banderas *m.* (Venezuela)

The prefix *cock-* in this item indicates that the animal is viewed as masculine. Again, this is typically African in conception.

Item	French Equivalent	Spanish Equivalent
cow-fish (Bahamas, Grenada, Montserrat, St Lucia)	coffre à cornes *m* **French Creole** kòf a kon (Martinique)	chapín *m*. (Cuba, Puerto Rico, Santo Domingo, Venezuela)

This fish is so called because of the cow-like appearance of its head.

Item	French Equivalent	Spanish Equivalent
duppy-ridin(g)-horse (Jamaica)	phasme *m*. (French Caribbean) cheval à diable *m*. (Guadeloupe) cheval bon Dieu *m*. (Martinique) **French Creole** chouval (a) djab (Guadeloupe) chouval-bondyé (Martinique)	mantis religiosa *f*. (Spanish Caribbean)

These are the Caribbean names for a praying mantis or a brown stick insect which can grow to about twenty-four centimetres long. Because of its stick-like appearance, its habit of remaining motionless and its ability to blend with the colour of the background, it is felt to be like a spirit, or duppy. It is likened to a riding horse because it looks like a matchstick toy horse.

Foods

Item	French Equivalent	Spanish Equivalent
cou-cou (anglophone Caribbean)	migan *m*. (French Caribbean)	cu-cu *m*. (Costa Rica)

Because of the wide occurrence of this dish in the southern Caribbean, a West African origin is highly likely, although sources are doubtful or unconvincing. Allsopp suggests Twi *nkuku*, "a species of yam", and Twi, Hausa and Yoruba *kuku*, "a cook" (from English) or "a European's cook".[13] However, the Twi *nkuku* seems most likely. The other name for cou-cou, *fungee*, found in Anguilla, Antigua, Barbuda, Jamaica, Nevis, St Kitts and the Virgin Islands, seems to have several sources in African languages, such as the Twi *fugyee*, "soft, mealy (of boiled yam)"; Kimbundu *funzi*, "cassava mush"; Congo *fundi*, "flour, porridge"; and Yoruba *funje*, "(something) given to eat". This dish is eaten across the territories of the Caribbean; it is made by boiling cornmeal, okra and butter together until firm enough to be shaped into a ball, using a wooden cou-cou stick. Flying fish and cou-cou is the national dish of Barbados.

Item	French Equivalent	Spanish Equivalent
dukuna (Antigua, British Virgin Islands, Montserrat, St Vincent)	doconon *m.* (French Guiana) doucoune *m.* (Guadeloupe, Martinique)	duckunoo *m.*, blue drass *m.* (Costa Rica)
	French Creole doukounou (Haiti)	

This item seems to originate from the Gã-Adangme *doko na*, "sweeten (somebody's) mouth"; or *doko nō*, "sweet thing"; or Twi *ɔdɔkono*, "boiled maize bread". The Gã-Adangme source seems to have influenced the form in the Eastern Caribbean, as evidenced by the variant spellings found (*doucouna, ducana, dukona*), while the Twi word seems to have influenced the form used in Belize.[14] The other names for this item in the non-standard English varieties of various territories are *blue-draw(er)s* (Jamaica), *boyo* (Belize, Jamaica), *cankie* (Guyana), *conchi* (Nevis), *conkie* (Anguilla, Barbados, St Kitts), *corn-dumpling* (St Kitts), *dokonu* (Belize, Jamaica), *pémi* (Tobago, Trinidad) and *stew-dumpling* (Barbados, St Vincent). It is a kind of pudding made of different mixtures of cornmeal, grated coconut, plantain flour, raisins, spices, sugar and essence, wrapped in either a piece of banana or plantain leaf or a sea-grape leaf and steamed. Made Caribbean-wide, it is popularly eaten in Barbados during independence celebrations.

Item	French Equivalent	Spanish Equivalent
calalu (Dominica, St Vincent, Tobago, Trinidad)	herbage de calalou *m.* (French Caribbean) calalou *m.*, kalalou *m.* (Guadeloupe, Martinique) calalou des morts *m.* (Haiti)	calalú *m* (Costa Rica) sopa calalú *f.* (Cuba)

This dish seems to have two African sources: Malinke *kalalu*, "many things", and Mandingo *colilu*, "an edible herb resembling spinach".[15] Albin Michel, in his book *Martinique: Produits du terroir et recettes traditionelles*, cites Dahomey as the place of origin of the recipe for this dish, which is a thick soup made of calalu, or dasheen leaves, mixed with many other ingredients such as okra, root vegetables, crabs, dumplings, salt beef or hambone, green peppers and herbs – all boiled together and served as a main meal.[16] Hence, both African sources cited above seem to have given rise to this item, which crosses all the major language barriers and cultures of the Caribbean. (See also the preceding discussion of pepperpot in the section on indigenous languages.)

European Languages

The third language group which was clearly of major influence on the lexicon of Caribbean languages was of course the European languages, namely, Spanish, French and Dutch. However, in this chapter we are concerned primarily with the first two. The following words are examples of the European influence.

Flora

Item	French Equivalent	Spanish Equivalent
African tulip-tree (anglophone Caribbean)	tulipier de Gabon *m.* (French Guiana, Guadeloupe, Martinique)	tulipán africano *m.* (Puerto Rico, Venezuela) amapola *f.* (Santo Domingo)

This tree is called "African" because it was first botanically recorded on the Gold Coast of Africa (in 1787), and "tulip" because of the colour, shape and texture of its flower.[17] The tulip-tree is known and cultivated in many Caribbean territories.

Item	French Equivalent	Spanish Equivalent
Barbados cherry (anglophone Caribbean)	cerise *f.* (French Caribbean) **French Creole** siriz (Guadeloupe, Martinique) siwiz (Dominica, St Lucia)	acerola *f.* (Puerto Rico) cereza *f.* (Cuba, Puerto Rico, Santo Domingo) cereza cimarrona *f.*, cereza del trópico *f.*, cereza de frutita *f.* (Santo Domingo)

Barbados cherry is a well-known fruit that is widely eaten or made into juice across the Caribbean territories. It is obviously called "cherry" because of the shape and colour of the fruit.

Item	French Equivalent	Spanish Equivalent
chil(l)i-plum (Antigua, Barbados, Grenada, Tobago, Trinidad)	prune d'Espagne *f.* (French Caribbean) prune du Chili *f.* prune jaune *f.* **French Creole** prinn (Guadeloupe, Martinique) pwinn (St Lucia)	ciruela campechana *f.* (Cuba) ciruela amarilla *f.* (Puerto Rico, Santo Domingo) ciruela morada *f.* (Santo Domingo)

This fruit is named after Nahuatl *chilli*, the name of a pepper. It is so called because of the small yellow plum's resemblance to a small yellow pepper, of which there are several varieties, and possibly used to distinguish this plum from the more common hog-plum, which is also yellow.[18] Some other names of this fruit are *plum* (Antigua, Montserrat, St Vincent), *hog-plum* (Bahamas, Belize, Jamaica, Turks and Caicos Islands), *August-plum* (Belize), *yellow-plum* (Belize, Cayman Islands, Jamaica, Trinidad) and *sugar-plum* (Guyana, Jamaica).

Item	French Equivalent	Spanish Equivalent
malacca-apple/pear (Antigua, Guyana)	pomme d'eau *f.*, pomme d'Haïti *f.* (Guadeloupe, Martinique) pomme rose *f.* (Haiti) **French Creole** ponm dlo (Guadeloupe, Martinique) ponm wòz (Haiti)	manzana de agua *f.* (Costa Rica, Santo Domingo) manzana malaya *f.*, pomarrosa malaya *f.* (Puerto Rico)

This fruit originated in the Moluccas Islands in the East Indies, from where it was brought to the anglophone Caribbean. Some other names are *pommerac* (Barbados, Dominica, Trinidad), *Malay-apple* (Belize, Bermuda), *otaheite-apple* (Cayman Islands, Jamaica), and *French cashew* (Grenada, Guyana). It is widely eaten in the Caribbean. Note that the words *apple* and *pear* are applied to this fruit, which is red in colour and has white flesh, similar to some varieties of apples, while *pear* refers to its shape, which is somewhat like that of the European pear. Such labels are used for many fruit names in the Caribbean because of what I have called the "appearance criterion",[19] which determined the names applied to fruits by the European colonizers as they confronted a new and unfamiliar environment.

Fauna

Item	French Equivalent	Spanish Equivalent
angel-fish (anglophone Caribbean)	demoiselle (grise) *f.* (French Caribbean)	pez angel *m.* (Puerto Rico) cachama (blanca) *f.* (Venezuela)
blackbird (anglophone Caribbean)	merle *m.* (French Caribbean)	chichinguanco *m.*, hachuela *f.*, quiebra *f.* (Cuba) mozambique *m.*, pichón prieto *m.* (Puerto Rico)

Note that the above bird is not the same species as the European blackbird (*Turdus merula*), which is also somewhat different in appearance from the Caribbean blackbird. Further, the female of the European species is brown, unlike the Caribbean species.

Item	French Equivalent	Spanish Equivalent
chub (anglophone Caribbean)	carpe *f.*, perroquet *m.* (French Caribbean)	loro *m.* (Cuba, Venezuela) guacamaya *f.* (Venezuela)

This fish is not the same species as the European chub, which is a freshwater fish. The Caribbean chub is a reef fish, also called *parrot-fish* because of the shape of its jaws.

Item	French Equivalent	Spanish Equivalent
cobbler (Barbados)	oursin diadème *m.* (French Caribbean)	erizo de mar *m.* (Spanish Caribbean)

It must be noted that the name of this item represents a semantic shift in Caribbean English, in that the sea-urchin, which is what a cobbler is, has been so named in Barbados because of the fact that its spines remind one of a cobbler's needle. It must also be noted that the name is peculiar to Barbados and is not found in other anglophone Caribbean territories, probably because Barbados is the only anglophone Caribbean territory that remained solely under the influence of the British throughout the era of colonization and slavery.

Foods

Item	French Equivalent	Spanish Equivalent
bread-pudding (anglophone Caribbean)	**bread pudding** *m.* (French Caribbean)	**pudín de pan y mantequilla** *m.* (Costa Rica) **pudín de pan** *m.* (Cuba, Santo Domingo)
grilled chicken (anglophone Caribbean)	**poulet grillé** *m.* (French Caribbean)	**pollo grillé** *m.* (Cuba) **pollitos asados a la parrilla** *m. pl.* (Puerto Rico) **pollo a la parrilla** *m.* (Santo Domingo)
meatballs (anglophone Caribbean)	**boulettes de viande** (French Caribbean)	**albóndigas** *f. pl.*, **bolitas de carne** *f.pl.* (Spanish Caribbean)
lemon meringue pie (anglophone Caribbean)	**tarte aux citrons** *f.* (French Caribbean)	**pastel de crema de limón** *m.* (Puerto Rico, Santo Domingo) **pastel de limón** *m.* (Venezuela)

These dishes indicate the spread of European influence across the Caribbean. They originated in Europe and came into Caribbean cuisine via the English. The terms then moved across the language barriers of the region.

It is clear from this sample of English words in the Caribbean lexicon that the items listed were so named because they were reminiscent of items in the European environment. The labelling of the Caribbean ecology indicates the tendency to associate new items with those already familiar to the European colonists, whether Spanish, French or British. It is for this reason that Caribbean languages abound in words which relate to a European reality.

Conclusion

Given all the examples set out in this chapter, it seems evident that the lexicon of the three European lexical-base languages of the Caribbean is undoubtedly cross-cultural. Items of flora from our indigenous heritage, such as *cassava*, are commonly used throughout the Caribbean. Items from our African heritage, such as *belly-ache bush* or *duppy-basil*, are also used in folk medicine across the region. Items of fauna, such as *blackbird*, from our European heritage are also known as such across Caribbean languages. Trans-Caribbean dishes from our African heritage, such as *dukuna* and *calalu*, demonstrate that the linguistic and cultural spread is Caribbean-wide. The entries in the *CMD* both define and inventory the multilingual and cross-cultural nature of the Caribbean environment and culture. It is this multiculturalism and cross-culturalism that so clearly demonstrate an unmistakable and vibrant Caribbean linguistic and cultural identity.

Notes

1. Margaret Kumar, "Postcolonial Theory and Cross-Culturalism: Collaborative 'Signposts' of Discursive Practices", *Journal of Educational Inquiry* 1, no. 2 (2002): 82.
2. Jeannette Allsopp, *Caribbean Multilingual Dictionary of Flora, Fauna and Foods* (Kingston: Arawak, 2003), xxxi–xxxii.
3. Richard Allsopp, *Dictionary of Caribbean English Usage* (Oxford: Oxford University Press, 1996), xli.
4. Walter F. Edwards et al., *A Short Grammar and Dictionary of the Akawaio and Arekuna Languages of Guyana* (Georgetown, Guyana: Amerindian Languages Project, University of Guyana, 1980), 20.
5. R. Allsopp, *Dictionary of Caribbean English*, 50.
6. A.J. Peralta and Thomas Osuna, *Diccionario Guaraní-Español y Español-Guaraní* (Buenos Aires: Tupa, 1950), 25.
7. Frederic G. Cassidy and Robert B. Le Page, *Dictionary of Jamaican English*, 2nd ed. (Cambridge: Cambridge University Press, 1980), 214–15; R. Allsopp, *Dictionary of Caribbean English Usage*, 274.
8. Francisco J. Santamaría, *Diccionario general de americanismos*, 2nd ed., vol. 3 (Mexico City: Gobierno del Estado de Tabasco, 1988), 315–16.

9. John P. Bennett, *An Arawak-English Dictionary* (Georgetown: Walter Roth Museum, 1989), 45; R. Allsopp, *Dictionary of Caribbean English*, 274.
10. R. Allsopp, *Dictionary of Caribbean English*, 279.
11. Raymond Breton, *Dictionnaire Caraïbe-Français du Révérend Père Raymond Breton, 1665* (Paris: CELIA/GEREC, 1999), 174.
12. R. Allsopp, *Dictionary of Caribbean English*, 207.
13. Ibid., 172.
14. Ibid., 206.
15. J. Allsopp, *Caribbean Multilingual Dictionary*, 119.
16. Michel Albin, *Martinique: Produits de terroir et recettes traditionelles* (Paris: Albin Michel S.A., 1997), 250.
17. R. Allsopp, *Dictionary of Caribbean English*, 12.
18. Ibid., 150.
19. If we take, for example, the Caribbean-English compound *blackeye-peas* we will find that the French Caribbean equivalent is *pois yeux-noirs,* or literally a calque of the English item. The fact that the peas have a black spot in the middle that looks like a "black eye" shows that an appearance criterion is at work here.

Part 2

Beyond Borders
Questioning the Canon

CHAPTER 5

Borders, Boundaries and Frames
Cross-Culturalism and the Caribbean Canon

SANDRA POUCHET PAQUET

This chapter explores issues of cross-culturalism and the Caribbean canon and the ways in which they are compatible and even collaborative signposts. Borders, boundaries and frames seem to encapsulate the crux of the ensuing argument because, as a system of thought, cross-culturalism destabilizes and challenges any notion of a Caribbean canon that can be defined by fixed geographical limits and conceptual frames. The broad strokes of this thematic are, of course, too large for a short essay, so I will restrict my focus to issues arising out of cross-culturalism and the shape of the Caribbean canon within the US academy and in South Florida, where new geopolitical configurations model what may yet prove a useful corrective to exploitative configurations of a core/periphery model.

I approach this task self-conscious about who I am and where I enter the debate about cross-culturalism and the Caribbean canon. While I was born, raised and educated in colonial and, later, independent Trinidad and Tobago, I was educated at a graduate and postgraduate level in the United States and have lived and worked there for twice as many years as I ever lived and worked in the Caribbean. I am part of the burgeoning Caribbean diaspora in the United States, and one who feels fortunate in having been able to maintain, without interruption, personal and professional ties to the Caribbean. Since 1992 I have lived and worked as an academic and educator in South Florida, a very different environment from my previous experiences in New England and the mid-Atlantic states, and before that in Jamaica. I stress the geopolitics of cultural knowledge because, for me, the pedagogical imperative changed with the geopolitical environment and institutional politics.[1]

For purposes of clarity, I would like to differentiate between imaginary and pedagogical canons as John Guillory has done, between the canon as "an *imaginary* totality of works" (that no one has access to as a totality) and the concrete "list of works one reads in a given class, or the curriculum, the list of works one reads in a program of study".[2] In Jamaica in the 1970s, nationalist and institutional politics shaped a pedagogical canon that privileged nation formation as an anti-imperialist, anti-colonialist enterprise; it was male-dominated and attuned to diversity after the imposed sameness of imperial domination, as a necessary prelude to nation formation.[3] In Connecticut in the 1970s, the Caribbean canon, whether imaginary or pedagogical, was largely unknown and aroused interest only as a subset of racial and ethnic minority politics in the New England states. In Pennsylvania in the 1980s, the Caribbean canon was a poor relation or subset of African-American literature and culture; when it diverged it became suspect. In the 1990s in South Florida, the sustained exodus of Cuban citizens that ensued after the Cuban revolution in 1959, and the liberalization of American immigration laws in the 1960s, which made emigration to the United States a viable alternative to emigration to Canada and Europe, gave rise to a creeping Caribbean presence that altered the pedagogical relationship of an imaginary Caribbean canon to the United States.

To put this enormous change into perspective, I would like to call attention to a truly admirable academic institution in the United States, the Society for the Study of the Multi-Ethnic Literature of the United States. Founded in 1973, the society endeavours to expand the definition of American literature through the study and teaching of Latino-American, Native American, African-American, Asian and Pacific American, and ethnically specific Euro-American literary works, their authors and their cultural contexts. For better or for worse, Caribbean-American literature was not listed in this expanded definition of American literature in 2003. In the context of a multiethnic United States, the different subject positions generated by a growing Caribbean-American phenomenon were not significant enough to be recognized as distinct in 1973.

In 2003, however, it was wrestling visibly with the challenge of naming what is Caribbean and American for purposes of recognition and inclusion,[4] a task daunting not only to the Society for the Study of the Multi-Ethnic Literature of the United States, but to academics and educators in the Caribbean as well.

As part of an ongoing and complex process of canon formation, what remains to be determined is what impact a flexible pedagogical canon may have on the shape of an imaginary canon that illuminates the ways in which racial, national, ethnic and gender positions construct aesthetic and cultural value within and beyond the finite boundaries of the Caribbean region. What I bring to this debate is shaped by my sense of urgency about South Florida as a geographical and cultural centre that wrestles, consciously and unconsciously, with the limitations and possibilities of a pan-Caribbean ethos that derives from an unprecedented mix of Caribbean populations among a majority immigrant population.[5] The narrative of community in this environment is plural and marked by distinct and overlapping pre-existing solidarities that might be determined by national origins, race, class, religion and ethnicity. The geopolitics of cultural knowledge in South Florida is of necessity cross-cultural, whether or not it qualifies as multicultural.

A distinguishing feature of the study of multi-ethnic literature in the United States is that it speaks to an integrative cultural exercise for purposes of national cohesiveness; it attempts to conceptualize the whole so as to recognize and include its many parts in terms that are compatible with nationalist politics. We might ask, is this an exercise in globalization in one sweeping gesture of Americanization? And if so, what does this mean to the many different subject positions in discourses of Caribbean life and culture? On the subject of canon formation and the African-American literary tradition, Barbara E. Johnson observed: "To be a subject means to activate the network of discourse from *where one stands*. Discourse is not a circle with one center, but more like a mycelium with many mushrooms. To be a subject also means to take nourishment from more than one source, to construct a new synthesis, a new discursive ragout."[6] This said, how much of the Caribbean is it possible to see from a Caribbean-American subject position? Is there an alternative to oppositional critical practices that distinguish between what is ethnic Caribbean in the United States and what is Caribbean as a site of critical investigation? How does one investigate the plurality of differences that constitutes the Caribbean, with all its contradictions and antagonisms, from an ethnic Caribbean perspective? Does this also mirror the dilemma of an imaginary canon from a Caribbean perspective? What are the thresholds of difference? And how much attention do we want to pay to them? After all, beyond Puerto Rico and the US Virgin Islands, there are Haitians and Haitian Americans, Cubans and Cuban Americans, Dominicans and Dominican Americans, Antiguans and Antiguan Americans, Jamaicans and Jamaican Americans, and so on. How do we speak, then, to and on behalf of such a diverse Caribbean cultural presence within and beyond the boundaries of the Caribbean region without losing control of the discourse? Is control consistent with the liberationist ethos of Caribbean literary culture? The proliferation of Caribbean subject positions necessitates paying a lot of attention to different points of origin in the Caribbean and in transnational spaces.[7]

A growing Caribbean-American constituency in the United States is nurtured by the exploitative economic power of the North American metropolis and perceptions of poverty, overcrowding and mismanagement in the geographically and economically small spaces of the Caribbean. The ensuing process of cultural interpenetration is lopsided at best in favour of Americanization. Historically, to recognize and include what is Caribbean in the United States is to cannibalize it, to repackage and rename it in the image and likeness of the continental United States. In any event, cultural adoption into multi-ethnic United States comes at a price, and results in an uneasy fit for some, though not for everyone who makes the transition; and, of course, the terms of the transition change with time and individual talents.

Key points of reference for an uneasy fit might be Eric Walrond (1898–1966) and Claude McKay (1890–1948), two black Caribbean writers and intellectuals who sought to impress black America with their difference. My concern is not whether they are loved, disparaged or rejected, but with the way their cultural contributions are read within a North American framework. Though Walrond is widely respected as a pivotal figure in the Harlem Renaissance, his value is inscribed (and appropriately so) in terms of when and how he contributed to the Harlem Renaissance, and this emphasis places minimal value on his Caribbean and Panamanian beginnings. His stunning *Tropic Death* (1926) speaks volumes to the poverty and ambition that drove intra-regional and extra-regional Caribbean emigration patterns before and after the First World War, but it is a largely discontinuous narrative within an African-American literary canon, which remains primarily interested in the parameters of race relations within the closed historical trajectory of black and white, slavery and freedom.[8]

It is interesting to note that there is no traumatic transfer of national loyalty from home to host in a writer, and sometimes in a black American, like Eric Walrond, who enters and exits black American letters with impressive completeness (1918–35). He appears to fit the stereotype of the celebrated West Indian wanderer, the man of the crossroads, who makes his home where he finds it, settling here and there – if not in the Caribbean, then Panama; if not Panama, then the United States; if not the United States, then southern France; if not there, then the United Kingdom – anywhere, in fact, but back where he originally started.

And what of Claude McKay, who arrived in the United States in 1912 and, despite his ongoing quarrels with the black American intelligentsia, chose black America as his homeland? In *A Long Way From Home* (1937), he characterizes his relationship with the United States as a stage performance on the one hand and, rather poignantly, he also uses the agricultural image of grafting to describe his immigrant desire to be recognized and valued for his contribution to black American life and culture.[9] The trauma in McKay's transfer of loyalty is evident in his studied rejection of his Jamaican beginnings in favour of his North American beginnings in so much of his writing. It can be argued that in McKay's case the dichotomy is a strategy of achievement/survival, since he determines that a free and open dialogue between the two worlds of Jamaica and black America is an impediment to achievement. It is interesting that McKay's most popular novel in the United States is *Home to Harlem* (1929), while his most accomplished work in the Caribbean canon is *Banana Bottom* (1933). The ideological positioning of these novels is so different as to be mutually unintelligible without a working knowledge of the social and cultural dynamics of both McKay's Caribbean and black America in the first half of the twentieth century. What makes McKay such an uneasy fit in the African-American literary canon is the profoundly Jamaican nature of his relation to the world, encapsulated in *My Green Hills of Jamaica,* a sentimental and idealized narrative of his Jamaican childhood.

A generation later, writers such as Paule Marshall and Audre Lorde, born in the United States and raised partly in "the ever-shifting and many-planed converging points" of Caribbean-American cultural worlds, inhabit distinct cultural spaces.[10] Paule Marshall appears equally comfortable in both the United States and in Caribbean worlds, in the hyphenated sense both African-American and Caribbean-American. However, the Caribbean is more an object of desire than a hard-won alternative site of identification in Lorde's *Zami: A New Spelling of My Name*. What Paule Marshall's upbringing in the United States anticipated – and what was not available to Lorde as a black feminist lesbian – was the growing role that Caribbean immigrant enclaves in post–civil rights United States would play in nurturing close cultural relationships with Caribbean territories. Fitting comfortably in both worlds, the ensuing double consciousness is not a site of psychic torment and alienation so much as a highly sophisticated analytical tool and a creative mechanism for new ways of seeing, so evident in novels such as Marshall's *The Chosen Place, The Timeless People, Praisesong for the Widow* and *Daughters*.

A host of Caribbean-American writers are now refocusing the values of the Caribbean and the United States; they add yet another dimension to a quest for free and open dialogue between the United States and the peoples and cultures of the Caribbean – among them, Cristina García, Julia Alvarez, Rosario Ferré and Edwidge Danticat. In the wake of a writer like Paule Marshall, these writers are something of a challenge because, like her, they have achieved great prominence in the United States with their distinctive mediation of North American and Caribbean worlds. While each of these writers privileges her North American vantage point, their work directly counters the invisibility of the Caribbean Other in their organic representations of a specific Caribbean reality. To read and explore their work is to penetrate distinctly Caribbean worlds in an aesthetic language that is widely accessible to North American and Caribbean audiences in their adopted language, and to others through translation, so that cultural interpenetration has an unprecedented integrity and authority in making a Caribbean social reality accessible to both worlds.

Orlando Patterson observes in "Global Culture and the American Cosmos" that there is no precedent in the United States for this kind of "colonization in reverse".[11] That may or may not be the case, but the point is that he describes a social and cultural phenomenon that marks a significant shift in subject position, from Caribbean to Caribbean American, and the flexible citizenship of the transnational:

> In structural terms, the mass migration of peoples from the periphery in this new context of cheap transportation and mass communication has produced a wholly different kind of social system. The migrant communities in the center are not ethnic groups in the traditional American sense. In the interaction between center and periphery, the societies of the periphery are radically changed, but so is the traditional immigrant community of the center. What has emerged is, from the viewpoint of the peripheral states, distinctive transnational societies in which there is no longer any meaningful identification of political and social boundaries.... The interesting thing about these communities is that their members feel as at home in the mainland segment as in the original politically bounded areas.[12]

The writers are themselves acutely aware of the distinctive space they occupy and have not retreated from the subject positions they occupy as contributors to Caribbean and US cultural life. For example, in an interview with Kim Dismont Robinson for *RG Magazine (Bermuda)* in 2000, Edwidge Danticat responds to an observation about her "hyphenated heritage" in the most straightforward and unapologetic manner. It is the worthy subject of free and open debate: "I'm always in the middle of this debate. Sometimes people are suspicious, and wonder if it means that people like me who write from the hyphen are 'less Haitian'." Danticat continues:

> This debate is important because there's a whole generation of people who came with our parents and are creating in another country.
>
> But I think they *should* struggle with that, because we are going to have to deal with that issue more and more. People are being raised between exile and assimilation.... I don't think it's tragic, it's just that people who are more on one side (e.g. people born and raised exclusively in one country) have trouble understanding.[13]

This is not dissimilar to the position that Julia Alvarez thematizes in *In the Time of the Butterflies* (1994) in the figure of the *gringa dominicana*, the investigative reporter and translator of Dominican experience into a Caribbean-American novel. This is also the subject of her essay "Doña Aída, with Your Permission", republished in her collection of essays, *Something to Declare*. Alvarez argues that she is neither a Dominican writer in the traditional sense nor a mainstream American writer. She adopts a descriptor "Dominican-American" to reflect her new cartography, a conflictual space in which she maintains internal and external views and where duality enables a new consciousness.[14]

A new place on the map is another world, one might say, of the creative imagination; it is also the lived reality of a Danticat and an Alvarez. But what does the Caribbean have to say about this Caribbean-American connection? Does it have something to fear in the context of continuing migrations from the Caribbean to the United States, increasing economic and cultural interpenetration, the steady erosion of the nation-state, national economies and national cultural identities? It is commonplace to observe that the Caribbean is a region in which all the continents of the world converge, that the Caribbean is a very modern sensibility and very self-consciously cosmopolitan. According to George Lamming,

> We were a global village from day one. We have a unique laboratory of the world because all the continents, at different times and for different reasons, deposited important portions of themselves here. The Caribbean sensibility grew up as a very modern sensibility, very cosmopolitan. There is hardly any theme that could be the subject of university literature that has not been the actual common experience of a Caribbean person. And that's one reason why Caribbean people have this extraordinary adaptability, whenever they move to any metropolis. It doesn't take us long to adjust. That's because the history of the Other has never been far from the history of ourselves.[15]

The reassurance with which writers like Danticat, Alvarez, García and Ferré lay claim to a hyphenated inheritance is testament to that. In their writing there is an open and free dialogue between worlds that was not available to a McKay.

Yet another subject position is that occupied by writers such as Derek Walcott, Kamau Brathwaite, Jamaica Kincaid, Maryse Condé, Michelle Cliff, Elizabeth Nunez, Patricia Powell, Antonio Benítez-Rojo, Édouard Glissant and Merle Collins. They are uncompromisingly Caribbean as a point of identification and return but earn their living and, in some cases, make their homes in the United States. Their contribution to Caribbean literary culture from the United States as a site of dissemination is immeasurable in its contribution to the deepening awareness the region has of itself. Thus, the United States and its economic and cultural institutions find themselves in the enviable position of mediating Caribbean literary and cultural production to the Caribbean region, to the United States and to the world – a position that was once the exclusive sphere of the United Kingdom and the European metropolis.

An interesting dimension to this complex process of cultural absorption and mediation is that Caribbean literary cultures arise out of precisely such adverse conditions. A quest for recognition and inclusion outside limited national boundaries has defined the cultural life of the region, even as it began to dream of political independence from colonial authority at different points in the region's history. This interdependence both facilitated and influenced cultural production in the past in ways that are yet to be documented and understood. In the context of José Martí (1853–1895), the hero of Cuban liberation from the yoke of colonialism who spent most of his twenty-four years of exile in the United States, Lamming identifies what he calls "the singular importance of the Caribbean external frontier. He lectured; he taught; . . . and above all he wrote . . . poet, a philosopher, playwright, and meticulous journalist. His voice became an essential part of the Cuban patriotic consciousness."[16]

Yet on the Caribbean side there is always anxiety about the globalization of US culture through television and other media and the cannibalization of the local by the superior resources of the Western metropolis. Such anxieties are repeated among Caribbean nationalists, though there is very little they can do about the scale of US influence and penetration. As Orlando Patterson observes, parts of the eastern United States are now integrated with the nation-states of the Caribbean "as deeply as or more deeply than those parts are integrated with other regions of America".[17] Yet the conflict of interest is there between those who make their homes in the Caribbean and those who emigrate. It invites, writes George Lamming, "a concept of Nation that is not defined by specific territorial boundaries, and whose peoples, scattered across a variety of latitudes within and beyond the archipelago, show their loyalty to the 'nation-state' laws of their particular location without any severance of cultural contiguity to their original worlds of childhood".[18] In an interview in 1998, Lamming, a champion of Caribbean sovereignty, responds with characteristic visionary logic to this issue of whether Caribbean culture can resist American influence: "Given our proximity to the United States and the very intimate interactions we have with the US, it is very difficult to find any Caribbean family that has no relations with America. So the question is not fighting off the influence, but how to develop a critical relation to that influence."[19]

The fact is that the United States fulfils a perceived need in Caribbean economic and cultural production. Lamming explains his position further: "Our writers are dependent on external promotion. We have not worked out in the Caribbean itself a publishing infrastructure. Most major Caribbean writers have publishers outside. And where you don't have the apparatus of literature in the community itself, there is no direct exchange between the writer and the reading class that you find in the United States or England."[20]

The dilemma for Caribbean writers and artists is not new. Before Americanization there was Europeanization, and Western/American cultural influence has generated enormous cultural production in the Caribbean. Cultural narratives of Caribbean community have a long history of mutually advantageous capitalist-style negotiation with metropolitan vendors of regional "indigenous" cultures. Patterson, in "Global Culture and the American Cosmos", argues that the Caribbean is not "a world of passive consumers, homogenized and manipulated",[21] and that "What has emerged is, from the viewpoint of the peripheral states, distinctive transnational societies in which there is no longer any meaningful identification of political and social boundaries".[22] If this can be said of the general population, how does it situate the creative imagination? To quote Maryse Condé:

> Are we condemned to explore to saturation the resources of our narrow islands? We live in a world where, already, frontiers have ceased to exist. . . . In new environments one faces new experiences which reshape the West Indian personality. For those who stay on the islands, changes occur also. As Glissant himself puts it, the Caribbean Sea, which he opposes to the Mediterranean, is not a closed area. On the contrary, it opens onto the world and its varied energetic influences.[23]

In a similar vein, beyond the necessity of ethnic groundings, Stuart Hall makes an interesting point about fluctuating tensions between the local and the global: "But just as, when one looks at the global post-modern, one sees that it can go in both an expansive and a defensive way, in the same sense one sees that the local, the marginal, can also go in two different ways. When the movements of the margins are so profoundly threatened by the global forces of modernity, they can themselves retreat into their own exclusivist and defensive enclaves . . . ."[24]

I am aware that the values of cross-culturalism in South Florida do not necessarily coincide with those that are current or deemed desirable in Cuba, Puerto Rico, Haiti, Trinidad and Tobago, Jamaica, Barbados or Guyana. In fact, that is my main point as I explore ideas of cross-culturalism and the Caribbean canon. Contributing elements of a Caribbean canon might be constructed for their value to nation formation, or as a reflection of elements of the regional cultural community, but for the life of me I cannot envision a Caribbean canon that is not shaped by cross-cultural enquiry of one sort or another, no matter where one is located in the Caribbean or the Caribbean diaspora. In the absence of fully articulated national canons within the region that might yoke literary and cultural studies to the idea of a national identity and a nationalist ideology, the idea of a Caribbean canon cannot be seen apart from the cross-cultural contexts in which the literature is produced, marketed, read and evaluated: first in relation to the colonial capitals of Europe, and subsequently in an exploitative/collaborative capital venture that has since been duplicated in Canada, the United States and the Caribbean.

If the Caribbean is not a single geographical place, but rather many places with fluid cultural boundaries that boast a multilingual, multi-ethnic, many-ancestored population, the Caribbean canon – to the extent that such a canon exists – is of necessity a place in the imagination, a mythic place linked variously to a multiplicity of origins and associations within and beyond the geographical limits of the Caribbean. The geopolitics of cultural knowledge makes cross-culturalism a logical pathway to communication and understanding within the Caribbean and in frontier territories like South Florida. As a system of thought, cross-culturalism facilitates dialogue among Caribbean peoples and cultures in the heartland and at the periphery, and complicates a sense of Caribbean identity that might be nation-based or race-based or language-derived, and perhaps determined by ethnic (race, religion, language) ancestry or political ideology, or a combination of any of these. Conceptually, cross-culturalism accommodates the historical and cultural specificity of Glissant's root and relation, as well as Brathwaite's inner and outer plantation.[25]

Clearly, the kind of flexible reading that cross-culturalism privileges does not necessarily coincide with rigid notions of national sovereignty, or even regional sovereignty, though it does not preclude them. The fact is that while cross-culturalism is an inclusive and open-ended process, it is but one construct among others that might be put in place to facilitate understanding of the social and symbolic systems that distinguish Caribbean cultures and societies. If this raises the spectre of aesthetics versus ideology, it should not; the constituent elements of evaluation and selection that go into canon formation make that kind of argument irrelevant. Given the multifaceted contours of Caribbean literary culture, new configurations of knowledge will inevitably appear to challenge pre-existing arrangements of imaginary and pedagogical canons. In this respect, one might argue as John Guillory has done, that "[i]t should be possible to understand the very divergence of canons and canonizers as a better ground than consensus for a defense of a literary culture". He continues:

> It is more practical, if not inevitable, that we consider what it means that "difference" has become our central critical category; at the least, this means the permanent difficulty of forming a canon acceptable to a consensus of the literary culture. This condition I would like to describe as the state of heterodoxy, where the *doxa* of literature is not a paralysed allusion to a hidden god, but a teaching that will enact discursively the struggle of difference.[26]

The absence of a working consensus on what constitutes a Caribbean canon, imaginary and pedagogical, after a century of extraordinary literary production, suggests that the entire corpus may have emerged as the project of criticism and theory.[27] As Guillory argues, the very divergence of canons and canonizers may be read as evidence of the disestablishment of consensus in recognition of the competing interests of divergent groups.

The absence of a regional institutional authority that can make its consensus of value felt wherever Caribbean literature finds a readership, and the absence of an adequate publishing infrastructure in the Caribbean and a reading class that can sustain that infrastructure, contributes to the idea of a Caribbean canon that remains an undetermined imaginary totality. One might argue that canon formation in the Caribbean, outside of regional and national institutions, is in the hands of individual writers and those institutions that contract to produce and market their work. Next in line would have to be those who consume and evaluate them as extensions of the same process.[28] In "Canon-Formation, Literary History, and the Afro-American Tradition: From the Seen to the Told", Henry Louis Gates Jr makes a strong case for the singular importance of comprehensive anthologies of literature and theory in this process: "A well-marketed anthology – particularly a Norton anthology – functions in the academy to *create* a tradition, as well as to define and preserve it."[29] But Gates speaks from a singular position of authority and influence that pertains to a rigorously mediated study of Afro-American literature and culture within the US academy that extends to the remunerative textbook industry in the United States. Nothing of the sort pertains in the widely scattered fields of Caribbean literary production and consumption, and one result is a relative freedom in the way pedagogical canons are constituted, whether or not they impinge on those sanctioned by national and regional institutions in the Caribbean.

For example, my institutional locus bears a direct relationship to the ideological content of what I teach and my emphasis on the historical circumstances of their production. Given the social function and institutional protocols of the academy that provides me with a forum for disseminating Caribbean literature, I choose to represent it as flexible and open, with the clear understanding that the changing shape of a Caribbean canon is finally beyond the individual control of any one scholar, teacher, anthologist, publisher or cultural or educational institution within or beyond the region's geographical boundaries, except where absolute governmental authority holds sway. In all this, it behoves us to remember that the masters here are the creative writers themselves; however subject to the vagaries of textual production and distribution, they continue to exert an influence on new generations of creative writers, beyond the assumed authority of required and recommended reading lists.[30]

In practice, each syllabus or series of readings I might construct reinvents the Caribbean canon in the rearrangement of a selection of its constituent elements, albeit with due respect for the particular talents of individual writers, their quirks of self-positioning, their ideological biases and their representative values, while operating always within the limitations of textual accessibility. If institutional protocol permits, I need not conform to the selections of anthologists who shape and reshape the canon at the behest of a publishing house with a target audience in mind. But one is limited, more often than not, by what is readily available at a reasonable cost through regular channels of cultural production and distribution.

But that emphasis sidesteps issues of cross-culturalism as a collaborative discursive practice that undertakes to examine diversity in time as well as geographical placement – or does it? One might argue that all Caribbean writers have direct experience of cross-culturalism, whether they choose to represent this as liberating or constricting or paradoxically so. If cross-culturalism entails inquiry into the local and culturally specific, a question might be whether this entails a comparative and/or an integrative multicultural vision. But cross-culturalism – differentiated from multiculturalism – privileges a comparative discursive framework beyond a national framework that encourages the integration of people of different ethnic groups and religions in all areas of a society.[31] I argue that the point at which cross-culturalism and the Caribbean canon come together involves the crossing of all boundaries, both conceptual and geographical, and this involves destabilization of the centre/periphery model as a discursive practice that sustains the values of the nation-state. I would also argue that cross-culturalism as a discursive practice does not in principle supersede other discourses so much as provide a meaningful alternative in its emphasis on a collaborative discursive framework. It is but one construct among others that might be put in place to facilitate an understanding of the social and symbolic systems that distinguish Caribbean cultures and societies.[32]

Notes

1. For a useful assessment of how geopolitics might be used as a mode of analysis, see Michael Klare, "The New Geopolitics", *Monthly Review* 55, no. 3 (July–August 2003), www.monthlyreview.org/0703klare.htm.
2. John Guillory, *Cultural Capital: The Problem of Literary Canon Formation* (Chicago: Chicago University Press, 1993), 30. As Guillory explains it, "the problem of what is called canon formation is best understood as a problem in the constitution and distribution of cultural capital, or more specifically, a problem of access to the means of literary production and consumption" (ix).
3. The oppositional values of Sameness and Diversity are a subset of Édouard Glissant's "Cross-Cultural Poetics", in *Caribbean Discourse: Selected Essays*, trans. J. Michael Dash (Charlottesville: Virginia University Press, 1989), 97–109.
4. "Home-Place, Identities, and the Political in US Ethnic Literature" (paper presented at the seventeenth annual conference of the Society for the Study of the Multi-Ethnic Literature of the United States, Florida Atlantic University, Boca Raton, Florida, 10–13 April 2003).
5. The following data is randomly drawn from the American Community Survey in 2002 (http://www.census.gov/acs/www/): In the ranking of large cities (with populations of 250,000 or more), the proportion of foreign-born persons in the city of Miami (60.6 per cent) was greater than for any other city in the nation; more than 74 per cent of all foreign-born Cubans reside in Florida, but Cubans represent just 22 per cent of Florida's total foreign-born population. The US 2000 Census estimated the Cuban population of Miami-Dade at 50.4 per cent, followed by Puerto Ricans at 6.2 per cent and Mexicans at 2.9 per cent. Also worth noting is that the 2000 US Census "Caribbean" category excluded those of Hispanic origin, those

who were in the country illegally or those visiting over long periods of time. With a conservative estimate of 200,000 in Dade County and 171,403 in Broward, 492,000 Floridians identify their primary ancestry as West Indian. In the 2000 US Census, in Florida there were approximately 17,339 people from the Bahamas, 1,800 from Barbados, 609 from Belize, 698 from the Dutch West Indies, 267,689 from Haiti, 163,190 from Jamaica, 18,115 from Trinidad and Tobago, 1,610 from the US Virgin Islands and 15,454 "Others".

6. Barbara E. Johnson, response to "Canon-Formation, Literary History, and the Afro-American Literary Tradition: From the Seen to the Told" by Henry Louis Gates Jr, in *Afro-American Literary Study in the 1990s*, ed. Houston A. Baker Jr and Patricia Redmond (Chicago: Chicago University Press, 1989), 43.

7. Yet, as Barbara E. Johnson, responding to "Canon-Formation", observes in respect to discourses of false universality, the "we" created can be empowering: "With its cognitive indeterminacy and its performative authority, it is both problematic and unavoidable for discourses of political opposition. For this structure of the stressed subject with an indeterminate predicate may well be the structure necessary for empowerment without essentialism. At the same time, it is an empowerment always in danger of presuming too much. But, then, can there be empowerment without presumption?" Ibid., 43.

8. This continues to be a factor in the contemporary scene. In a recent interview with Emily Apter, Maryse Condé observes in respect to the marketing and reception of her own work in the United States: "Editors [in the United States] tend to see everything in black and white . . . . But this really doesn't work, since my books are concerned less with race and much more with the complexities of overlapping cultures, with conditions of diaspora, and with cross-racial, cross-generational encounters." "Crossover Texts/Creole Tongues: A Conversation with Maryse Condé", *Public Culture* 13, no. 1 (2001): 93.

9. Claude McKay, *A Long Way from Home* (1937; New York: Harcourt, Brace and World, 1970). See chapter 1, in particular, 1–4.

10. The phrase belongs to Gayatri Chakravorty Spivak, "Three Feminist Readings: Mc-Culler, Drabble, Habermas", *Union Seminary Quarterly Review* 35, nos. 1–2 (Fall–Winter 1979–80). She observes that "the sense of a 'world' [in this case, read the United States and Caribbean worlds] is the ever-shifting and many-planed converging points of interminable determinations; and even a 'change' conceived of as a restructuring must be called again and again into question" (15).

11. Orlando Patterson, "Global Culture and the American Cosmos" (Andy Warhol Foundation for the Visual Arts: Paper Series on the Arts, Culture and Society, no. 2), 9, http://www.warholfoundation.org/paperseries/article2.htm. "Colonisation in Reverse" is the title of a poem by Louise Bennett, Jamaican poet. It was published in *Jamaica Labrish* (Jamaica: Sangster's Bookstores, 1966), 179.

12. Patterson, "Global Culture", continues: "Thus, more than a half of the adult working populations of many of the smaller eastern Caribbean states now live outside of these societies, mainly in the immigrant enclaves of the United States. About 40 per cent of all Jamaicans, and perhaps half of all Puerto Ricans, live outside of the political boundaries of these societies, mainly in America" (9).
13. Kim Dismont Robinson, "The Immigrants' Storyteller", *RG Magazine* (Bermuda) 8, no. 8 (August 2000): 21.
14. Julia Alvarez, *Something to Declare* (Chapel Hill, NC: Algonquin, 1998), 172–73.
15. George Lamming, "Damning Lamming", interview with Knolly Moses, *Panmedia*, http://www.panmedia.com.jm/features/lamming.htm.
16. George Lamming, *Coming, Coming Home: Conversations II* (St Martin: House of Nehesi, 1995), 44–45.
17. Patterson, "Global Culture", 6. He continues: "The separate units [Caribbean societies] are legally autonomous, but sovereignty becomes merely a resource to be used in interaction between the main collective actors. In spite of legal restrictions on the movement of peoples, there is a vast flow in both directions – legal and illegal migrants from the periphery, tourists and investors from the center. There is no simple flow of cheap labor to capital in this system [the Western Regional Atlantic Cosmos], as in the classic colonial regimes. Skilled and cheap labor flow in both directions. Legal and illegal capital also moves in both directions" (7).
18. Lamming, *Coming Home*, 32.
19. Lamming, "Damning".
20. Ibid.
21. Patterson, "Global Culture", 3.
22. Ibid., 9.
23. Maryse Condé, "Order, Disorder, Freedom, and the West Indian Writer", *Yale French Studies* 2, no. 83 (1993): 130.
24. Stuart Hall, "The Local and the Global: Globalization and Ethnicity", in *Culture, Globalization and the World System: Contemporary Conditions for the Representation of Identity*, ed. Anthony D. King (Minneapolis: University of Minnesota Press, 1997), 36.
25. Édouard Glissant, *The Poetics of Relation*, trans. Betsy Wing (Ann Arbor: Michigan University Press, 1997); Edward Kamau Brathwaite, "Caribbean Man in Space and Time", *Savacou* 11–12 (September 1975): 1–11, 106–8.
26. John Guillory, "The Ideology of Canon-Formation: T.S. Eliot and Cleanth Brooks", *Critical Inquiry* 10, no. 1 (September 1983): 195–96.
27. Gayatri Chakravorty Spivak, *Outside the Teaching Machine* (New York: Routledge, 1993). On the subject of literary canons, Spivak makes this important point among many: "There can be no general theory of canons. Canons are the conditions of institutions and the effect of institutions. Canons secure institutions and institutions secure canons" (271).

28. A striking example of the disconnect that can occur between the national, the regional and diaspora communities, and the transnational publisher as canon maker is noted by Kwame Anthony Appiah, *In My Father's House: Africa in the Philosophy of Culture* (New York: Oxford University Press, 1992), where he concludes that the editors of the Heinemann African Writers Series "constitute in the most concrete sense the pedagogical canon of Anglophone African writing" (55).
29. Henry Louis Gates Jr, "Canon-Formation, Literary History, and the Afro-American Literary Tradition: From the Seen to the Told", in *Afro-American Literary Study in the 1990s*, ed. Houston A. Baker Jr and Patricia Redmond (Chicago: Chicago University Press, 1989), 37.
30. In "What Is at Stake in the 'Battle of the Books'?", *New Criterion* 8, no. 1 (September 1989), a hostile response to John Guillory's 1987 essay "Canonical and Non-Canonical: a Critique of the Current Debate", Christopher Ricks makes an interesting point about canon formation: "But the most important and enduring rediscovery or reinvention of a book or a writer comes when a subsequent creator is inspired by it to an otherwise inexplicable newness of creative apprehension" (44). In the same vein, Derek Walcott cites Malraux's *The Psychology of Art*: "What makes the artist is the circumstance that in his youth he was more deeply moved by the sight of works of art than by that of the things which they portray." *Another Life* (Washington, DC: Three Continents, 1982), 3.
31. David Baronov and Kevin A. Yelvington, "Ethnicity, Race, Class, and Nationality", in *Understanding the Contemporary Caribbean*, ed. Richard S. Hillman and Thomas J. D'Agostino (Kingston: Ian Randle, 2003). My point of reference here is their idea of Caribbean nationhood as variations of four essential frameworks: *"mestizaje-creolite* (racial/mixing/creolism), racial democracy, national race, and multiculturalism" (224).
32. Margaret Kumar makes an important point in this respect: "Moreover, in a complacent acceptance of culturalism, the suffix 'ism' may also be taken as a process of movement that calls for a replacing of one construct of thought with another. It also connotes an adherence to a conscientious direction and perspective that coerces total acceptance and adoption of one set of values over another. If such is the case, then culturalism becomes anachronistic and antithetical." "Postcolonial Theory and Cross-Culturalism: Collaborative 'Signposts' of Discursive Practices", *Journal of Educational Inquiry* 1, no. 2 (2002): 84.

CHAPTER 6

Mutual Ground
Post-Empire Canons of Art in Britain and the Caribbean

▶ LEON WAINWRIGHT

A rough survey of the art history of the past three decades might lead to the conclusion that there has always been a canon debate at the heart of controversies over visual representation, in both Britain and the Caribbean. Evidence is there in the vocabulary of any artists who have ever found themselves at art history's margins and so joined the drive for "inclusion" and "remembrance" and demanded to be "visible". Such are the terms of canonicity: the simultaneously physical and visual collecting of art and artists in a way that confers upon them the status of the best and most representative known to the history of art.

The canon as a mechanism for legitimizing the artistic past has become prone to intensive critique in art history as a discipline. If such concerns have recently lessened, as in the UK spaces where I have taught and researched art history, there is a sense that debate about the canon is something that has already happened, and so deserves no further attention. I became conscious of this attitude in 2004 when preparing to speak in the Caribbean on the topic of art canons.[1] My colleagues saw me about to make a long journey only to deliver a paper focused on an apparently rather outdated inquiry. I was charitably told that however anachronistic the canon debate may seem, nonetheless, "*They* have to go through that, just the same as *we* did."[2] It would be too easy, however, to accept that countering – or even "firing" – the canon should be passé for some people and hot news for others. As I make obvious in the following, I feel uncomfortable with the assumption that something was in fact achieved in Britain when canon debates were at their height. And I find the related idea unacceptable: that perhaps debates about canons or along similar lines have never taken place in the Caribbean before now. The implication is an "us and them" divide, of two art histories with little, if anything, in common. It is a distinction casually made without the benefit of comparing the regions where struggles around canonization have condensed.

What I am about to outline unsettles these perspectives of absolute difference and anachronism by emphasizing the historical pervasiveness of canons. Well after the 2004 conference, with the benefit of time in the Caribbean to trace out critical questions about contemporary art there, I have taken the opportunity to reflect on that region and on Britain with the canon idea at the centre of analysis. This chapter tackles the assumption of a time lag or delay between the two regions, deriving from some unquestioned notion of art's historical "progress", with Britain undoubtedly in the lead. It also serves another, no lesser aim: to demonstrate the implicit benefits of swapping notes on two seemingly distinct regions in which canon questions about art history have been raised. For artists in particular, these are questions that address the possibilities and obstacles around their historical remembrance. Why, it is worth asking, has this desire for self-definition surfaced in British and Caribbean settings? As I show, if in each place it is a desire shaped by the mobilization of difference as a political category and a means of overcoming exclusion, then it would be good to know what particular character this has taken, and how it has changed.

To say a little more by way of introduction about the prehistory of the past few decades, it was the argument over creolization in the Caribbean that incorporated concerns about the canon, which it takes little imagination to see the current focus on the canon now incorporating in turn. In the most generous analysis, accounts of creolization would amount to a democratic *description* of racial, ethnic or cultural elements regarded as making up a distinctively Caribbean zone, or at least one comprising nations with certain cultural affinities, expressed and ordered according to their relative importance. In a less generous, more critical view, creolization had nothing to do with plain description. Its founding motivation was to manage difference as a political commodity in a region vigorously negotiating the process of decolonization (and thus much dependent for its architecture on the selections made by those doing the describing). In the area of "creole nationalism" especially, official stipulations would show some forms of difference – reified ethnic ones – to be more contextually legitimate than others.[3]

Such a designation of roles to ethnicity and difference in the building of anti-colonial nationalisms closely informs the cultural politics of the present question of Caribbean canons. Creolization talk has given rise to the subsequent conversation about the Caribbean's "repeating", heterogeneous cultural canon. Significant discontent and fallout around the uses of culture as a political commodity have focused on the extent to which its particular emphasis on difference has made for a stubborn fixity in art and representation. In this view, by exchanging its once lively and transformative potential for a hoary notion of "unity through difference", cultural nationalism maintains a stranglehold on alternative terms of cultural self-definition and sets the parameters of any sort of Caribbean canon. The currently expressed need to break away from such lingering, stifling "nation narratives" offers a riposte to that more orthodox emphasis on hegemonically scripted national identities. We find these being refused, for instance, by the artists associated with what Annie Paul has called an alternative group (as well as a wider cohort of contemporaries) in favour of a more complex embrace of apparently progressive differences. These include generational ones and a nascent outer/national conversation with and through post-colonial difference, in which art and artists of the Caribbean enter creative historiographic and critical relationships with the wider world. Their riposte has been issued as a departure from the more orthodox emphasis on hegemonically scripted national identities as the foundation for a Caribbean cultural canon.

With the benefit of a Caribbean lens, the history of British entanglements in canon wars begins to show some features for comparison. I remark on British attempts to make an impact upon the art history canon – taken as a mutually defining network of related institutions of display, collecting, patronage, reception, recording and so on. How did the agitations of an ebullient group of arts activists during the 1980s in Britain come to shape and be shaped by institutions that could no longer ignore their resounding pleas for canonical inclusion? I have made my response to this question on a negative note by outlining what has resulted, and what has failed to result, from those artists' agitations around the canon idea. The overall picture tacitly undermines any myth of British multiculturalist progress. It makes transparent the reproduction of older exclusions in a new, perhaps less easily contestable form, as well as faith in canonicity itself as some sort of lasting, once-and-for-all "redemption" of the marginalized.

The history of cultural politics subsequent to the end of Empire is consequently just as contradictory as Kamau Brathwaite anticipated in his seminal work on creolization. This is indicated by the way that present-day battles are being fought in the Caribbean over the art historical record, whether they be to strengthen the backbone of national spaces of aesthetic meaning or a contingent group of artists struggling free from the circumscriptions of older national canons. It may be interesting therefore to see how counter-canonical discourses – such as the British ones around "Black Art" and a "diaspora aesthetic" – have met with pitfalls which Caribbean artists and commentators might benefit from knowing about. The institutional co-option of what were once vitally radical terms of cultural identification and analysis reveals the mutual ground of art and its canons to be continually shifting while its core concepts reproduce. But it is equally valuable to recall how long such shifts and patterns have been endured in the Caribbean, and what strategies have emerged in order to cope.

British "Black Art" and Managing Difference

When, in 1992, Anne Walmsley published her account of the Caribbean Artists Movement (CAM) – a generation of West Indian artists and writers in Britain who came together from 1966 to 1972 – she wrote forcefully of the need for their presence to be "fully documented and made public".[4] Yet, despite a purpose to have "deliberately avoided theoretical analysis of CAM, in the belief that this would constrict and distort it", taken as a whole, Walmsley's stance and the book it generated are inherently and complexly theoretical. They make transparent how the outlook and common concerns of CAM were often focused on its own historiography, as evidenced in their meetings and correspondence and manifest in their art and writing. Placing at its centre the matter of historical remembrance, Walmsley's is a group biography but also a CAM project, extending the influence of the movement beyond its 1972 dissolution.

Walmsley's study offers a starting point for discussion about the contingencies of historiography and artists' groupings represented by contemporary contexts for negotiating the canon and the art history record. During the 1980s in Britain, prior to her account, there was little remembrance of artists of the Caribbean who were active during the previous two decades in contesting Britain's postwar art history. Artists mainly of the second generation of Caribbean migration made much of what they shared with artists of several other diasporas, largely those of Africa and South Asia, and to a lesser extent East Asia and the Middle East. Their commonalities were represented in a range of art forms, including filmmaking, photography, performance, painting and drawing, installation and other media. It was a group, like CAM, at pains to reflect on their situation within a historical frame, and so invested heavily in historical inscription. Preoccupied with their promotion and recording around and through their art, they organized to curate exhibitions, publish, write about art and archive the evidence.

It is instructive to relate to this broad base of practices primarily as an assault on the art history canon, and to understand the canon as a record or measure of contents which has often taken the form of a narrative detailing selected elements of the artistic past. For artists of several diasporas in Britain who have claimed exclusion from the canon – which resembles for them the mainstream of a British national art history – the 1980s has to be considered the period of the most ebullient statements of this kind. The consequences this has for the present day, and for a discussion of the Caribbean, rest in the detail of how many of its artists have seen fit to target the environment touched by the canon, namely the gallery network and art criticism. In so doing they have taken artistic activity, or what has been called "arts activism",[5] as the basis for a sort of canon "counter-formation", as artist Keith Piper explained in 1984:

> You see, today what we are looking for is a Black visual aesthetic, a way of making works that is exclusive to us, in the same way as our musicians have invented many musical forms which are totally "Black". We need a Black visual aesthetic because as Black artists we still depend on forms and ideas about art borrowed from European art history. It is that history, and the dominance of its values over us, which we need to reject because they cannot serve us in our struggle.[6]

In Piper's statement we can identify an artist for whom the authority of "European art history" had to be discarded, its being thought synonymous with a colonizing force that entrapped "Black" artists into dependence, and a particular obstacle in their "struggle". By contrast, Piper was more intent on a reverse kind of exclusion, a self-selected one, which shaped the early years of his practice during what became more widely exemplary of the entire "critical decade" of the 1980s.[7] With fellow artist Eddie Chambers, he organized the first "Black Art" exhibition at Wolverhampton Art Gallery in 1981,[8] and a year later used the First National Black Art Convention at Wolverhampton Polytechnic to form the BLK Group, a collection of art students and recent graduates from the West Midlands that staged exhibitions from 1982 to 1984.[9] They were followed by a run of largely group "survey" exhibitions of topic- or issue-focused art under the sign of Black Art, which was closely defined as made by black artists to speak to a black community and address "Black issues". Such events included reference – such as in their titles – to an ongoing drive for self-definition and a sense of needing to drastically intervene against racism. Making this possible was a curatorial concern to name, chart and document an excluded black presence while highlighting the institutional obstacles in the way of these artists' wider and lasting recognition.[10]

Black Art stood to emphasize some leading related themes. It drew its imagery from the facts of racial violence and disadvantage faced by communities of immigrants to Britain and their descendants. In particular, it signalled the fraught matter of national belonging that they were having to negotiate firsthand. A single work might touch on one or more of such themes, such as the circumstances of young black Britons in Tam Joseph's *UK School Report* (1984),[11] which plays on the roots of disaffection and "deviance" in the passage through school and college. His *Spirit of the Carnival* (1988)[12] responds to mistreatment by the British establishment, visualizing a reminder of the police violence and clashes at the annual celebrations in London's Notting Hill.[13]

Black Art themes would also be handled in other ways, most notably by artists such as Claudette Johnson, Joy Gregory, Veronica Ryan, Chila Burman, Ingrid Pollard and Lubaina Himid, who led many of the group shows. A central strand was their robust, often disturbing introduction of femininity as a complicating aspect of difference, using topics of domesticity and intimacy to confront connections among ideas about family, kinship and British nationhood. The complicities of popular imaging with racism and stereotype became a signature concern in the multimedia work of Sonia Boyce, such as her *From Someone Else's Fear Fantasy to Metamorphosis* (1987).[14] A four-part self-portrait with montage and sketched additions, it brought satire to the double oppression of black women by their prevalent fetishism in film, advertising and photography. Boyce's preference at that time for figurative pastel drawing showed how women artists could develop radical positions at variance with those of their male counterparts. The frequently collaborative practices of women refused to replicate the masculinism of artists such as Piper and Chambers, questioning their sense of the artist as an autonomous male author[15] while refusing to rehearse a commensurate rhetoric, often drawn from the US Black Arts Movement and pan-Africanism.[16]

A key characteristic of British Black Art was its close involvement with artists of the South Asian and other diasporas,[17] a development that distinguishes the UK context from better-known formations of artistic "blackness" elsewhere, such as the United States. It saw the "Black" concept as a political identity (rather than an indicator of African descent) being embraced in a widely enjoined critique of the canon. Some of the women I have named were of this kind, together with a group that included Zarina Bhimji, Allan de Souza, Shaheen Merali, Sunil Gupta and Sutapa Biswas. A painting and collage by Biswas, *Housewives with Steak Knives* (1986), became iconic of this "Asian" participation.[18] Its loose canvas depicts a modern-day multi-limbed Kali with henna-stained hands and protruding tongue, who indicates her status as a goddess of destruction by threatening decapitation with kitchen utensils. A necklace of heads, including those of the right-wing politician Enoch Powell and other white males, marks out the targets of her aggression. By way of such "Indian" references, Biswas made it obvious that Black Art, in Britain at least, could come from many ethnic quarters and be a common focus for mobilizing a counter-canon.

My interest in Britain has tended to pivot on this unique assembling of artists of many ethnicities and to promote a keen sense of the subtle differentiations to be made between the voices and positions of that historical moment. This important diversity among artists has been generally unnoticed in recent accounts, which has a lot to do with deeper questions about the political ground on which artists cope with the terms of their description. They were not all in fact pursuing the same political goal of a separate "Black visual aesthetic" as expressed in Piper's statement, and Black Art was far from a singular category. The position taken by Rasheed Araeen, a Pakistan-born member of the Black Panthers and founder of *Black Phoenix* magazine, in which he published a rousing "Black Manifesto",[19] made this obvious. The publication was later incorporated into the international journal *Third Text*,[20] and with Araeen as its founding editor, its readers could compare his views on the situation of "Black" artists with a range of other outlooks, the oppositionalism of Piper and Chambers included.

Embracing the term *Black Art* and arguing as forcefully for a militant critique of the canon, Araeen saw such art as closely bound up with the history of artistic modernism – indeed, as continuous with it – no matter how much this was overlooked in the art history record. The sort of opposition to the canon which claimed that Black Art came out of a discrete cultural history, somehow removed from a shared modern story, was for him a denial of its provenance and continuing connections. As he explained, with a note of concern, in 1988:

> The term "black art" is now being commonly used by the black community as well as by people in Britain in general. But this common usage is often a misuse, as far as the work that might be called "black art" is concerned. It may be a convenient term to refer to the work of black artists, but it also implies that their work is or should be different from the mainstream of modern culture. . . . "Black art", if this term must be used, is in fact a specific historical development within contemporary art practices and has emerged directly from the joint struggle of Asian, African and the Caribbean people against racism, and the art work itself explicitly refers to that struggle.[21]

Despite the diversity of perspectives among the Black Art artists, it was common by the mid 1980s for commentary to refer to this community as if they stood, with consensus, for a single purpose. More gravely, given what overlapped in their aims, it was generally ignored that they had only identified themselves as black in response to their shared circumstances of racism and exclusion from art history. An explicit language of resistance – typical of Black Art – was not evident in all art made by those who found themselves marginalized. The photography of Vanley Burke, for example, which predates Piper, Chambers and their peers, has frequently been conflated with the Black Art activities of the 1980s. In Burke's own words, his photographs present a sort of "histograph", "capturing the personal, social and economic life of black people as they arrived, settled and became established in British society".[22] His largely monochromatic images bring attention to the workplace, to delicate portraits of children, to worshippers and days at the fair. But the dimensions of "Black experience" he drew from everyday life differed from the agitations of Black Art proper, with its demands on the canon. If there is a tendency for canons to oversimplify, to discourage complexly plural or fragmented narratives, this brought the consequence of artists' being matched with others on the basis of ethnic difference, regardless of their individually held interests, and to frustrate their demands on the canon.

Effectively two leading paradigms of Black Art were adopted by those claiming a marginal position in relation to the canon. Piper and his immediate colleagues offered the strategy of declaring an absolute separation from the "European values" which alienated them, declaring their own cultural parameters in the face of exclusion. Araeen's approach, by contrast, was to assert a presence allegedly integral to twentieth-century and British modernism, being no "different from the mainstream of modern culture", and thereby constitutive of it. However, at the time they were asserting these differing positions (in the early 1980s), it was the separatist attitude that won the most attention. BLK Group events and Lubaina Himid's show at the Institute of Contemporary Arts led to greater exposure of protest-based work. It was the sort which offered a line of attack on the canon that was all too easily incorporated by art institutions; when taken as a licence to marginalize these artists further, their separatist posture posed a paradox. It energized the very spirit of generalization which had excluded all artists, of whatever "ethnic" background, from the white mainstream.[23]

Initially the sort of gallery and exhibition spaces that Black Art was given were mostly separate from mainstream commercial or prominent public galleries. There had been so-called community-based projects such as the Greater London Council anti-racist mural project of 1985,[24] and places like the Black Art Gallery and 198 Gallery, with a narrow remit to promote "ethnic Art". But these were less known and little accessed by a general art audience, and so attracted the criticism that these artists were being deliberately kept apart from their white peers.[25] The support first given in 1988 by the prominent Whitechapel Gallery carried the association of its location, in an area of London's East End which has traditionally been a place of immigration. Such adaptations by art institutions towards the end of the 1980s, described in the then official vocabulary of "ethnic minority arts", served to distance artists from valued spaces of national display.

On the surface, blanket promotion of "ethnic" artists, regardless of how they each identified themselves, would seem to suit the separatist attitude. Yet artists such as Eddie Chambers were angrily disappointed that the 1980s were so short-lived, since the decade's properly "critical" period of bona fide Black Art exhibitions and arts activism ended in 1986.[26] Those with fundamentally radical investments in Black Art would be grouped together with artists who were not party to such debates through arts programmes and art commentary. And in public life more widely, the growing status of the notion of "Black Britishness" came to be applied to mean all "non-whites" in general, thereby robbing it of its meaning as a term of political affiliation. As Araeen had forewarned, when the priority for arts policies became redistributing resources to minority ethnicities in general, this would frustrate ambitions for wider "visibility". Rather than responding to direct arguments about the racial dimension of the art canon, and concomitant ethnicizing values in national art historiography, the trend became one of misrecognizing the constitutive role of black people within the art history canon.[27]

The contribution of academic thought during the late 1980s is at first sight an analytical reflection and clarification of the two positions shared among practitioners of Black Art. It was probably conceived to reconcile them; it dwelled less on the trope of blackness and particular points of view about art and politics, in favour of attention to the field of cultural production in general. Paul Gilroy, writing in 1988 from within the discipline of cultural studies, asserted the idea of a "diaspora aesthetic", which was developed further by Stuart Hall in connection with Caribbean cinema,[28] by the curator and arts organizer Gilane Tawadros[29] and by academic Kobena Mercer. They took an ambivalent stance on the matter of difference and ethnicity, producing what Ien Ang has noted of post-colonial intellectuals as their "double focus",[30] deeming the "diaspora aesthetic" idea useful for understanding artists of any diaspora whatsoever and designed to engage a positive change in their circumstances.

One line of approach would find agreement with Piper's. The diaspora aesthetic partly stood for the idea that being diasporic indicated a fixed, easily identifiable experience typical of people of African, Asian and Caribbean descent alike, distinguishing them as a common group with an essential connectedness capable of withstanding their changing circumstances. A second critical strand was a more properly analytical attitude emphasizing the style of "diaspora culture" as a far more ambiguous phenomenon. This usage fleshed out Araeen's arguments, although in a vocabulary then unfamiliar to art history, by referring to the "dialogic strategies and hybrid forms"[31] of diasporas and "the hybrid, transitory and always historically specific forms in which questions of 'race' and ethnicity are articulated".[32] This aspect of commentary thereby turned away from essentialism in order to characterize the diasporic as itself heterogeneous and formed by contingency with history.[33]

These initiatives from cultural theory altered the landscape of discussion by intervening in the factional schisms among the Black Art interlocutors. They also broke away from the mechanistic official language of "ethnic minority arts" and exerted particular influence on national organizations such as the Arts Council of England, as well as local galleries. It was a set of circumstances that caught my attention in 1997 as a doctoral student conducting archival work and interviews with a range of participants in those spaces. I asked how and why the diaspora aesthetic had achieved such currency. It was felt that the concept was deemed more satisfactory than the Black Art idea as a definition of the cultural, social, political and historical experiences of those creative individuals who felt shunned by art institutions. It articulated a rationale for their practices, affirming their value as products of these complex histories of migration, settlement, exclusion and resistance. As an intellectual development, talk of a diaspora aesthetic promised a systematic look at what "diaspora people" were making in any field of cultural production, as evidence and affirmation of their "diaspora lives". Artists, arts organizers, theorists and critics alike were now able to speak broadly about "Black" cultural practices, from fine art to popular culture, as all bearing similar signs of their diaspora.

In the face of such interests, public art institutions were the first to absorb criticism about the exclusions they were practising, and some of these reflections would feed into discussions about how best to grant artists support. By the 1990s, and with the founding of the publicly funded Institute of International Visual Arts (inIVA) in 1995,[34] the official language of promotion had dispensed entirely with the notion of ethnic arts in favour of a firmly multiculturalist emphasis on "diversity" and recognition of "difference".[35] It was similar to what had been around during the previous decade through the work of the Institute of Contemporary Arts,[36] and identical to some of the terms of the diaspora aesthetic.

This can still be seen in the recent priorities declared by Arts Council

England (ACE) that "cultural diversity" with "specific reference to ethnicity" ought to predominate among the funding and job opportunities for artists and curators. In May 2003 a national network of organizers was put in place to launch Decibel, an ACE initiative directed to "ethnic diversity resulting from postwar immigration, with a focus on arts and artists from African, Asian and Caribbean backgrounds", promising "to profile arts practice ... and to develop opportunities for increased access into the mainstream".[37] But, like the proposed ACE Year of Cultural Diversity – postponed from 2001 to 2002, rebranded as "The Big Idea" and then subsequently scrapped – Decibel's agenda met with the criticism that it marks a "current tendency towards a segregated visual arts sector".[38] Despite its declared aims to ensure that "the landscape is changing",[39] one critic noted that it "has failed to spark debate about art world pathologies" typical of the "institutional racism"[40] signalled in the 1999 MacPherson Report on the Stephen Lawrence Inquiry and the Race Relations (Amendment) Act.[41]

In the most severe critique, institutional change in Britain has proved to be little more than the ability to "manage" difference and artistic production and to limit the possibilities for how artists may identify themselves. Kobena Mercer has suggested that such "multicultural managerialism" and "multicultural normalisation" had fully taken hold by the end of the millennium,[42] when ideas of diversity, heterogeneity and hybridity became accommodated under institutional conditions in which "the subversive potential once invested in notions of hybridity has been subject to pre-millennial downsizing".[43] In 2006 the series of four talks "Re-constituting a Black British Canon", organized at Tate Britain with speakers selected and chaired by the gallery's cross-cultural curator, Mike Phillips, coincided with a major rehanging of the Tate's collection, and suggested a separate art history of blackness and diaspora as detached from modernism.

One might conclude that the current official vocabulary of arts funding and promotion, in line with that associated with the diaspora aesthetic concept, has been put to some uses that fail to match with the ambitions of the Black Art movement. It is an outcome that confirms Araeen's warning of 1994 that, "in the West, [multiculturalism] has been used as a cultural tool to ethnicise its non-white population in order to administer and control its aspirations for equality. It also serves as a smokescreen to hide the contradictions of a white society unable or unwilling to relinquish its imperial legacies. In this context one can understand the British fascination and celebration of cultural difference."[44] Apprehensive about such institutional change, in 1991 Valerie Brown set about making her photo and graphic piece *Encounters*, in which a white hand caresses a black backside above a fringe of enjoined hands. This fringing imagery was taken from the publications and letterhead of the Commission for Racial Equality.[45] I first wrote about this image as a visual comment on the fear of "inter-racial" sex and of miscegenation as the possible basis for a historical colour bar.[46] But Brown's piece has far more to do with the suspicion that equality struggles would fail, since black artists were being noticed by white authorities but only as fascinating in some very one-sided ways.

Caribbean Alternatives

The starting point for a comparison of the institutional dimension of art canons in the Caribbean appears on the surface not to have anything to do with the terms of difference used in Britain. Being so many islands and territories rather than one state seems to mitigate against any true comparison if designed as an evaluation of corresponding national units with equating structural conditions. And yet the idea of British black artists as outsiders to art history who have been routinely overlooked, or as insiders whose constitutive role within art and modernity has also been denied, has found a similar currency within the history of Caribbean canons and counter-canons. Canonical categories in the Caribbean have been quite strikingly dominated by related anxieties over "outsider" values about art, only here the terms are reversed: alien, outsider features are those that threaten to invade the region and jeopardize the formation of something recognizable and sovereign about its art. As categories that have remained doggedly concomitant with issues of national scope, they have encouraged artists in the Caribbean to resort to strategies that parallel those used in Britain.

The translation of an outsider designation because of marginalized identification (as found in Britain) into a label for foreign impositions and colonial interference (as in the Caribbean) has profound significance for how canons are generated. Trinidad's state-sanctioned accounts of national culture have indirectly derived from ever-sharpening distinctions between the metropolitan or overseas versus local or indigenous components for making art. Indeed, such literal isolation has long been considered to enable national distinctiveness; a major concern is the need to press art into the service of "domestic" rather than "foreign" interests. A leading proponent of this view was Trinidad and Tobago's first prime minister, Eric Williams, who expressed the terms of this relationship in his many addresses, interviews and publications, such as in the following: "Dependence on the outside world in the Caribbean in 1969 is not only economic. It is also cultural, institutional, intellectual and psychological. Political forms and social institutions, even in the politically independent countries, were imitated rather than created, borrowed rather than relevant, reflecting the forms existing in the particular metropolitan country from which they were derived. There is still no serious indigenous intellectual life."[47]

In the face of this still-present ideology it may seem impossible to think of addressing the questions I have raised with input from an "outsider" and through "outside" examples, although evidently this is a view I would reject by encouraging attention to Britain. Examining concerns about art's reception and historiography – again, perhaps primary locations for canon formation – Gabrielle Hezekiah has drawn attention to the continuing effects of such divisions, evidenced in the salient critical issues around the canonization of "Caribbean art": "the dynamic and often unspoken/unnamed tensions that exist in the discussion of territory, stakes and belonging in the visual arts in several areas of the English-speaking Caribbean".[48] Ultimately, Hezekiah supposes, such tensions cluster around two questions. The first is, "Who has the right to write an art history of the Caribbean?" – which involves "unspoken issues of race, ideological position, artistic/institutional affiliation and insider/outsider status". The second is about the choice of an appropriate language of art and art criticism that would be deemed suitable for "the local context/contest" and a need to be critically aware of "the introduction of a 'newfangled', 'outsider' language".[49] These are summed up by three resolutions: "There is such a thing as Caribbean Art"; "We must develop a language for dealing with it"; and "We must take ownership of it (before somebody else does)."[50]

Hezekiah assumes that, like chattel, to be owned, art discourse has the status of a commodity. This is a synecdoche of a larger argument about ownership of art criticism being the first step towards ownership of art and its histories, since the matter of who manages to speak will largely decide what is understood about the object of discourse. The institutions of creole nationalism helped to push this view, with the adverse circumscription of art as a national "sign". This presents particular challenges for artists, such as Christopher Cozier, who are "uncomfortable"[51] with the options this leaves available for contemporary practice. They are among what Cozier identifies as the "Boom Generation" in Trinidad, struggling to enter and shape the island's growing contemporary art milieu.[52] The sort of canon they construct is quite at odds with the earlier nationalist tendency to cast art in the role of a foundation for the larger edifice of a Caribbean creole canon. My contact with Trinidad from 2004 was during a time of transition in its art sector towards wider participation, in a move to foreground these relations through contemporary practice. One measure of the artists' activity was that fine art can no longer be correlated entirely with any one of the island's ethnicities; it encompasses a wider social makeup through growth of interest beyond its traditionally upper-class core. As such, artists have rethought the older intersections of visual creativity, regional identities, status, ethnicity and national belonging.

In 2006 there was firm evidence of this change with the launch of "Galvanize", a series of artists' projects and events based in Trinidad and spearheaded by artist Mario Lewis, who with support from the leading London gallerist Victoria Mirò had earned a master's degree in fine art at Goldsmiths College the previous year. The event happened alongside Carifesta but was not part of its official programme and did not receive any of its allocated public money. The changes that it signalled have to do partly with increased promotion of the arts in general, such as the commercialization of carnival as a corollary of the Caribbean tourist, leisure and cultural industries.[53] Galvanize organizers were able to make use of an existing media infrastructure, including daily television interviews during the programme's opening weeks, a mutually annotating web of Internet sites designed and written by publishing professionals, and features in magazines with global distribution.[54] A glowing editorial in the *Trinidad Guardian* praised the resourcefulness and slick organization of Galvanize, drawing a sharp contrast between it and Carifesta and the debacle caused by the latter's poor execution – a topic which frequently captured headlines during September of that year.[55] An alternative contribution in the visual arts to Carifesta had in fact been debated for some time, for example, in the polemic given in 1999 by Cozier, a member of the Galvanize steering team:

It has been my experience and view that events such as Carifesta, which were about us coming into being and knowing ourselves after the competitive agendas of the colonial space, have now become tired and exclusive. The idea is perhaps too heavily guided by the agendas of nation building and its cultural programming with its narrative of the "folk" versus the Afro/Indo Saxon. It is, perhaps, now drifting along as either a forum for communal despair or decorative eloquence, or both. Today the poles are different. It may be the "ownership class" of the nationalist dream versus an unknown internal other that is no longer satisfied to remain as just voyeurs. It is time to support and encourage the participation of new names and ways of responding to this space.[56]

Much of the thinking behind Galvanize was done by a group of artists who have explored over the past two decades the divisions of "inside" and "outside" that it broached. Annie Paul's interest in Trinidad, set out in her essay "The Enigma of Survival: Travelling Beyond the Expat Gaze", focuses on this group, a community that in a moment of typographical wordplay she calls "alter-NATIVES" – namely Christopher Cozier, Steve Ouditt, Eddie Bowen and Irenée Shaw – who, to quote her, "represent a category of artists from the Caribbean . . . [who] find themselves on the wrong side of nation stories in opposition to majority groups that assert ownership of the national or Caribbean space".[57] Travelling beyond the expat gaze (and its expert "expatese") means recognizing these "natives without narratives, or perhaps with unpopular or inconvenient narratives", in order to subvert the manner in which, "in privileging discourse about the self and other exclusively, the expat gaze overlooks identities ostracized or exiled by the national".[58]

By framing this group in terms of their refusal of expatriate desire, Paul's essay is addressed to northern settlers in the Caribbean and the wider international body of art historians and critics. Such an observation about the expat overseeing/policing the Trinidad art scene is less prescient than for the other islands that she has written so forcefully about.[59] Nonetheless, Paul is justified in showing that models of art criticism in the Caribbean region have rested heavily on accounts of the nation and the national, the hybrid, the indigenous, the native and the anti-colonial, the self and the Other, and thereby deny ground to the experiences and practices of artists who remain unconvinced about the expediency of such distinctions. The origin of those terms is less the expat, perhaps, than the strident "owners" of the Caribbean's national spaces, by whose terms the current generation of artists refuses to be limited, delimited or "troped". As Cozier puts it:

> Since the mid eighties in Trinidad, and by the mid nineties in the rest of the anglophone Caribbean, the threat of artist-led initiatives to define or come to terms with different objectives or responses to the Caribbean space has caused much anxiety. The new enemy of the nationalist has shifted from the colonizer to the perpetual "next generation" whose allegedly ambiguous relationship to the national space is not understood. At the outer edge of this sacred space is the "foreign head". The shift to process and method opens up the idea that the boundary between what is defined as local and what is supposed to be foreign (alien to us) has become unapologetically permeable and that the thematic and conceptual concerns of the artist are not already fixed. So the contemporary space can be interpreted as part of an ongoing evaluative or investigative look at the local, as well as the broader domain of artistic activity globally.[60]

If the expat and the "majority groups that assert ownership of the national or Caribbean space" do so with adverse effects through "nation stories", this raises the question of what might be the concrete alternatives. In one point of view, the artists of the alterNative group, as well as many more who cast themselves in a similar role of contesting such narratives, have opted not to abandon difference at all, but have reincorporated difference on their own "alternative" terms and of their own kind. These differences are not inclined to articulate the features of racial, ethnic and colour particularity that shape anti-colonial nationalisms; they have more pointedly to do with their aftermath: differences of generation, and a dynamic re-evaluation of the globalizing processes that had originally prompted "Third World" nationalisms but were masked or unheard beneath the national anthems and the other songs championing the national and the local. An illustration of this is Cozier's video piece staging the inculcation through a radio broadcast of Trinidad and Tobago's anthem and a flickering cinematic repetition of the social housing units built throughout the islands – each strands of social planning of a portentously "unfamiliar" and "scripted" future.[61]

This generational aspect of Caribbean cultural canons may appear to form a helpful parallel for understanding Britain's battles with the canons of its art environment. Accounts of these have on the whole tended to remain insular, or else best explained through comparison with the United States.[62] The division of generations into anti-colonial and post-colonial in the Caribbean goes some way towards illuminating the generational patterns among Britain's community of art practitioners of African, Asian and Caribbean descent. It may also seem to index them, rather neatly, to a much debated division about modernist and post-modernist attitudes to the visual.[63] But this generational chronology is cut across by further differences that in turn make it premature to herald a burgeoning alternative to the "sacred space", as Cozier put it, of modernist, anti-colonial art canons. A generational scheme of historical change oversimplifies both the Caribbean and the diasporic story in Britain alike. The artist Shastri Maharaj, for instance, was not among the coterie of artist-educators who practised around the time of independence, nor does he see himself among the generation of artists who offer a more tangential relationship to self-representation and ethnicity than he did during the 1980s and 1990s.[64] In the United Kingdom, many artists who have featured in developments of the past three decades were in fact born abroad, but they share contemporaneity and peer group with British artists who have immigrant parents.[65] The differences between the experiences of the two generations has often been a matter of face-to-face debate,[66] but it is unfair to relegate the outlook of artists of the older, "arrivant" generation to a time slot in art's historical past when they continue to adapt and produce work in and of the present.[67]

Getting to know art and artists of the Boom Generation in the Caribbean is also about recognizing the elective outer-national affinities they draw upon. Cozier has pointed to the significance of a "list of Trinidadian artists who have produced bodies of work in and about places like southern Africa",[68] which includes Marlon Griffiths, Wendy Nanan, Dean Arlen and Cozier himself, all of whom were hosted by the Bag Factory in Cape Town, South Africa, and displayed their work there.[69] He notes that "[t]hese works have embarked on a new axis of comparative investigations between us and other southern locations, and what some have called 'post-colonial' cultural experiences". Such fruitful "South–South conversations", with Caribbean artists and thinkers corresponding across the political geography of former colonies, are perhaps best encapsulated in Tejaswini Niranjana's archival and book project, in which she gathers and analyses music of the South Asian diaspora in Trinidad to facilitate an investigation around gender, generously posting online some music samples to annotate her conclusions.[70] It would be a serious mistake to see in Niranjana's project an Indo-nationalist alignment of the Asian subcontinent with its Caribbean diaspora rather than the sophisticated contribution that it promises. Hers is just one of the new collaborative networks raising questions about canons of cultural meaning that transcend the balkanized cultural geography of the Caribbean.

Another example of how outer-national partnerships may point the way to similar advancements was offered on the occasion of the Jamaican National Biennial, which I had the privilege to visit in 2004 and in a review essay dubbed it "the proudest, most vibrant art show of Winter 2004–5 in the Anglo-Caribbean".[71] It saw the emphasis on cultural diversity and inclusivity brokered in the United States and Britain (in the way I have outlined) playing a part in the Caribbean itself through the running of the Biennial. Significantly, it demonstrated how official notions of difference and diversity can be celebrated according to more than one model or any single means, that is, through creating a whole experience of visiting the event rather than directing attention to the individual selections of the artist participants. As I noted,

> Talking to people inside and outside the Biennial I realised what far larger issues of inclusivity are being debated in relation to the National Gallery's future. The first mainly has to do with artists: it links every spark of the curators' energies given to allowing artists, as if from a great Jamaican family tree, to come together under one roof. They range from those born, based or settled on the island, to Jamaicans mainly or solely resident abroad (New York City–based Anna Henriques and Peter Wayne Lewis), to the English expat Rex Dixon who has since resettled in Trinidad. The second conception of inclusivity is largely about audiences: the administrative drive toward a radically more appealing and inclusive Gallery that can draw in the typical Jamaican, the kind who passes perhaps daily by the door, but seldom, if ever, finds it appropriate to enter.[72]

The exhibition hinted at two perhaps competing senses of how "Jamaicanness" and aesthetics can be put on national public display and engaged with. Previous attention to the same space – the National Gallery of Jamaica – had shown a sharp pathology of the curatorial authority instituted there.[73] In 2004 this was challenged from above by a notable change in the running of the gallery, which brought to its biennial an ethos of outreach and widening participation similar to that of major public spaces such as the Brooklyn Museum, from which the gallery's new executive director comes. Considerations of this sort had in fact been made by the gallery's principal curators at the turn of the millennium, highlighting the obstacles to unlocking its educational resources.[74] This more recent development illuminated ways of making the academicism that the institution is known for work even harder to address its contemporary role; the fresh programming of events that followed has continued on this track. The Biennial also indicated how much could be gained through a more global sort of outreach designed to change the architecture of art canons in the region. This, and the outcomes of Niranjana's time in Trinidad, suggests that art and its histories in the Caribbean are negotiating various conversational alternatives by engaging in novel forms of collaboration.

Canons and Futures

Questioning the dominant, hegemonic canon is a crucial project, and one revealing of the still embattled beliefs invested in art practice as a critical site of transformation. Both the Caribbean and British contexts offer examples of the motivations and pressures for seizing the intellectual resources on offer to assemble canons – or counter-canons – and for contestation through art and its historiography. During the 1980s and early 1990s, these were much more conspicuous in Britain than they are at present; nowadays, exhibition organizers, curators and critical commentators are on the whole less inclined to name a stable corpus of art practices, and to describe any selection of artists as a coherent group sharing common outlooks and experiences.

If artists of diverse backgrounds in Britain no longer focus their energies on "becoming visible" but think more about the terms of their visibility – the manner in which they are promoted and received – this is some indication of the shifting yet constant demands over representation in art and its histories. Canonizing the work of artists of African, Asian and Caribbean backgrounds in Britain has not been without its mixed outcomes and discontents. The canon debate has happened without delivery of the guarantees of acceptance and understanding sought by the formation of artists and artworks of recent decades, and we are left with some harrowing difficulties for writing a history of this art. Clearly canons have a troubling presence; living with and without a canon are equally problematic, and never tenable for all of the time. A canon for a diverse community of identities has to negotiate in a sustained manner the double bind of emphasizing ethnicity, nation and inflexible notions of culture as grounds for affinity.

It may be less appropriate to wonder about future canonical scenarios that break with past canons. The more pressing question is: What are the alternatives to the apparently ceaseless jockeying for competition and preoccupation with visibility and canonization? A genealogical interest in such developments, especially a better sense of the history of failures around the canon, would better establish the grounds for this sort of departure. The canon debate is both enabling and yet problematic; the advantage of knowing its history is in locating and learning from its problems: how to have a canon that is self-reflexive and aware of its exclusions.

One such route to self-reflexivity has been opened up by the recent critique of how cultural criticism conceives of the art object and the artist. Regardless of claims that "Black cultural politics insists upon the ascendancy of a broader aesthetic and political project",[75] the weight of interest has rested unmistakably on the latter, as perhaps one might expect of a consciously politically led project to contest the dominant narratives of art history. Under these circumstances, however, alternative understandings of the histories of art remain very difficult to elucidate, so much so that, as artist Juginder Lamba has put it, simply "[t]he work itself has become secondary".[76] Or as Gabrielle Hezekiah suggests, commenting on a similar situation in the Caribbean, the outcome is "the subsequent relegation of the work itself to relative obscurity and isolation in the midst of so much rhetorical fluff".[77]

While it claims to bind a framework of critical analysis onto a particular history of art, the diaspora aesthetic idea has in fact delivered few definitions which reference actual works of art. The caveat widely issued among commentators is that, like the artists they have described, their accounts adopt "postures of indiscernibility"[78] thought to be deeply enabling of a diasporic politics of knowledge and representation. For Hall in particular, such a viewpoint is germane to the emergence of a potentially redemptive notion of ethnicity and identity formation[79] that is intended to renew our sense of the importance of the diasporic as an intellectual construct. As such, the common canonical ground for diaspora artists is defined as a space of ongoing self-definition and identification through conventions of picturing held to have wider implications for the symbolization of race, difference and nation. Common to accounts within this counter-canon is that the role of art is primarily one of communicating or symbolizing in the manner of (visual) texts and signs.

As with much of the discussion around canonicity, it is this vocabulary from poststructuralist theory after its "linguistic turn" which has gained the most prominence in Britain. The linguistic and textuality paradigm, however, would suppose that art objects have the ability to codify narratives or to offer a didactic "voice" in a wider political struggle, each of which requires the command of a visual language in which art does the work of a signifying cultural text. Hal Foster recognized in his essay "The Artist as Ethnographer?" that this renders the practitioner of art as "a paragon of formal reflexivity, sensitive to difference and open to chance, a self-aware reader of culture understood as text".[80] But for artist and critic Jean Fisher, thinking in this way tends to suggest that "art is more a cultural product than a dynamic process or complex set of immanent and sensuous relations".[81] This complaint is enlarged by Rasheed Araeen: "As for the dominant discourse, it is so obsessed with cultural difference and identity, to the extent of suffering from an intellectual blockage, that it is unable to maintain its focus on the works of art themselves."[82] The *aesthetic* in "diaspora aesthetic" operates as a blanket term for styles of visual meaning and how they are conveyed – that is, in a hybrid, syncretic or creolizing way. It thereby indicates the process of signification and communication rather than aesthetic experience as perceptual or phenomenological "sense". In such a scheme, representation threatens to render the notion of aesthetics obsolete, so that artworks become nothing more than media: encoded signs (of nation, ethnicity, culture or diaspora) ready to be decoded.

Such criticisms presage a larger project which would investigate the implications for the canon of the prevailing theoretical attitude typified by the diaspora aesthetic idea. A methodology which seeks to emphasize the textuality of visual objects, once applied to this context, has brought some adverse outcomes for artists such as Piper and his peers. Their works have been made into signifiers, named as cultural products, transformed and translated into signs and representations. That this elaborately skirts around the art objects themselves becomes obvious when the constructed, discursive objects of art criticism (the objects of post-structuralist thinking) predominate at the expense of attention to the tactile and visually apparent physical ones which emerge under the hands of artists – art objects with a material dimension, with textures and colours. Indeed, canonical claims have risked becoming complicit in what Barbara Stafford sees as the "ruling metaphor of reading", "the intellectual imperialism of collapsing diverse phenomenological performances, whether drawings, gestures, sounds or sense into interpretable texts without sensory diversity".[83] As the historian of philosophy Martin Dillon has remarked, "One way not to see the world is to read it as text."[84]

The recent histories of art in the Caribbean and in Britain both emphasize the textual codification of racial, ethnic and colour difference. As a result, it would appear that the vitality and material presence of art and the experiences and ambitions of contemporary artists have remained largely undisclosed, with commentators preferring instead to debate canonization in the currently familiar ways I have been describing. Granting value to the art of "excluded" individuals or communities requires considerable energy to maintain in the face of the shifting, hegemonic territory of art display, reception and commentary. A particular challenge is how to conceive of a role for art historiography, which is transparent about its stake in the current environment: one shaped by common, often competing, claims of marginalization. As I have outlined, the groups involved in commentaries that unquestionably support campaigns for counter-canons risk finding themselves reaffirming the status of the very mainstream, centre or norms they set out to enjoin or critique.

The really awkward but necessary question to ask of these Atlantic histories is why the communities that shape them should continue to burden themselves with self-perceptions of cultural marginality and exclusion. How sustainable is the "war of position" entailed in canon debates? Zygmunt Bauman's suggestion about the recent interest in "identity crisis" is that "[m]ilitant assertion of group identity will not remove the insecurity which prompted it".[85] This points to the idea that any future strategic position on art canons would benefit from reflecting on how and why the range of options between "alterNATIVISM", separatism and "constitutive insiderism" has emerged as the only effective modes of resort, and how to imagine other futures.

The current political pressure on art criticism to assert a cultural (counter-) canon of marginalization has not been matched by vigorous analysis of further concepts of cultural production beyond the play and contestation of differences. This is ironic, given that the possible decoupling of art from other forms of political representation is precisely what arguments over the canon had seemed to promise, favouring instead some inscrutable measure of artistic and historical value. Although criticism continues to insist on framing art objects as significations of national place, political position or ethnic belonging, it still has to account for why the same visual practices continually refuse the singular role of being media of political representation alone. What is the sovereign place of art in otherwise overdetermined landscapes of visual meaning, such as the ones I have been describing in Britain and the Caribbean? The consequences of struggles around the canon and the terms they have engendered (whether "Black Art", the diaspora aesthetic idea, the lexicon of Caribbean biennials or the attempted departure from "nation narratives"), when taken up for analysis, show the limits of applying the category of aesthetics as if it were interchangeable with that of representation. By their inscription as themes of primarily ethnic and national discourse, linguistic units and commodities of exchange, artworks as tokens in "canon wars" have been drained of their aesthetic depth, their visual texture, intentionality and peculiar phenomenal presence. The art history of the Caribbean and Britain, however unable to live with or without canons, has still to reclaim that mutual ground.

Notes

1. This is where the first version of this chapter was presented in January 2004 at the conference "Cross-Culturalism and the Caribbean Canon", University of the West Indies, St Augustine, Trinidad. Some of the details of this chapter first appeared in my essay "Canon Questions: Art in 'Black Britain' ", in *A Black British Canon?*, ed. Gail Low and Marion Wynne-Davies (Basingstoke: Palgrave Macmillan, 2006): 143–67, before being substantially reworked to take account of the Caribbean context. My thanks go to the University of Sussex and the Leverhulme Trust for the fellowship, including support for fieldwork, that enabled me to initiate this work during 2004–5, and to those who gave generous feedback at that University of the West Indies conference. Thanks also to Christopher Cozier and Anne Walmsley for their comments, and to Patricia Mohammed, who kindly reviewed a subsequent draft.
2. It was a reference to the enthusiastic interest shown among art historians in Britain, typified by Griselda Pollock's study of "firing the canon" in art history's "culture wars", *Differencing the Canon: Feminist Desire and the Writing of Art's Histories*

(London: Routledge, 1999), and Nanette Salomon, "The Art Historical Canon: Sins of Omission", in *(En)gendering Knowledge: Feminism in Academe*, ed. Joan Hartmann and Ellen Messer-Davidow (Knoxville: University of Tennessee Press, 1991), 222–36.

3. I am condensing much here, although I return to this later in the chapter. The anglophone debate on creolization is extensive in Caribbean studies. For a recent overview and anthology of perspectives, see Verene A. Shepard and Glen L. Richards, eds., *Questioning Creole: Creolisation Discourses in Caribbean Culture, in Honour of Kamau Brathwaite* (Kingston: Ian Randle, 2002); Edward Kamau Brathwaite, *Contradictory Omens: Cultural Diversity and Integration in the Caribbean* (Kingston: Savacou Publications, 1974); Derek Walcott, *What the Twilight Says: Essays* (London: Faber, 1998); and Daniel Miller, *Modernity: An Ethnographic Approach: Dualism and Mass Consumption in Trinidad* (Oxford: Berg, 2007), 51.

4. Anne Walmsley, *The Caribbean Artists Movement: 1966–1972* (London: New Beacon Books, 1992), xviii.

5. Edward Anthony Chambers, *The Emergence and Development of Black Visual Arts Activity in England between 1981 and 1986: Press and Public Responses* (PhD diss., Goldsmiths College, University of London, 1998).

6. Keith Piper, press release, Black Art Gallery, London, 1984, unpaginated.

7. For example, David A. Bailey and Stuart Hall, eds., *Critical Decade: Black British Photography in the 1980s* (Special Issue), *Ten 8*, no. 3 (Spring 1992); Issac Julien and Kobena Mercer, "De Margin and De Centre: The Last 'Special Issue' on Race?", *Screen* 29, no. 4 (1988): 2–11; Paul Gilroy, "Cruciality and the Frog's Perspective: An Agenda of Difficulties for the Black Arts Movement in Britain", *Third Text* 5 (Winter 1988–89): 33–44; David Chandler, ed., *Keith Piper: Relocating the Remains* (London: inIVA, 1997); and the artist's own writing: Keith Piper, *A Ship Called Jesus* (Birmingham: Ikon Gallery, 1991). The essays noted above partly respond to Piper's photo-text collages: Keith Piper, "Body and Text", *Third Text* 2 (Winter 1987–88): 53–61.

8. Wolverhampton Art Gallery, *Black Art an' Done: An Exhibition of Work by Young Black Artists* (Wolverhampton: Wolverhampton Art Gallery, 1981).

9. Eddie Chambers et al., *The First National Black Art Convention to Discuss the Form, Functioning and Future of Black Art* (Wolverhampton: Wolverhampton Polytechnic, 1982).

10. See: Mappin Art Gallery, *Into the Open: New Painting, Prints and Sculpture by Contemporary Black Artists* (Sheffield: Mappin Art Gallery, 1984); Creation for Liberation, *Creation for Liberation Open Exhibition: Art by Black Artists* (London: Creation for Liberation, 1985); Lubaina Himid, *The Thin Black Line* (Hebden Bridge: Urban Fox Press, 1985); Institute of Contemporary Arts, *The Thin Black Line* (London: ICA, 1985); Black Art Gallery, *Some of Us Are Brave, All of Us Are*

Strong: An Exhibition by and about Black Women (London: Black Art Gallery, 1986); Black Art Gallery, *From Generation to Generation (The Installation)* (London: Black Art Gallery, 1986); Eddie Chambers, ed., *Black Art: Plotting the Course* (Oldham: Oldham Art Gallery, 1988); Eddie Chambers, Tam Joseph and Juginder Lamba, eds., *The Artpack: A History of Black Artists in Britain* (London: Haringey Arts Council, 1988); Rasheed Araeen, *The Essential Black Art* (London: Kala Press, 1988); Stoke on Trent City Museum and Art Gallery, *Black Art: New Directions* (Stoke-on-Trent: Stoke-on-Trent City Museum and Art Gallery, 1989); Eddie Chambers, ed., *Let the Canvas Come to Life with Dark Faces* (Sheffield: Herbert Art Gallery and Museum, 1990).

11. Tam Joseph, *UK School Report* (1984), acrylic on canvas, 141 inches × 76 inches. Collection of Sheffield City Art Galleries.
12. Tam Joseph, *Spirit of the Carnival* (1988); reproduced in Chambers, Joseph and Lamba, *Art Pack*, 30.
13. See Eddie Chambers, ed., *Us an' Dem: A Critical Look at Relationships Between the Police, the Judiciary and the Black Community* (Lancashire: Lancashire Probation Service, 1994); Kwesi Owusu and Jacob Ross, eds., *Behind the Masquerade: The Story of the Notting Hill Carnival* (London: Arts Media Group, 1988); Arts Council of Great Britain, *Masquerading: The Art of Notting Hill Carnival* (London: Arts Council, 1986).
14. Sonia Boyce, *From Someone Else's Fear Fantasy to Metamorphosis* (1987), mixed media on photograph; reproduced in Gilane Tawadros, *Sonia Boyce: Speaking in Tongues* (London: Kala, 1997), 43.
15. For further elucidation, see Boyce's own views expressed at that time in John Roberts, "Sonia Boyce in Conversation with John Roberts", *Third Text* 1 (Autumn 1987): 55–64.
16. Note, for example, the similarities between the earlier quote from Piper and Larry Neal's writing of 1968: "The Black Arts Movement is radically opposed to any concept of the artist that alienates him from his community. Black Art is the aesthetic and spiritual sister of the Black Power concept. As such, it envisions an art that speaks directly to the needs and aspirations of Black America. In order to perform this task, the Black Arts Movement proposes a radical re-ordering of the western cultural aesthetic. It proposes a separate symbolism, mythology, critique, and iconology. The Black Arts and the Black Power concept both relate broadly to the Afro-American's desire for self-determination and nationhood. Both concepts are nationalistic. One is concerned with the relationship between art and politics; the other with the art of politics." Larry Neal, "The Black Arts Movement", in the "Black Theatre Issue" of the *Drama Review* 12, no. 4 (Summer 1968): 29. Compare this with the special issue of *Callaloo* 23 (Winter 1985), dedicated to Larry Neal of *Callaloo*. For further British parallels see Eddie Chambers, *Run Through the Jun-*

gle: Selected Writings by Eddie Chambers (London: inIVA, 1999), and a concise review of that anthology: Niru Ratnam, "Run Through the Jungle: Selected Writings by Eddie Chambers", *Third Text* 48 (1999): 78–80.

17. See, for example, the overview in Amal Ghosh and Juginder Lamba, eds., *Beyond Frontiers: Contemporary British Art by Artists of South Asian Descent* (London: Saffron Books, 2001). For listings by artist and year, see Melanie Keen and Elizabeth Ward, *Recordings: A Select Bibliography of Contemporary African, Afro-Caribbean and Asian British Art* (London: Institute of International Visual Arts and Chelsea College of Art and Design, 1996).

18. Sutapa Biswas, *Housewives with Steak Knives* (1985), oil, pastel and acrylic on paper and canvas, 96 × 108 inches, Bradford Art Galleries and Museums; reproduced in Chambers, Joseph and Lamba, *Art Pack*, 8; Mora J. Beauchamp-Bird and M. Franklin Sirmans, eds., *Transforming the Crown: African, Asian and Caribbean Artists in Britain 1966–1996* (New York: Caribbean Cultural Center, 1997), 29.

19. Rasheed Araeen, "Preliminary Notes for a Black Manifesto", *Black Phoenix* 1 (1978): 3–12; reprinted in Rasheed Araeen, *Making Myself Visible* (London: Kala, 1984).

20. The nature of this incorporation is explained in Rasheed Araeen, "Why 'Third Text'?", *Third Text* 1 (1987): 3–5.

21. Rasheed Araeen, *Essential Black Art*, 5. Araeen's definition can be compared with the larger pattern of political organization outside the art community, evident from an earlier statement by the Organisation of Women of Asian and African Descent: "When we use the term 'Black' we use it as a political term. It doesn't describe skin colour, it defines our situation here in Britain. We're here as a result of British imperialism, and our continued oppression in Britain is the result of British racism." *Race and Class* 27, no. 1 (1985): 32.

22. Mark Sealy, ed., *Vanley Burke: A Retrospective* (London: Lawrence and Wishart, 1993), 12.

23. This clash of priorities and what could be discerned of their immediate effects is set out in one of the most valuable documents of this period, a discussion between Araeen and Chambers. Rasheed Araeen and Eddie Chambers, "Black Art: A Discussion", *Third Text* 5 (Winter 1988): 51–62.

24. Greater London Council (GLC), *Anti-racist Mural Project* (London: GLC Race Equality Unit, 1985); Greater London Council, *New Horizons: Exhibition of Arts* (London: GLC Ethnic Arts Sub-committee, 1985).

25. Rasheed Araeen, "A History of Black Artists in Britain" (typescript, GLC Race Equality Unit, London, 1986), and "From Primitivism to Ethnic Arts", *Third Text* 1 (1987): 6–25. These contributions from Araeen respond to as well as anticipate the prevailing official outlook and practices typical during the period from Khan, 1976, until 1989. Some primary and secondary sources include Arts Council, *The*

Arts and Ethnic Minorities: Action Plan (London: Arts Council of Great Britain, 1985); Kwesi Owusu, *The Struggle for Black Arts in Britain: What Can We Consider Better Than Freedom* (London: Comedia, 1986); Owusu and Ross, *Behind the Masquerade*; Richard Cork, Balraj Khanna and Shirley Read, *Art on the South Bank: An Independent Report* (London: Greater London Council, 1986); Mark Fisher, "Black Art: The Labour Party's Line", *Modern Painters* 2, no. 4 (1989): 77–78.

26. See Chambers, *Emergence and Development*, and Eddie Chambers, "The Black Art Group", *Artrage* 14 (Autumn 1986): 28–29.
27. Rasheed Araeen, "The Success and the Failure of Black Art", *Third Text* 18, no. 2 (2004): 135–52.
28. Stuart Hall, "Cultural Identity and Cinematic Representation", in *Black British Cultural Studies: A Reader*, ed. Houston A. Baker, Manthia Diawara and Ruth A. Lindeborg (Chicago: Chicago University Press, 1996), 220.
29. Gilane Tawdros, "Beyond the Boundary: The Work of Three Black Women Artists", in *Black British Cultural Studies: A Reader*, ed. Houston A. Baker, Manthia Diawara and Ruth A. Lindeborg (Chicago: Chicago University Press, 1996), 240.
30. Ien Ang, "Identity Blues", in *Without Guarantees: In Honour of Stuart Hall*, ed. Paul Gilroy, Lawrence Grossberg and Angela McRobbie (London: Verso, 2000), 1–13.
31. Stuart Hall, "What Is This 'Black' in Black Popular Culture?", in *Black Popular Culture: A Project by Michele Wallace*, ed. Gina Dent (Seattle: Bay Press, 1992), 29.
32. David Morley and Kuan-Hsing Chen, eds., *Stuart Hall: Critical Dialogues in Cultural Studies* (London: Routledge, 1996), 9. Compare with Stuart Hall, "New Ethnicities", in *Black Film/British Cinema*, ICA Documents 7, ed. Kobena Mercer (London: ICA, 1988).
33. Hall's use of the term *diaspora aesthetic* was tied to these two perspectives. On the one hand, he advocated critical work that "allows us to see and recognise the different parts and histories of ourselves, to construct those points of identification, those positionalities we call a 'cultural identity' ". See Stuart Hall, "Cultural Identity and Diaspora", in *Identity: Community, Culture, Difference,* ed. Johnathan Rutherford (London: Lawrence and Wishart, 1990), 237. On the other hand, Hall concurred with Mercer's observation that "across a whole range of cultural forms there is a 'syncretic' dynamic which critically appropriates elements from the master-codes of the dominant culture and 'creolises' them, disarticulating given signs and rearticulating their symbolic meaning . . . . [a] hybridising tendency". Quoted in Hall, "Cultural Identity", 220.
34. Established in 1995 under the rubric of internationalism in art practice, the Institute of International Visual Arts (inIVA), based in London, is funded largely by the Arts Council of Great Britain to provide a continuing programme that includes publications, exhibitions, schools education, a Web presence, commissions of artwork, art writing, artists in residence and open lectures.

35. Arts Council of Great Britain, *The Arts and Cultural Diversity* (London: Arts Council of Great Britain, 1989); Ria Lavrijsen, ed., *Cultural Diversity in the Arts: Art, Art Policies and the Facelift of Europe* (Amsterdam: Royal Tropical Institute, 1993); Sam Walker, "Black Cultural Museums in Britain", in *Cultural Diversity: Developing Museum Audiences in Britain,* ed. E. Hooper Greenhill (Leicester: Leicester University Press, 1997); Black Arts Alliance, *Black Arts Alliance Report* (Manchester: BAA, 1999); Greater London Authority, *Without Prejudice? Exploring Ethnic Differences in London* (London: Greater London Authority, 2000).
36. See, for example, Institute of Contemporary Arts, *Thin Black Line*; David A. Bailey and Kobena Mercer, eds., *Mirage: Enigmas of Race, Difference and Desire* (London: ICA and inIVA, 1995); Homi Bhabha, ed., *Identity,* ICA Documents 6 (London: ICA, 1987); Kobena Mercer, ed., *Black Film/British Cinema,* ICA Documents 7 (London: ICA and British Film Institute, 1988).
37. Richard Hylton, "The Politics of Cultural Diversity", *Art Monthly* 274 (March 2004): 20.
38. Ibid.
39. Arts Council of England, "Decibel", http://www.decibel-db.org (accessed 1 November 2004).
40. Hylton writes in "The Politics of Cultural Diversity", 22: "The notion that some people are more culturally diverse than others is as spurious as it is to consider some people as being more ethnic than others. . . . 'Ethnic minority' and 'culturally diverse' are terms that privilege a limited notion of difference based on race. Such euphemisms are unhelpful because they presuppose normality to be white and everything else to be diverse."
41. Her Majesty's Stationery Office, *The Stephen Lawrence Inquiry: Report of an Inquiry by Sir William MacPherson of Cluny* (London: Home Office, 1999); Commission for Racial Equality, *The Stephen Lawrence Inquiry: Implications for Racial Equality* (London: Home Office, 1999); Home Office, *Race Relations (Amendment) Act 2000: New Laws for a Successful Multi-Racial Britain* (London: Home Office, 2001).
42. Compare Kobena Mercer, "A Sociography of Diaspora", in *Without Guarantees: In Honour of Stuart Hall,* ed. Paul Gilroy, Lawrence Grossberg and Angela McRobbie (London: Verso, 2000), 234: "To the extent that the postcolonial vocabulary, characterised by such terms as 'diaspora', 'ethnicity' and 'hybridity', has displaced an earlier discourse of assimilation, adaptation and integration, we have witnessed a massive social transformation which has generated, in the Western metropolis, what could now be called a condition of *multicultural normalization*"; and Stuart Hall and Sarat Maharaj, "Modernity and Difference: A Conversation between Stuart Hall and Sarat Maharaj", in *Stuart Hall and Sarat Maharaj: Modernity and Difference,* ed. Sarah Campbell and Gilane Tawadros (London: Institute for International Visual Arts, 2000), 46.

43. By "downsizing" Mercer indicates the systematic absorption and circumscription of initiatives towards diversity by public and other institutions, a meaning given special inflection by this borrowing of vocabulary from a corporate ethos of productivity and efficiency. See Mercer, "Sociography of Diaspora", 235.
44. Rasheed Araeen, "New Internationalism, or the Multiculturalism of Global Bantustans", in *Global Visions: Towards a New Internationalism in the Visual Arts*, ed. Jean Fisher (London: Kala Press, 1994), 9.
45. Valerie Brown, *Encounters* (from the series; 1991), colour photograph/montage; reproduced in *Four x 4: Installations by Sixteen Artists in Four Gallery Spaces* (Harris Museum and Art Gallery, Preston; Wolverhampton Art Gallery, Wolverhampton; The City Gallery, Leicester; Arnolfini, Bristol, 1991), 16.
46. Wainwright, "Canon Questions", 150.
47. Eric Williams, *From Columbus to Castro: The History of the Caribbean, 1492–1969* (London: André Deutsch, 1970), 501.
48. Gabrielle Hezekiah, "Conceptualizing the Boundaries of Nation-Space: Some Thoughts on Art, Criticism and the Creation of a Canon", *Small Axe* 6 (September 1999): 80.
49. Ibid., 82.
50. Ibid., 90.
51. A term of description he has used to indicate this complex experience. See the documentary work made by Trinidad-born film maker Richard Fung, *Uncomfortable: The Art of Christopher Cozier* (2005); and Nicholas Laughlin, "Discomfort Zone", *Modern Painters* (June 2006): 102–3.
52. Compare Christopher Cozier, "Boom Generation", *Caribbean Review of Books* 11 (February 2007); and Christopher Cozier, "Between Narratives and Other Spaces", *Small Axe* 6 (September 1999): 23.
53. Gerard Aching, *Masking and Power: Carnival and Popular Culture in the Caribbean* (Minneapolis: Minnesota University Press, 2002), 3–4, with attention to Trinidad, has documented how contemporary Caribbean carnivals and popular festivals "constitute sites and events where local governments carry out the duplicitous role of facilitating 'national culture' for foreign consumption on the one hand, and scrutinizing, controlling, and policing public spaces where manifestations of that culture are exhibited on the other. This duplicity is particularly evident in islands where carnival is considered the principal national festival." See also Garth L. Green and Philip W. Scher, eds., *Trinidad Carnival: The Cultural Politics of a Transnational Festival* (Bloomington: Indiana University Press, 2007); Philip W. Scher, *Carnival and the Formation of a Caribbean Transnation* (Gainesville: Florida University Press, 2003); Errol Hill, *The Trinidad Carnival: Mandate for a National Theatre* (Austin: Texas University Press, 1972); Peter van Koningsbruggen, *Trinidad Carnival: A Quest for National Identity* (London: Macmillan Caribbean, 1997).

54. The Galvanize project made use of a detailed and creatively presented website in the format of a rolling diary of events and documentation; see http://projectgalvanize.blogspot.com/. This would be cross-referenced at the locally authored site of Caribbean contemporary art, "Art Papers" (http://artpapers.blogspot.com/) and the programme of film screenings (http://studiofilmclub.blogspot.com/), as well as on numerous other sites globally. Philip Sander, "Talking It Through", *Caribbean Beat* 83 (January–February 2007); Courtney Martin, "Galvanize, Port of Spain, Trinidad", *Flash Art* 251 (November–December 2006).
55. See "Editorial: Carifesta Must Engage Artists, Not Just Audiences", *Trinidad Guardian*, 28 August 2006; Lisa Allen-Agostini, "For the Benefit of Art", *Trinidad Guardian*, 2 September 2006; Attillah Springer, "Galvanizing Our Culture", *Trinidad Guardian*, 16 September 2006.
56. Cozier, "Between Narratives", 28–29.
57. Annie Paul, "The Enigma of Survival: Travelling beyond the Expat Gaze", *Art Journal* 62, no. 1 (Spring 2003): 49.
58. Ibid., 65.
59. See, for instance, her comparison of a European expatriate presence in Jamaica and Barbados; Annie Paul, "Uninstalling the Nation: The Dilemma of Contemporary Jamaican Art", *Small Axe* 6 (September 1999): 57–78.
60. Cozier, "Between Narratives", 22.
61. Aspects of the video are taken up in later work by Dean Arlen, and it is tempting to read Cozier's description of these as a comment on his own initial use of the motif: "Ranks of little generic house shapes symbolise government-provided housing developments and imply the discomfort of the economically displaced, who also face new, unfamiliar social relations and environments" ("Boom Generation", 21).
62. See Ian Baucom, David A. Bailey and Sonia Boyce, eds., *Shades of Black: Assembling Black Arts in 1980s Britain* (London: Duke University Press, inIVA and AAVAA, 2005).
63. See Stuart Hall, "Assembling the 1980s: The Deluge and After", in *Shades of Black: Assembling Black Arts in 1980s Britain* (London: Duke University Press, inIVA and AAVAA, 2005), 4–5.
64. I have written in further depth on this through a profile of the artists' career. See Leon Wainwright, "Indian Art in Trinidad? Ethnicity at Material Limits", *Journal of Creative Communication Studies* 2 (August 2007): 163–86.
65. Some examples to note include, in the Caribbean case, Veronica Ryan, who came to the Caribbean as a baby, and Denzil Forrester and Hew Locke, who came as adolescents; in the case of Africa, Yinka Shonibare and Sokari Douglas-Camp, who continue to move between Nigeria and Britain, Juginder Lamba and Zarina Bhimji from Uganda, and Johannes Phokela and Gavin Jantjes from South Africa; in the

case of South Asia, Rasheed Araeen of Pakistan and Balraj Khanna of India; in the case of the Middle East, Mona Hatoum of Palestine; and from elsewhere in Europe, Zineb Sedira of France.

66. Such as at the seminar organized by Creation for Liberation in Brixton in 1987, when Aubrey Williams addressed younger, British-born artists of a range of ethnicities. See Walmsley, *Caribbean Artists Movement*, 320, 340.
67. One such is the Guyana-born artist Frank Bowling, who continues to work energetically and to enjoy enormous success. An outline of his recent exhibitions and a brief overview of his career are given in Maya Jaggi, "The Weight of Colour", *Guardian* (UK), 24 February 2007, 11.
68. Cozier, "Boom Generation", 21.
69. The most recent of these visits was by Dean Arlen, whose summary exhibition of his time there in 2006, "Cape Town Chronicles", was held at the National Museum in Port of Spain, Trinidad, in December 2006.
70. See: http://mobilizing-india.cscsarchive.org/ and Tejaswini Niranjana, *Mobilizing India: Women, Music, and Migration between India and Trinidad* (Durham, NC: Duke University Press, 2006).
71. Leon Wainwright, "Art and Inclusion at Jamaica's National Gallery: The 2004 National Biennial", *Jamaica Journal* 29, no. 1–2 (June–October 2005): 24–25. An earlier version of that review article appears as "Jamaica National Biennial: Contradictions in Coherence", *Art Fairs International* 1, no. 5–6 (2005): 45–47.
72. Wainwright, "Art and Inclusion".
73. Annie Paul, "Legislating Taste: The Curator's Palette", *Small Axe* 4 (September 1998): 65–83.
74. See David Boxer and Veerle Poupeye, "National Gallery of Jamaica: A Research and Educational Institution", *Caribbean Journal of Education* 22, no. 1–2 (April–September 2000): 9–21. I am grateful to Annie Paul for bringing this article to my attention.
75. Tawadros, "Beyond the Boundary", 274.
76. Satjit Rizvi, "Here and Now 2: Juginder Lamba in Conversation", in *Beyond Frontiers: Contemporary British Art by Artists of South Asian Descent,* ed. Amal Ghosh and Juginder Lamba (London: Saffron Books, 2001), 256.
77. Hezekiah, "Conceptualising the Boundaries", 79–80.
78. Tawadros, "Beyond the Boundary", 274.
79. Stuart Hall, "On Postmodernism and Articulation: An Interview with Stuart Hall", in *Stuart Hall: Critical Dialogues in Cultural Studies,* ed. David Morley and Kuan-Hsing Chen (London: Routledge, 1996), 131–50. Compare with Stuart Hall, "New Ethnicities".
80. Hal Foster, "The Artist as Ethnographer?" in *Global Visions: Towards a New Internationalism in the Visual Arts,* ed. Jean Fisher (London: Kala Press, 1994), 14.

81. Jean Fisher, ed., *Global Visions: Towards a New Internationalism in the Visual Arts*, (London: Kala Press, 1994), 33.
82. Araeen, "New Internationalism", 9.
83. Barbara M. Stafford, *Good Looking: Essays on the Virtues of Images* (Cambridge, MA: MIT Press, 1995), 8.
84. Martin C. Dillon, *Semiological Reductionism: A Critique of the Deconstructionist Movement in Postmodern Thought* (New York: State University of New York Press, 1995), 104.
85. Zygmunt Bauman, *In Search of Politics* (London: Polity Press, 1999), 197.

Part 3

Negotiating Subjectivities, Finding Ease

CHAPTER 7

Coping with the New Culture
The East Indian Advisory Board as Mediator, 1937–1945

▸ BRINSLEY SAMAROO

On 1 January 1920, Indian indentureship formally ended in the British Empire. This meant the end of the system worldwide, since the British government, as rulers of India, had banned the recruitment of Indians on the subcontinent in 1917. Thus the French and the Dutch, for example, could no longer source *girmityas* (agreement-signers) from Pondicherry or Calcutta. By this time, just over half a million indentured Indians had been brought to the Caribbean island colonies and the British, French and Dutch colonies on the northern rim of South America. Of this total, about 144,000 had arrived in Trinidad, and a quarter of them had availed themselves of the return passage to India. At the time of Indian emancipation, the East Indian population (both those born in India and those born in Trinidad) stood at 121,420 of the colony's total population of 366,000.[1] About 84 per cent of these were Hindu, 14 per cent Muslim and 2 per cent of other religions (Christian, Buddhist and tribal). Even before this community attained freedom in 1920, its leaders had already started the process of hacking out a space for themselves in the New World. They were the last of the major immigrant groups which had started coming in the sixteenth century; most of those had already claimed their own spaces.

What were some of the early East Indian organizations? It is important that we look at these groups, because it was from these organizations that the state drew the membership of the East Indian Advisory Board (EIAB) from 1937. The groups existed at two levels. On the one hand, there were Hindu and Muslim religious organizations which catered to the specific spiritual needs of adherents of these two faiths; on the other hand, there were larger, secular bodies whose leaders were a combination of religious and non-religious activists in the emerging East Indian population. These secular bodies agitated to settle grievances of the whole East Indian population.

Let us look initially at the Hindu religious organizations. In 1881 the Hindu Sanatan Dharma Association was formed; this group secured full incorporation in 1932. In 1932 the Sanatan Dharma Board of Control was created. In 1952 both these religious bodies combined to form the Sanatan Dharma Maha Sabha. These groups all represented the orthodox Hindu tradition, but all Hindus in the colony did not belong to this orthodoxy. In 1934 the Arya Prathinidhi Sabha was formed, which was the local branch of the India-based Arya Samaj, whose views challenged the majority Sanatanist theology. In 1937 the state recognized and gave representation to the Arya Prathinidhi Sabha on the EIAB.

The Muslim community, too, organized themselves into a number of religious groups. In 1898 came the formation of the Islamic Guardian Association and in 1926 the Tackveeyatul Islamic Association (Society for the Strength of Islam) was founded. The Anjuman Sunaat al Jamaat Association was incorporated by Ordinance 24 of 1935, and 1938 saw the formation of the Tabligh-ul-Islam for the propagation of Islam through education. The latter group merged with the Tackveeyatul Islamic Association in 1943. Finally, in 1947 came the formation of the Trinidad Muslim League.

All of these religious groups, both Hindu and Muslim, concentrated on the religious concerns of their respective communities as they struggled to chart a new course of spiritual growth in a different environment that lacked the support system which had existed in the ancestral place. At the secular level, Hindu, Muslim and Christian leaders joined hands to form the Princes Town–based East Indian National Association in 1886. Some two decades later, in 1909, Indian leaders from North and Central Trinidad banded together in the East Indian National Congress, which was based in Couva. During the mid 1930s the East Indian National League was formed under the leadership of Port of Spain businessman A.C.B. Singh.

All of these groups were valid non-governmental organizations whose activities took place in full public view. Government officials were often invited to attend and the press reported extensively on meetings, festivals and a host of other activities. From 1937, however, the state decided to make a serious intervention into the organizational life of the East Indian community. The ruling class was clearly reading the writing on the wall, and it had decided to take proactive precautions. The Great Depression of the post–First World War period had left lingering hardship among the colony's working class. At the same time, the workers could plainly see the splendour in which the oil and sugar barons lived. To add insult to injury, the owners of the oil industry had brought in white South Africans as managers, since such people knew how to deal with "niggers". What was even more ominous for the ruling oligarchy was the fact that the situation had produced two national leaders – Butler and Rienzi – who were now actively mobilizing the two major races in the colony's two major industries. In this deteriorating industrial and social climate, the white elite saw black plotters behind every fig tree and loudly complained to the imperial headquarters when they felt that the colonial administration was not being sufficiently repressive. In July 1937, for example, George F. Huggins, chairman of the Associated West Indian Chambers of Commerce, led a thirteen-man delegation from Trinidad to confer with the ruling class in Britain. Huggins claimed that the unrest in Trinidad had nothing to do with wages, but rather with "colour feeling" and Bolshevist propaganda. He was fearful because there were only a few thousand Europeans against 425,000 coloured and Indian people, and demanded permanent establishment of a white garrison.[2]

These generally intolerable conditions combined with a particularly harsh dry season in 1934 to ignite the opening salvo of the disturbances in 1937 and 1938.[3] In their efforts to stem the onrushing tide of dissent, the colonial authorities embarked on a many-pronged initiative. They maintained severe restrictions against worker combination in trade unions, deported non-Trinidadian "troublemakers", curtailed the flow of "seditious" literature into the colony and socialized the various communities into a feeling of great pride that they belonged to an empire "upon which the sun never set". In May 1937, for example, Goberdhan Pandit, a Hindu leader in the Siparia area, was requested to play a major role in the coronation celebration scheduled for Siparia. Other members of the newly appointed EIAB in other parts of the colony were sent a similar directive. Among the items on the programme were the following:

1. Ringing of Joy Bells, 6 a.m., 12 noon and 6 p.m.
2. Christian Church services 9:30 a.m.
3. Parade of Siparia school-children on recreation ground 10:30 a.m. with:
   March Past and Salute the Flag
   Song – Land of our Birth [that is, Britain]
   Coronation Song – Let Trumpets Sound
   Address –
   Song – Here's health unto his Majesty
   Three cheers for His Majesty the King
4. Treat for school-children at their respective schools
5. Planting of trees
6. Bounty to the poor[4]

The organizers of the event saw no problem in requesting Hindu and Muslim members of the EIAB to participate in Christian church services to the exclusion of Hindu or Muslim religious participation. Nor did they have any difficulty in asking Christian ministers in the celebration centres to bring together the Christian poor to receive the king's bounty. Joseph Hardath Dube, the Arya Samaj representative on the EIAB, complained that this practice was particularly offensive to the people of Chaguanas, the vast majority of whom were non-Christian. Many of the recipients, Dube added, could hardly be described as paupers.[5]

Members of the Board

The formation of the EIAB was an attempt on the part of the colonial authority to separate the East Indians from the rest of society by selecting a representative group of community leaders and advertising this group as the spokesmen for the East Indian community. The administration's hope was that the board would be the agency to keep their compatriots a docile, loyal and non-protesting group. The selected members, on their part, seemed to understand the quandary in which they were placed. Sitting on the board could mean loss of their influence, since they were perceived by some as puppets of the state. Refusal to sit, however, would mean giving up an opportunity to seek improvement for the lives of less fortunate East Indians. The colonial records do not indicate who was asked and who declined state selection for the EIAB. What we have is a list of those who accepted and a record of their advocacy at the monthly meetings of the board.

During February and March 1937, prospective members were contacted by the colonial secretary, who stated that the mandate of the proposed board was "to advise on all matters relating to East Indians in the colony".[6] Further clarification on the role of the board was given in November 1938, in response to questions raised by C.W. Julumsingh:

Q.1. What are the terms of reference of the East Indian Advisory Board?
A. The Board is advisory and consultative on East Indian matters which the Government may submit, and does not have any executive or administrative function.
Q.2. Whether the business of this Board can be discussed with persons other than members, when the occasion warrants it?
A. The business of the Board should not be discussed outside; members may obtain information on questions raised provided that it be in the best interest of the Board, but should do it in such a manner as not to jeopardise the confidential aspect of the subject.
Q.3. Whether members are in order to introduce matters of importance to the East Indian community for the consideration of the Board?
A. No objection to members presenting questions for the consideration of the Board.[7]

The first meeting of the board was held on 5 April 1937 at the warden's office, Port of Spain, under the chairmanship of the protector of immigrants, W.F. Knowles. At this meeting, eight prominent East Indian leaders were present; seven of them were to form the core of the board until it ceased to function around 1945. Let us look at these eight board members, seeking to understand the possible reasons for their selection.[8]

Al Haj Moulvi Ameer Ali (1898–1973) was born in Pointe-a-Pierre, Trinidad. At the age of twenty-five he was sent to Lahore (then a part of British India) and Egypt, where he studied Islamic theology. Upon his return to Trinidad in 1931, he was appointed *mufti* (spiritual leader) of the recently formed Tackveeyatul Islamic Association. Subsequently he was aggressive in promoting the interests of the Muslim community, joining with Hindus and Christians when he considered this strategically necessary. In this way he was instrumental in securing state recognition of Muslim marriages in 1936. Additionally, as a member of the colony's Board of Education and of the EIAB from 1937, he proved to be an able and incessant advocate of equal educational opportunity for all, Christian and non-Christian. It is significant that the first non-Christian school to be recognized by the state (in 1948) was the El Socorro Islamia, built by the Trinidad Muslim League, which was co-founded by the Moulvi.

Joseph Hardath Dube (1894–1948) was born in Princes Town, where he was educated at the Canadian Mission School. An active member of the East Indian National Association and of a number of literary and debating societies in the south of Trinidad, he obtained employment with the law firm of Hobson and Company in San Fernando. He was an active member of the Arya Prathinidhi Sabha and their constant advocate at meetings of the EIAB.[9]

Goberdhan Pandit was born in Couva in 1882. His public education was at the California Canadian Mission School, but his parents ensured that he was equally trained in Hindi and Sanskrit. Through self-training, he qualified as a land valuator and settled in the southern village of Siparia Old Road in Oropouche. There he became involved in a wide range of community activities. By the early thirties he had become president of the Hindu Sanatan Dharma Association, founded the Nirdhan Daya Upkar (Society for the Upliftment of the Poor) and secured election as vice-president of the East Indian National Congress. He was a justice of the peace for the Siparia area and a member of the government-appointed Agricultural Rent Board. Goberdhan Pandit appears to have been the major consultant to the state on the question of recognition of Hindu marriages, which finally became effective in 1945. Before that, in 1939 he was one of three delegates from the EIAB to the Moyne Commission; the others were Moulvi Ameer Ali and Syed Mohammed Hosein, about whom we shall speak presently.

Hosein Bocus Syne was a transport contractor from Siparia. A pioneer in opening the deep south of Trinidad, he is remembered in the name of his ancestral (Trinidad) birthplace: Syne Village, just outside Siparia. The minutes of the EIAB do not reflect significant output from this member, and his position on the board was terminated after the first year (1937–38).

Ramsamooj Persad was a Hindu leader from Penal who was actively involved in a number of religious and cultural groups in the Debe–Penal area. An executive member of the South Trinidad Cane Farmers' Association, he appeared before the Moyne Commission in 1939 as one of the cane farmers' representatives.

Albert Sobrian was a Presbyterian who owned large cocoa estates in County St Patrick. He was a nominated official of the Legislative Council in 1924, and in 1925 unsuccessfully contested the St Patrick seat in the colony's first Legislative Council election. In 1937 he was appointed to the EIAB, and two years later he appeared before the Moyne Commission as a representative of the Cocoa Growers' Association.

Dalton Chadee was born in a Presbyterian home in San Fernando in 1900. He completed his formal education at Naparima College, after which he took employment as a law clerk while pursuing legal studies. During the 1930s he was an active member of the San Fernando Borough Council (as councillor and alderman), a patron of the East Indian Literary and Debating Association and an ardent advocate of increased educational opportunities for the East Indian population.

Lionel Ramjit Lalsingh was born in 1896 in Balmain Village, Couva. Educated at Balmain C.M. School, Naparima College and Queen's Royal College, he enlisted as a soldier in the British West India Regiment and saw active service in Egypt during the First World War. A devout Hindu, he was the first secretary of the SBDC and secretary of the East Indian National Congress from 1930 to 1943. At the time of his appointment to the board, he was one of Couva's leading merchants.

After its first year of operation, that board was modified and expanded. Replacing H.B. Syne was Syed Mohammed Hosein, a San Fernando–based Muslim activist. Born in 1888, Hosein was one of the founders of Anjuman Sunaat al Jamaat Association, and in 1934 he was part of a Trinidad Muslim delegation sent to India to establish contact with Islamic leaders and organizations on the subcontinent. He was also a film distributor. As a licensed Hindi interpreter and a Muslim divorce officer, he was particularly helpful in the board's deliberations. During the first year, there were two Muslims, four Hindus and two Christians on the board. In 1939 two additional Christians were added, bringing the board's membership to ten nominated members and the protector of immigrants, who was the permanent chairman.

Charles Washington Julumsingh, the son of India-born parents, was born in Tacarigua in 1873. He was educated at the Tacarigua C.M. School, after which he entered the Presbyterian teaching service as a pupil teacher. By 1891 he had attained the position of headmaster of the Arouca C.M. School. In 1891 he joined the civil service and was posted to Cedros, where he embarked on a programme of energizing that distant fishing village. He became secretary to the local health authority, manager of the government school and president of the Agricultural Society and the Indian Literary League, as well as secretary of the Cedros Anglican Missionary Board. By 1937, at age sixty-five, he had retired from the public service and settled at Riverside Road, Curepe.

The other Christian leader chosen was Reverend Charles David Lalla (1890–1958), a Presbyterian minister from Couva. He was one of the founders and the first president of the East Indian National Congress. Ordained in 1915, he became the first local moderator of the Presbyterian Church, in 1931. A keen constitutionalist, he discussed proposed changes before the Moyne Commission in 1939. He was appointed in 1941 as a member of the colony's Franchise Committee, which was charged with drafting major political reform. Between 1920 and 1924 he served as a nominated member of the Legislative Council. He served for many years as a government examiner for prospective Hindi interpreters.

With these two additions in 1939, the board was now made up of two Muslims, four Hindus and four Christians. Two of the ten nominated members were from the north of the island (Ameer Ali and Julumsingh), two from the central region (Lalla and Lalsingh), three from San Fernando (Chadee, Hosein and Dube) and three from the deep south (Goberdhan, Sobrian and Persad). No women were included, although the East Indian community had by this time produced some highly qualified women. Dr Stella Abidh, for example, had qualified in medicine at the University of Toronto and had joined the civil service in Trinidad in 1937. From the date of her return to Trinidad in 1936, she had taken a special interest in public health, a field which she pioneered in the colony. There were other very suitable women: Gladys Ramsaran had qualified as a barrister and was an activist among Indian women in the south, and Margaret Samaroo was a cinema proprietor in San Fernando. She was a pioneer in the soft-drink industry in the colony and a livewire in a number of women's groups in San Fernando.

How did the EIAB function during its tenure? Most members of the board took their responsibilities seriously, attending meetings regularly, participating in debate and sitting on subcommittees appointed to deal with particular issues. The state soon came to realize that the members possessed the necessary experience and had learned to advise properly; it therefore increasingly relied on the board for advice. Despite this reliance, however, the colonial authorities felt it necessary to keep a tight rein on the activities of the board. In order for the members to advise properly, they were constrained to discuss some board matters with knowledgeable members of the public. Most often these matters could hardly have been confidential: legislation of Hindu marriages, legalization of cremation, a level playing field for all denominations, preparation of a petition to the Moyne Commission. In June 1940 the chairman wrote a stern letter to the board:

> It has been brought to my notice that the Minutes of the meetings of the East Indian Advisory Board are being made available to members of the public. This is a most undesirable procedure particularly so as in these minutes are recorded important matters in the interest of the East Indian community. . . . In the event of a recurrence of same, I shall be forced to stop the distribution of copies of the minutes.[10]

This was Crown Colony government at work: subject peoples had to be constantly monitored and guided. They were not yet ready for self-government.

The Issues

What were the issues which took up the board's time? Some matters occupied years of discussion and heated debate before being resolved; quite often these were the issues which spilled out into the public arena, to the chairman's annoyance. One such issue was recognition of non-Christian marriages. The British government's failure to legalize Hindu and Muslim marriages was the cause of a sad legacy for the wives and children of Indians, who had no inheritance rights. This was one of the platforms upon which Mahatma Gandhi had mobilized the Indians in South Africa and the subject of many a resolution passed by the Indian National Congress in its campaign for *swaraj* (freedom). In Trinidad and Tobago, Muslims successfully agitated for recognition of their marriages in 1936, and by 1938 the colonial government seemed determined to bring positive closure to the Hindu matter. In August the chairman of the board wrote to Goberdhan Pandit that he had drafted a bill in connection with the Hindu marriage registration legislation:

> I am anxious that a satisfactory and final decision be arrived at when we meet on the 19th instant as a matter has been long pending. To this end I have requested Mr. Dube to forward at an early date a copy of the draft bill prepared by yourself and Mr. Dube, so that I might be in a position to study it before the meeting of the 19th instant.[11]

But this matter was not finally resolved until 1945. Sanatanist views were not always shared by the Arya Samajists. Advice had to be constantly sought from India on the complex theological issues which governed Hindu marriages, and internecine disagreements among factions of the Hindu community proved a major hindrance. Quite often the government was caught in a quandary of conflicting advice and had to lean heavily on Goberdhan Pandit. Nevertheless, it is to the board's credit that it kept this matter continuously on its agenda until it was successfully resolved.

Another matter on which there was unanimity on the board was the urgency of the provision of equal educational opportunity for Hindus and Muslims. A definite aspect of British policy in its colonies was the spread of "civilization", which for European rulers meant, of course, Christian civilization. In India and in Africa, in China and in the Caribbean, bands of missionaries descended to "save" heathen souls from their various non-Christian ontologies – that view persists even today. It was this aggressive proselytizing by Christian missionaries in India which goaded large sections of the Indian population into the revolt of 1857. The British colonial mission to India was a very Christian mission, aimed at spreading the light of Jesus to people whom they considered benighted by heathenism. Missionaries took their cue from senior British Indian administrators such as Thomas Macaulay, whose famous minute of 1835 decreed the end of British support for Sanskrit and Arabic studies in India and stated the aim of English education. According to this minute, what was needed in India was "a class who may be interpreters between us and the millions whom we govern: a class of persons Indian in blood and colour, but English in taste, in opinions, in morals and in intellect".[12] Towards that end, the British government placed full support behind the Christian missionaries, who could now be found on street corners and in the bazaars of Dacca and Murshidabad, offering conversion packages which included not only Christian salvation but equally secure jobs with the English *sarkar* (government).

An English missionary who lived through the 1857 revolt recalled that the real fight in India was the Christian struggle against Islam: "I have no doubt but that the grand aim of the Mohammedans was, not only to annihilate the British power in India, but also to extirpate Christianity; for Mohammedanism can cope with heathen religions, because of the many truths it contains, but it cannot stand before Christianity: as little as the Crescent, i.e. the moon, can stand before the sun."[13] The same missionary interpreted the British victory over the Indians as God raising up "saviours for us, as he had done in ancient times".[14] In the Caribbean, efforts to create non-Christian institutions of learning were strongly resisted by the ruling classes, and the persistent pleas of non-Christian communities for state recognition of their schools were constantly rejected. In these circumstances, the non-Christian East Indians could either attend state schools or Christian denominational institutions or start their own schools. In this latter regard, a number of efforts were made. In 1929 the Arya Samaj started a school in the Marabella–Gasparillo area and in 1931 it joined hands with other East Indians to create the Hindu–Muslim School in Chaguanas. But both these attempts withered on the vine because the founders could not sustain the costs of paying teachers and maintaining the buildings. The absence of state approval for the programmes being offered was a final nail in the coffin. From the thirties, therefore, the East Indians continued, as they had done before, to conduct *maktabs* (Islamic religious teachings) and *satsanghs* (Hindu religious discourses) in their mosques and mandirs scattered all over the face of the land.

Frustrated by this continuing discrimination in education, members of the board decided to use this forum as their next stage for agitation. The minutes of the EIBA are filled with references to this question; a summary is attempted here. At the board's meeting of 7 June 1937, Syed Hosein raised the question of appointment of Hindus and Muslims to the colony's Board of Education so that the matter could be raised at that level. The debate continued after this request until June 1939, when Moulvi Ameer Ali moved a carefully worded resolution indicating that the East Indian community had grown tired of government's prevarication:

> Whereas the non-Christian population of the Colony, which, with very few exceptions are East Indians, forms 1/3 of the entire population of the island.
>
> And whereas in Section 18(1)a of the Education Ordinance the term "a religious denomination" is interpreted to mean *any Christian religious denomination.*
>
> And whereas Non-Christian East Indians under the Ordinance do not enjoy the same facilities and privileges as the various Christian denominations and are suffering grave disadvantages in their endeavour to establish schools.
>
> Be it resolved:
>
> 1. That this Board prays that Government be pleased to make provision in the Education Ordinance to give the various non-Christian communities the same status, recognition and privileges . . . so as to enable them to establish their own respective schools on the same principle as the several Christian denominations have established or are establishing their own respective schools.[15]

In that same year, of course, Moulvi Ameer Ali took up this matter with the visiting Moyne commissioners and obtained the support of that decisive body. Thus it was that in 1948, the El Socorro Islamia was granted government recognition and assistance, and with this green light there was a flurry of school-building activity. In October 1952 the colony's governor, in reviewing the activities for the past year, noted that

> [d]uring the past year four Hindu bodies and three Muslim bodies were approved for the purpose of establishing and conducting schools in the Colony, and they have made a considerable contribution to the relief of overcrowding by providing schools at their own expense at sixteen different sites in the country. In addition a large and well-constructed Hindu school has been erected at Aranguez with Government assistance and funds have been provided for the completion this year of a Muslim school at Five Rivers, Arouca.[16]

So far we have looked at the successful campaigns for the recognition of Hindu marriages and for the achievement of parity of educational opportunity. A third activity which occupied the attention of the board for almost a year was its investigation and recommendations regarding serious factional disputes in areas of concentrated East Indian settlement. The two major areas of such discontent were Tableland (east of Princes Town) and a large swathe of County Caroni, from Felicity on the western coast to Bejucal to the east. The Tableland dispute, which appears to have started in late 1937, was the easier of the two problems. Visits by board members during the second half of 1938 (who mediated between the warring factions) and increased police surveillance restored peace. The Caroni fighting, on the other hand, reached murderous proportions very quickly and needed lengthy investigation and mediation. As early in the board's life as May 1937, members were apprised of "[f]action fights and other differences among East Indians residing in Bejucal – Charlie Village, Cumberbatch, Pierre and Kakandi villages".[17] In June 1937 the board appointed an investigating committee whose mandate was to enquire into the factional disturbances in Caroni and to suggest solutions to this problem. Members of the committee were H.B. Syne, Moulvi Ameer Ali, J.H. Dube and Goberdhan Pundit. The committee deliberated for about ten months; its members made many trips to the area and interviewed faction members, community leaders and the police. In February 1938 they presented a majority report, as well as a minority report by Dube.[18]

According to both reports, the trouble started in 1934 when Radhia, sixteen years old, of Tahadil Road, Felicity, eloped with Rajkumar, age eighteen, a dancer from Bank Village, Carapichaima. At the time of the elopement, Radhia had been estranged from her husband for about a year. At the annual Ram Lila festival, held on the open savannah near Radhia's residence, Rajkumar had entranced the young lady with his superb dancing. She willingly abandoned the protection of her uncle Outim and made off with Rajkumar. Outim took offence at this unauthorized departure because, as he claimed, Rajkumar was a chamar and of a lower caste than his niece Radhia. Thereupon, in true Ramayanic tradition, Outim and his landlord, Akhnath Maharaj, gathered a band of their kinsmen and undertook a mission to rescue Radhia from the clutches of Rajkumar.

The pity of this was that the combatants were all Hindu and members of both camps were closely related to each other. As the war raged, a member of each faction was killed, many people were beaten and injured and many houses were stoned and burnt. In the police investigation and court trials that followed, one combatant was hanged and eight were convicted and jailed. At the time the committee reports were submitted, the investigators were fearful that upon the release of those imprisoned, the war would continue: "14. The Committee has met the leaders and prominent members of both factions and have persuaded them to remedy their ways. They related to the Committee how terribly they have suffered during recent years on account of quarrels and fights and they have assured the Committee that they have no desire for quarrelling and fighting again."

Dube's minority report also felt that trouble was ahead: "13. I am in agreement with the majority report that there is good reason to believe that there may be trouble ahead, as the youths of both sides are given to idling when not actually working." Both reports made a number of useful recommendations, most of which were taken up. Among them were that the police force at Chaguanas should be strengthened, that a police station should be located in the affected area, that religious work should be encouraged and that the government should appoint a committee to "devise ways and means to keep the young people engaged in healthy outdoor sports and other recreations". Other recommendations were that influential people in the area should be approached to exert their influence and that aid should be provided to deserving people in the area, subject to the approval of the warden.

The lengthy engagement of the committee with this serious problem, their frequent presence in the area and their mediation and counselling, as well as their sensible recommendations, did much to ease the tension. The police presence was increased, Hindu and Presbyterian leaders strengthened their presence in the area and the government took a more active interest in improving the infrastructure of the community. Had the EIAB not intervened, the situation would surely have deteriorated further.

Besides these major activities of the EIAB, numerous other relevant matters were brought to the attention of the government. There was frequent enquiry regarding the inability of Hindus to cremate their dead on open pyres. After years of debate in the East Indian press, the EIAB followed up with representation to the Moyne Commission in 1939 and further agitation after the Second World War; the necessary legislation was finally enacted in 1953.[19] The Muslim leaders on the board pressed for the appointment of more marriage officers and for the allocation of land for their educational and religious activities. The board was unanimous in constantly pressing for access to the institutions of the larger society: for permission for Hindu and Muslim religious leaders to visit prisons, hospitals and orphanages; for Hindu and Muslim festivals to be declared holidays; for Hindu interpreters in hospitals and government offices; for appointment of Hindus and Muslims to the Cocoa Subsidy Board and the Board of Education; and for improvement of the infrastructure on the estates where East Indians lived.

At the board's meeting on 9 August 1937, Syed Hosein raised the following matters:

(a) That this board respectfully desires to draw Government's attention to the disgraceful and insanitary conditions of barracks in which labourers on the Sugar Estates are housed, which are worse than the most insanitary slum areas which the Government with the assistance of the City Corporation are about to clear.

(b) That this board also respectfully suggests that Government consider the advisability of appointing an Official (with a thorough knowledge of the Hindu language) to visit the sugar estates periodically, with a view to enquire into the grievances of the labourers and making suggestions to improve the standards of life and the cultural level of these workers.[20]

In September 1937, Charles Julumsingh, seconded by C.D. Lalla, petitioned the government for appointment of East Indians to the colony's Executive Council "as has been done in the neighbouring colony of British Guiana".[21] All members of the board were in agreement that the importation of ganja should be gradually reduced until a total ban had been effected. The government took this advice, inadvertently giving rise to a flourishing local agricultural enterprise and bringing prosperity to many a neglected village. From time to time members of the board raised matters of particular concern. Goberdhan Pandit frequently raised questions about flooding in the Oropouche lagoon and about stricter controls on goldsmiths who were unscrupulous in the practice of their trade.[22] Syed Hosein was keen that the Nariva Swamp should be irrigated and given out in parcels to prospective rice farmers. During the Second World War, Ramsamooj Persad was particularly concerned that an East Indian be appointed to the Control of Commodities Committee.

The East Indian community came out in their numbers to listen to their representatives before the Moyne Commission. The *Trinidad Guardian* reported that many came from far distances. There were Indian women in "their flowing *orhanis*, their arms bedecked with dozens of silver ornaments", Muslim men with long beards and Indian men in traditional Oriental dress.[23] The EIAB delegation comprised its chairman, Captain Meaden, Moulvi Ameer Ali, Syed Mohammed Hosein and Goberdhan Pandit. These delegates sat together with another group, the Indian Evidence Committee. Together they raised many issues which had been aired at meetings of the EIAB since 1937.[24] A major concern of the delegation was the condition of former indentured labourers and their children who still lived on plantations, where living and working conditions were very poor. On most estates the labourers had to work from 7 a.m. to 4 p.m. for an average of fifty cents per day. The increase to fifty cents had been the first in ninety-three years, and had come as a result of the agitation of 1937.

The commission was told that forty thousand Indians were living in barracks which were poorly served in regard to medical facilities and proper housing, with few facilities for rearing animals on adjacent estate property. Child labour was rampant on the plantations, "scale robbery" was a normal practice when farmers' canes were being weighed, and the labourers' tasks were often arbitrarily increased by unscrupulous drivers. The delegation recommended that more state land should be made available to East Indian farmers so that they could grow more rice and make the island self-sufficient. The delegation also complained about the relative absence of East Indians in the government service, the scarcity of teachers in existing schools, the non-recognition of Hindu marriages and the illegality of cremating their dead. They wanted to see more East Indian doctors in Indian areas so that cultural differences could be bridged.

The Moyne Commission agreed with some of the complaints: "Few East Indians hold appointments to government posts in relation to the numbers in the East Indian community. We strongly recommend that the possibility of the appointment of suitable East Indians to posts be carefully borne in mind by the Colonial governments."[25] The commission's report also recommended an increase of East Indian teachers in primary schools and supported the demand for legitimization of marriages: "We find ourselves in full sympathy with the complaints regarding the arrangements for legitimisation and validation of East Indian marriages and recommend that these marriages should so far as the law is concerned, be put exactly on the same footing as other marriages."[26]

Noting that the East Indian population – numbering 151,000 – comprised one-third of the total population, the report stated that every effort should be made to encourage this segment to feel comfortable and secure in the new place. In this regard, steps should be taken to legalize the position regarding the grievance about cremation. The commission did not agree with setting up a separate enquiry into the conditions of East Indians. These people, it declared, should be encouraged to think of themselves as part of the larger West Indian population and not as a separate group. In any event, the report added, the general recommendations for the whole population regarding physical infrastructure and social services applied equally to the East Indian population.

It should be noted that the EIAB was not the only body representing East Indians. There was also the East Indian Evidence Committee and the Sanatan Dharma Board of Control. Even before the full Moyne Report was released (in 1945), its recommendations were released during the war. Members of the EIAB were cognizant of this fact, and in June 1940 Hosein moved a resolution that the government should give early consideration to the report's specific recommendations.[27] As has been previously noted, recognition of Hindu marriages took place in 1945 (Act No. 13 of 1945), Hindu and Muslim schools were recognized from 1948, the cremation issue was settled in 1953, and in 1943 Adrian Cola Rienzi was appointed to the Executive Council. From this time too, East Indians were increasingly appointed as Hindu and Muslim marriage officers, their holy men could visit state institutions, and they found increasing employment as teachers and probation officers. In the wave of post-Moyne constitutional change, East Indians became increasingly active at the county council level and at the central legislative level, which the 1946 constitution allowed.

How, then, can we judge the work of the EIAB? In the first instance, the board was set up as a means of controlling the East Indian population through incorporation of some of its most prominent leaders. These were all men with strong vested interests who could, hopefully, be depended upon to keep their restless compatriots in check. In this the government was not disappointed. The minutes of the meeting of July 1937 make this significant statement: "3. The Chairman conveyed the thanks of His Excellency the Governor to the members who had convened a special meeting in San Fernando, during the recent strikes, in which they pledged their support to Government."[28] The same can be said about the restoration of peace in Tableland and Caroni.

However, for all their influence, board members were patently unable to hold back the labouring East Indian poor from joining hands with their African brethren as they brought the oil and sugar industries to a standstill in 1937. Indeed, it was the Indian sugar workers – women and men – who had started the disturbances in central Trinidad. In this revolutionary phase it was Rienzi (with Butler) who took precedence in leadership. At the same time, there were matters which needed longer and more painstaking deliberations than the immediate grievances of the thirties. In this regard the board served as a most useful intermediary between the state and the East Indian. Here was a repository of experience and of individual achievement through the long and tedious process of persistence and unceasing effort.

Concerned about long-term solutions to long-outstanding problems, the board raised a number of crucial issues which were of concern to an East Indian population desperately trying to create its own space in the New World. The board was not particularly interested in ideological issues such as the manner of cremation or doctrinal differences between Hindus and Muslims. Its members were far more concerned with practical problems such as the privilege of cremating their dead, the establishment of Hindu or Muslim schools, the legalization of non-Christian marriages, appointment of East Indians to state boards, improvement of hiring conditions on the sugar estates and the provision of infrastructure for those who produced rice and vegetables. For this reason they were held in high regard by the public, and this moral authority enabled them to go unguarded into territory where even the brave dared not go.

The state on its part felt severely threatened by the onrushing revolution and sought allies among the various communities. Hence it paid heed to the recommendations of the board. In the circumstances, therefore, the board served as an effective bridge, assisting the transition of a people from the Orient to the Occident. Had the board not intervened at this crucial transition period, the process of adaptation to the New World would have been much longer and more traumatic. The EIAB was thus a beacon in troubled waters.

Notes

1. Colony of Trinidad and Tobago, *Census 1946* (Port of Spain: Government Printery, 1946), 31.
2. Huggins to Neville Chamberlain, 3 July 1937, CO295/599, File 70297, Public Record Office (PRO), London.
3. For a detailed description of the 1935 unrest see S. Basdeo, *Labour Organisation and Labour Reform in Trinidad 1919–1939* (Trinidad: Lexicon, 2003), 115.
4. Minutes of the EIAB, Senior Assistant Warden Victoria to Goberdhan Pandit, 7 May 1937.
5. Minutes, 3 May 1937.
6. Minutes, G.W. Seymour to Goberdhan Pandit, 19 March 1937.

Coping with the New Culture   169

7. Minutes, 7 November 1938.
8. These biographies are drawn from Murli J. Kirpalani, Mitra G. Sinanan, S.M. Rameshwar and L.F. Seukeran, eds., *Indian Centenary Review: One Hundred Years of Progress, 1845–1945 Trinidad, B.W.I.* (Port of Spain: Indian Centenary Review Committee, 1945), 131; also from Bridget Brereton, Brinsley Samaroo and Glenroy Taitt, *Dictionary of Caribbean Biography* (St Augustine: Institute of Caribbean Studies, University of the West Indies, 1998).
9. James Dubay, interview by author, 15 December 2003.
10. Minutes, H. Meaden to all members, 12 June 1940.
11. Minutes, H. Meaden to Goberdhan Pandit, 11 August 1938.
12. S. Hay, ed., *Sources of Indian Tradition* (New York: Columbia University Press, 1988), 31.
13. C. Leupolt, *Indian Memoirs* (London, 1884), 351.
14. Ibid., 359.
15. Minutes, 5 June 1939. The parent ordinance referred to in the resolution was Ord. 23 of 1933.
16. *Hansard*, Trinidad and Tobago, 1952–53 session, col. 13. Among the school builders was the Arya Prathinidhi Sabha, which started off with two schools in 1952 and reached nine schools by 1972.
17. Senior Assistant Warden, St Patrick, to Goberdhan Pandit, 25 May 1937.
18. Minutes, Majority and minority reports of Investigating Committee, February 1938. The account which follows is drawn from these sources.
19. *Hansard*, Trinidad and Tobago, 1952–53 session, col. 1568–97.
20. Minutes, 9 August 1937.
21. Minutes, 6 September 1937.
22. Minutes, 7 September 1938.
23. "Indians Have Their Say to Commission", *Trinidad Guardian*, 14 March 1939.
24. These issues are taken from reports in the *Trinidad Guardian*, 14 March 1939, and the *Port of Spain Gazette*, 14 March 1939.
25. His Majesty's Stationery Office, *West India Royal Commission Report*, Cmd. 6607 (London: HMSO, 1945), ch. 24, para. 88.
26. Ibid., para. 90.
27. Minutes, 3 June 1940.
28. Minutes, 5 July 1937.

CHAPTER 8

Reflections on the Imaging of Africa in the Calypso of Trinidad and Tobago[1]

▸ Louis Regis

Introduction

Despite its demonstrably African character[2] and the African personality of many of its practitioners,[3] the calypso has traditionally presented an ambivalent picture of Africa. Although the mass movement of the late 1960s and early 1970s employed Africa symbolically in its rediscovery of a nationalistic cultural identity, deployment of newly constructed images was not powerful enough to completely eradicate images and stereotypes which had been cultivated for centuries. Even some of the more Afro-conscious calypsonians who championed the movement were unable to escape the conditioning of an earlier period. The phrase "back to Africa" still exerts tremendous psychic hold on Afro-Trinidadians and Tobagonians, for most of whom Africa remains simultaneously a source of psychic strength and romantic appeal and an area of darkness, a site where pastoralized images of tribal life compete with images of incomprehensible ethnic violence.

This chapter surveys the calypso's depiction of Africa rather than that of the African presence in the Caribbean and its extended family of themes. A study of the representations of Africa in the calypso allows for observations on the many interrelated elements which impact the study of the calypso itself and affect how the calypso can be used in pedagogy. The unchanging view of Africa revealed in the comparatively small corpus of calypsos on Africa challenges the researcher to search for explanations. In pursuing this, the study appreciates that the lyrical texts are but one element in production of the commodity and performance artefact that is the calypso. Success in the entertainment industry depends on popular response, which is a function of more than just literary text. Awareness of this shapes the tone and tenor of songs and is a major factor in the development of particular calypso themes. Answers to the questions which prompted this study, then, sometimes defy rigorous interrogation of the calypso texts themselves; they can be found inside the social and cultural contexts within which the calypso operates. The study will pay close attention to the more popular, that is, audience-acclaimed songs. Examination of their lyrical texts and the circumstances of composition and performance will shed light on the theme of Africa in the calypso, on the nature of the parent society and, just as important, on the nature of calypso itself.

Darkest Africa

Calypsonians generally have had little contact with Africa and, lacking firsthand experience, substitute fantasy and media-sponsored inscriptions for knowledge. Exposure to Africa and to Africans has yielded results which vary from calypsonian to calypsonian and are clearly the products of individual personality and imagination. We can take a brief look at the experiences of individual calypsonians who either have made the pilgrimage to Africa or have encountered Africans in Europe.

In the 1950s, Kitchener, temporarily in self-exile in England and obviously in touch with Africans also temporarily residing there, recorded "Africa My Home" (1951), "Nigerian Resistance" (1954) and "Birth of Ghana" (1955).[4] These calypsos demonstrate familiarity with West African place names and leaders, something which cannot be said for the vague expressions of other Caribbean Basin diasporeans. The infectious antiphonal choric lines of "Birth of Ghana" evoked more positive public response in Ghana than did the song commissioned by the national government, and Kitchener was lionized for his spontaneous unsolicited paean of praise to the Ghanaian people. The persona of "Africa My Home" is the transplanted exile longing for return to his familiar landscapes. His voice is generic West African – albeit anglophone – rather than tribal or national. Kitchener's return to the Caribbean in 1963, however, severed the cord which tied him to that consciousness of Africa; complete amnesia set in after he had retraced the last leg of the triangular trade.

Brynner, the modern Ibn Batuta and perhaps the only calypsonian of his and any other generations to travel extensively through West and East Africa, sublimates the physical experience of climbing Mount Kilimanjaro into a mystical one. The narrator of his "Uhuru Harambee" (1969) ascends the sacred space of Kilimanjaro and communes there with illustrious militants, martyrs of different battles in different places, who now congregate on the Mountain of the Moon, which is venerated by the ancient Egyptians as the birthplace of their race:[5]

> I met Marcus Garvey, Malcolm X and Patrice Lumumba
> Nat Turner, Albert Luthuli and Martin Luther King Junior
> They ask 'bout my people
> If we continuing the struggle
> Well I tell them what is the score
> Saying we are stronger now than before.[6]

In the context of the cycle of consciousness and militancy of the late 1960s, this was indeed a valid proposition.

Sparrow's appearance at the inaugural Festival of African and Caribbean artistes (FESTAC) hosted in Nigeria in 1977, a visit insisted upon by the organizers, produced quite a different song result. "Du Du Yemi" (1978) celebrates with typical Sparrow flair a sexual encounter with the nubile Natasha. However, Sparrow's numerous visits to Nigeria and Ghana since FESTAC have produced nothing. Gypsy and Lady Wonder have not made significant statements since their return. Surprisingly, neither did the prolific Chalkdust, whose great work was done before his visits.[7] Watchman's stay in East Africa generated "Lessons from Africa" (1999), which tries to inculcate in the Afro-Trinidadians and Tobagonians who were embroiled in the ethnic wars of the 1990s respect for the culture of the Indian Other. Ironically, Watchman was silent in song about the experience of Rwanda, where ethnicity had taken a killing turn, which was the reason for his being posted in East Africa in the first place. David Rudder's nine calypsos on South Africa deserve special mention because they all appear on one album (1990)[8] and reflect a range of concerns not encountered elsewhere in the calypso of the day.

On tour in Europe in 1987, Rudder met musicians from southern Africa, and from this limited contact he wrote nine songs which present a variety of South African responses to apartheid: the seeker after truth who dismisses equally the black and white propaganda of Radio Pretoria and Radio Soweto ("Good Morning South Africa"); the militant freedom fighter ("Amandla Ngawethu"); the peace-loving patriot who is forced into violence ("Fire in the Laager"); the poet who exhorts the children of South Africa to work together in the interests of freedom and unity ("Pull Together"); the escapists at the watering hole revelling in the illegal rights manufactured by illegal alcohol ("Down at the Shebeen"); the lover reassuring his frightened woman ("Johannesburg Woman"); the migrant miner bewailing his dark destiny ("Working on the Join"); the prophet who proclaims the imminent end of the drawn-out conflict ("Victory Is Certain"); and finally Nelson Mandela ("New Day Dawning").

Listening closely to these songs, one gets the impression that the personae are natives of Rudder's spirit, which soars above the black and bloody of Watchman's "Gun Religion" (1988), for example, and tries to grapple with the complex realities confronting those "frightened foolish men of Pretoria", as Rudder styles those trapped in the South African nightmare ("Haiti", 1988). "New Day Dawning", which concludes the suite,[9] belongs to the small tradition of "I"-narrator songs on Mandela, a tradition which includes Sparrow's "I Make No Apology" (1991), Marva's "I Mandela" (1991) and Stalin's "Ah Fit" (1996). Mandela holds a special place in the imagination of Afro-Caribbeans who marvel at the strength of courage and resolve he demonstrated during his long imprisonment, a quality of endurance alien to practice in the anglophone Caribbean:

> My struggle
> Is the struggle of the African people
> Against all domination
> Black or white
> Never giving up on my dream
> Of a free and just society
> Don't they know we want the harmony
> Just as day melts into night
> Equal opportunity is the dream that I live for

> Lying these long lonely nights in my cell
> The dreams grow stronger
> *Amandla ngawethu* [power to the people]
> For this dream I am prepared to die
>
> *Chorus*
>
> I see a brand new day a-dawning
> I see a bright new shining star
> I feel the magic of the morning
> Soon we will all know where we are
> In South Africa.[10]

In this song, in one of those mystical transfers of consciousness and power inexplicable outside the realm of spirituality, Rudder personifies in Mandela the finest qualities of the African spirit, those very qualities which Stalin celebrated in "No Other Man" (*ca.* 1971). One gets the impression, however, that the "I"-narrator of this song is as much Rudder, longing for an equitable Trinidad and Tobago, as Mandela yearning for an equitable South Africa. For Rudder, as for several of his personae, the ideal South Africa is a place of love, not a laager, a place where African and Afrikaner dance together to the rhythm of unity and freedom. One hears in "Pull Together", for example, the appeal for Caribbean unity of "Haiti" (1988), "Rally Round the West Indies" (1988) and "One Caribbean" (1994). "Pull Together" and "New Day Dawning" suggest that Rudder may well be employing South Africa as a metaphor for Trinidad and Tobago. "Heaven" (1996) provides further evidence of this aspect of the Rudder metaphor. Beginning with a compassionate survey of the "human abattoir" of Rwanda, the calypso extends to consider the global and universal phenomenon of man's inhumanity to man. Humanity had denied Auschwitz in Europe and so had to face Cambodia in Asia. This in turn humanity denied, and so had to confront Kigali in Africa. The lessons seem clear enough for all other polities, and especially so for Trinidad and Tobago, which was peopled by emigrants from these three old continents and which is in a permanent state of denial.

> Ever since Time began man has searched for his heaven
> Sometimes seeking it in the reflection of his neighbour's blood
> He'll say, "Mirror, mirror on the wall
> Who's the fairest of us all

Don't spoil my vision, my heaven is waiting"
Foolish men will declare
"It can't happen here"
Don't you know tribal war is one dark emotion away
Oh the horror, the horror, the horror.[11]

In recalling Conrad's *Heart of Darkness*, Rudder locates the impulse to barbarism not only in nineteenth-century Europe but also in twentieth-century Trinidad, as it had manifested itself earlier in Europe, Asia and Africa in what poet Eric Roach has called "this grisly century".[12] "Heaven" is one of the few songs about black-on-black violence in Africa. Calypsonians' bewilderment at the carnage in African states has been reflected in their general silence on the matter. Within a decade of independence, the confederation of Nigeria was shaken by the Biafran secession, and a unitary state was restored only after an Ibo bloodbath. Brynner's "Trouble in the Congo" (1961), of which only a fragment remains in memory, is the only calypso commentary on this episode, just as Rudder's "Heaven" stands out as the only surviving commentary on a similar happening in Rwanda a quarter-century later. It may be that calypsonians are ignorant about the salience of ethnicity and tribalism in these newly constituted states, which were arbitrarily created by the colonial rulers for administrative convenience to rationalize the looting of the continent. One view articulated in calypso is that Africa should unite. Valentino's "Africa Unite" (1979) and Kinte's "United Africa" (*ca.* 1994) appeal for this unity, while Stalin, with characteristic optimism, boldly prophesies that "one day Africans will be living under one flag" ("More Come", 1986).

Zimbabwe's independence in 1978 was celebrated in fine style in Valentino's immensely popular "Stay Up Zimbabwe" (1979), but Zimbabwean president Robert Mugabe's appropriation of white-owned farms and sweeping suppression of dissent in the late 1990s did not arouse calypsonians to song. One surmises that there might be a vague feeling of a historical injustice being righted in the despoiling of the white farmers, but no one has condemned Mugabe as openly as Sparrow did Uganda strongman Idi Amin ("Idi Amin", 1978).

At best, then, most calypsonians and other Caribbeans see Africa through a Western glass, darkly. Africa remains a distant symbolic ancestral homeland, more a trope than a reality, yet happenings in Africa periodically reawaken a latent consciousness in the West Indies, where Africa is revived cyclically in the popular Afro-Trinidadian consciousness by dramatic social and political occurrences. Commentary on happenings in Africa, however, is restricted to Trinidadian interest in events there as reported in Western media, and is the product of an unclear Trinidadian gaze on distant African situations.

In commentary, calypsonians deploy characteristic voices and reasoning. The Growling Tiger's classic "The Gold in Africa" (1936) voiced anger at Italy's 1935 invasion of Abyssinia which ignited Caribbean combustions of the late 1930s, including the Butler Riots in Trinidad.[13] This calypso also offers an excellent analysis of the Italian invasion, all articulated in recognizable Trinidadian idiom as Tiger condemns Mussolini's bullying as the action of "a beast / A thief, a highway robber / And a shameless dog for a dictator" before concluding, in calypso style, that "I do not know he making so much strife / The man must be want Haile Selassie wife."[14]

Similarly, Cypher's "Rhodesia Crisis" (1966) offered a calypso-style punishment for Ian Smith, the white supremacist who had seized power in the then British colony of Rhodesia: "I say they should pull down he pants / Open it wide and light Jack Spaniard inside".[15] One cannot help comparing Cypher's success against the comparative "silence" of Zebra's eminently sober and serious "Rhodesia: Calypso Commentary" of the same year. Both songs condemn Smith for his actions and the British government for its lack of action; both compare the situation of the 1960s to that of the 1930s; and both, recognizing that Italy's aggression helped spark the Second World War, warned of a similar conflagration over Rhodesia. Cypher's calypso, however, may have been the more popular because of the element of *picong* in his treatment of the subject.

Apartheid, South Africa's peculiar institutionalized racism, inspired over a hundred songs, many excellent and in some cases very popular. Among these are Maestro's "Over Yonder" (1977), Commentor's "Children of Soweto" (1977), Stalin's "More Come" (1986), Duke's "How Many More Must Die" (1986), Bally's "Shaka Shaka" (1988), Sparrow's "Isolate South Africa" (1982) and "Invade South Africa" (1986) and, of course, Rudder's nine songs. Bally's "Shaka Shaka" converts the South African situation into an African family concern: "Shaka, Shaka, talk to me / In one happy family / Anytime yuh touching one / Bes' yuh hit all and done."[16] From this the threat logically issues: "Tell them if they touch Mandela / They better hit all o' we". This recalls the *badjohn* rhetoric used in the early carnivals, when masqueraders chanted, *"Jour vert barre eux / Pa mete la main la sou yeux* [Daybreak bar them / but don't put your hands on them]", a clear warning to the police against attempting to arrest any of their band who may have been wanted on criminal charges.

The image of Africa as an area of darkness is projected in Valentino's "Third World" (1972). Here calypso's poet and prophet for Trinidad's and the National Joint Action Committee's (NJAC) black nationalism[17] gave voice to his vision of the future:

> Meditating in my house just the other day
> Is like Ah charge up mihself and Ah trip away
> Way over yonder I did behold
> Because in front of mih eyes was a brand new world
> But like a wheel the world turn around
> And all the people who was up they come right back down
>
> *Chorus*
>
> Now I no longer see the African
> A primitive man with a spear in his hand
> But I see an intelligent civilised man walking that proud land
> And I see that Ethiopia go rise again
> And in the Third World the African will reign.[18]

Two years after 1970, Africa remained as dark as before, and Africa's "primitive man with a spear in his hand" can evolve into "an intelligent civilised man" only in a ganja-induced vision ("Ah charge up mihself"). This is the image of Africa that NJAC hoped to eradicate in its adult education series, Black Truth, in the mid 1970s; this continues to be the liberating mission of the Emancipation Support Committee.

This stereotypical image of tribal Africa was reinforced by Merchant's tremendously popular escape fantasy "Umba Yao" (1978), which presented a Tarzan-Phantom portrait of life in traditional Africa as the experience of a dream:

> I dream I was in Africa
> And I was a warrior
> Hunting lion and tiger
> Brave as my forefather
> And when the darkness gather we sit around a fire
> Telling of the bravery and courage

> Of our great ancestor
> And we chanting
> Umba ya ya o
> O o o o o o
>
> Beauty and freedom surround me
> Food and wealth in a quantity
> If I could go back to Africa
> Where I could be a great hunter
> Running swimming climbing
> Or round a fire dancing
> Women washing and singing
> You can hear their voices echo in the wind.
> And they chanting
> Umba ya ya o
> O o o o o o[19]

The only shadow over this pastorale is the duel between the son of the dead chief and a challenger for the chieftainship.

What is remarkable about Merchant's calypso is that it was performed at a time when NJAC was in the middle of its education drive, which reconstructed Africa as the home of great civilizations. The beautiful melody of "Umba Yao", its agreeable tempo and exciting beat encouraged even NJAC personnel to dance to it at their happenings. This draws attention to the fact that a calypso can engage an audience through its music even more than through its messages. The mid-year release of the song may also have contributed to its popularity, because it gave the public something fresh, something that had not been trampled on in the carnival dust. "Maebo" (1980), the sequel, was totally overlooked, perhaps because it was presented on the carnival album *"D" Hardest*, which features the acclaimed "Who Squatting", "Morne Diablo" and "Down at the Disco"; however, one cannot play down the fact that many sequels do not generate the response of the original hit.

By contrast with "Umba Yao", Maestro's intelligent and rational "Over Yonder" (1977), which comments bleakly on the anomaly of white rule in southern Africa, remained a "silent song" that never won the popularity it should have achieved. This too could have been a function of timing and placement. "Over Yonder" was released posthumously when the public was still grieving over

Maestro's untimely death and finding typical Trini consolation for this tragedy in "Bionic Man", which was interpreted as Maestro's foreshadowing of his death. "Over Yonder" thus remained lost in that excellent album *The Anatomy of Soca*, whose major track beside "Bionic Man" was "Tanty", a highly compressed "I"-narrative of an adulterous relationship which ends in Tanty's death. The relative silence of Maestro's celebration of the warrior ethos, "Son of a Warrior" (1976), is underscored by the popularity of his "Savage" (1976–77), which purports to celebrate the sexual potency of the Caribbean male. Although "Savage" seems to critique the stereotype of the Caribbean male as a sexual savage, one wonders if its popularity owed something to public perception of its being an update of Sparrow's "Congo Man" (1965).

It was a dark day for Africans everywhere when Sparrow and/or his songwriter fastened upon stories of the alleged rape of white nuns in the war-savaged Congo (now Zaire) and composed "Congo Man", a calypso which reduced the agony of the newly independent people to a lurid black-on-white sexual fantasy. Trinidadian audiences lapped up this song, delighting in the melody, beat and skilful use of double entendre ("Ah never eat a white meat yet"), as well as in the stage performance of calypso's greatest showman, then at the height of his amazing career and clearly in love with "Congo Man".[20] One cannot say how much importance audiences attached to the psychosexual dimension of black/white sexuality. Few seemed aware of the shock, horror or anguish of the Africans, who were appalled that one of their own could subscribe to the stereotype of the African as a "cannibal head-hunter" lusting for a taste of "white meat".[21] "Congo Man" has provided a seemingly indelible negative stereotype of African sexuality, one which added a savage tattoo to the pastoral vision of the African.

For Sparrow, Africa seems to be an erotic if not erogenous zone. His appearance at FESTAC 1977 generated "Du Du Yemi". Two years after this, he recorded "Gu Nu Gu" (1980), the story of a woman who found in the torrid lovemaking of an African witch doctor the truth of everlasting youth, and "Love African Style" (1980), a celebration of African sexuality. These two, as well as "King Kong" (1977), contribute to the conclusion that Sparrow subscribes to the stereotype of African sexuality rather than subverts it.

Reconstructing Africa

In the middle of the 1970s, NJAC began an adult education campaign which featured dissemination of the work of Chancellor Williams, Josef ben Jochanan, John Jackson, Cheikh Anta Diop and Ivan van Sertima, among other scholars on Africa. Chalkdust, a University of the West Indies–trained historian, was in the vanguard of the calypsonians who later developed the calypso response to the traditional portrait of Africa. Initially Chalkdust had subscribed to the traditional perception of Africa as an area of darkness. In "We Is We" (1972) he had dismissed Africans as people who "only know 'bout tom-tom and spear". "We Is We" was critical of the "colour-crazy" youth of 1970 who were wearing fatheads (afros) and dashikis – the outward symbols of the Black Power movement – and seeking to know more about India and Africa.[22] By the close of the decade, however, Chalkdust had seen the light of Africa and was an advocate of NJAC's Ethiopianism.

The protagonist of Chalkdust's "Black Child's Prayer" (1983), the ten-year-old Mamba, thanks God for the history teacher who has inducted him into the secrets of millennia of greatness on the Mother Continent. The mass of information presented imaginatively as the work of one class session is a panoramic survey of the history of the entire continent, from the ancient Nile Valley high cultures, through the medieval savannah empires and post-medieval forest kingdoms of West Africa, to the modern states of southern Africa.[23]

Chalkdust's "White Man's Plan" (1985) immediately challenged Johnny King's statement in "Nature's Plan" (1984), which had spotlighted the blacks in South Africa as a people doomed to servitude by what King called nature's plan:

> Down in South Africa whiteman with gun power
> Have the natives in subjection
> The Black majority live in poverty
> All because they ent strong
> Black man life is a thoroughfare
> Nature make him a slave
> South Africa is a nightmare
> For coloureds from cradle to the grave.[24]

Several Afro-Trinidadians had responded in anger to these sentiments and to the lack of racial pride demonstrated by unthinking descendants of Africa who revelled in the song, whose musicality made it so popular that audiences at the Dimanche Gras show demanded an encore. Like "Umba Yao" before it and "Jahaahji Bhai" after, the musical text of "Nature's Plan" may have appealed more to the audiences than the lyrical text. "White Man's Plan", versifying the monumental work of Chancellor Williams, sought to redress what Chalkdust perceived as the imbalance created by "Nature's Plan":

> They have they facts upside down
> They philosophy is wrong
> Condemning Black men in song
> Saying they weak they not strong
> In Calypso they keep singing
> That Nature keeps on killing
> The humble, feeble and weak
> So is strong Blacks that Nature seek
> Is time that they understand
> That civilisation
> In Black Africa it all began
> But it took white barbarians, Muslims, Jews and Christians
> To subdue Black Africans
>
> *Chorus*
>
> Nature's plan didn't change Black man
> Chinese gunpowder caused that destruction
> Nature's plan didn't change Black man
> Chinese gunpowder caused that destruction
> They came with Bible and Koran
> Left us the books and kept the land
> Nature's plan didn't change Black man
> Chinese gunpowder caused that destruction.[25]

Succeeding stanzas in the calypso spell out details of the empires which were destroyed not by nature's plan but by the supremacist agenda of the white man armed with a superior military technology. The song also supplements the catalogue of great African leaders listed in "Black Child's Prayer":

> It is true that the Blacks were meek
> But, friends, they were never weak
> Them white Arabs King Menes rout

> Khamose drove the Hebrew out
> Shabaka and Taharqa
> Assyrians they massacre
> Candace of Ethiopia
> Stopped the Greek Alexander
> Kalydosos in the Sudan
> Halted Arab invasion
> Nzinga kept Portugal from her land
> Down in Monomotapa
> The great King Mutota
> Drove Arabs from the Empire.[26]

One is intrigued by the line "It is true that the Blacks were meek", which is aimed directly at Johnny King. Meek people do not found states and/or maintain them vigorously against alien aggression. It does seem somewhat disingenuous of Chalkdust, as a historian, to extend to people of obvious force of personality – and in many cases ruthlessness – the meekness credited hypothetically to the race as a whole (in Stalin's "No Other Man"). However, mythologizing requires selectivity, and Chalkdust chooses to be selective in dissociating the world's great men of colour from the towering arrogance of European monarchs, just as he chooses to ignore the complicity of the *asantehenes*, *alafins* and other autocrats in the Atlantic slave trade.

The lessons of NJAC's education programme were invoked in 1997 in GB's response to Bro Marvin's sweeping condemnation of African cultural nationalists in "Jahaaji Bhai" (1996). After complimenting and congratulating the Indian community and appealing to the spirit of unity that sustained the shipmates of indentureship (and their descendants), Marvin had launched an unprovoked assault on African cultural nationalists:

> For those who playing ignorant
> Talking 'bout true African descendant
> If yuh want to know the truth
> Take a trip back to yuh roots
> And somewhere on that journey
> Yuh go see a man in a *dhoti*
> Saying he prayers in front a *jhandi*
> Then and only then you'll understand
> What is a cosmopolitan nation.[27]

This gratuitous insult had not excited unfavourable public comment until Pearl Eintou Springer, a pan-African activist and Orisa worshipper, challenged the song and the singer:

> Brother Marvin cannot make statements that are so personal to him, and those like him, who are *dougla*, with the full connotations of the meaning of the word, and expect them to apply to all African people.
>
> Nowhere in my African past would I find anyone praying in front of a *Jhandi*. Nowhere in that calypso is there any credit, glory, any reference to anything significant and African; nowhere in the language, nowhere in the music, nowhere in his clothing, nowhere in the lyrics is there any recognition of Africa. The music is beautiful, the underlying sentiment of unity laudable.
>
> The perpetuation of the foolishness of no Mother Africa or Mother India must also stop.[28]

Springer's views about the total absence of anything African are contested by Keith Smith, editor of the *Express*: "Washing off the last of the Carnival germs in the coldness of the Lopinot river I heard the Yoruba chant in the song being carried along the river, the chant beginning somewhere upstream, the wind carrying it downstream and sundry voices picking it up in the pool where I happened to be."[29] Smith is neither musician nor musicologist, but being rooted in the Laventille community, with its heritage of Yoruba and Rada religious rituals, he would have recognized the melody of "Jahaaji Bhai" as being familiar. If he speaks true, the Africans who loved the song would have been charmed by a melody that they have carried along in their collective unconsciousness; if the melody is not Yoruba, they would have been reacting naturally to the power of music.

GB's "Jahaaji Blues" (1997) is the best-known of the fifteen songs which took Marvin to task:

> Jump off African business, jump off
> Harambee, jump off African business, jump off
> Dr JD Elder and the whole clan must be blue
> In this age of enlightenment, boy, don't misconstrue
> The first trace of humans is in Tanzania
> And through Adam God showed us his brown clay and woolly hair
> So evolution or creation
> Everyone came from the Black man.[30]

Although "Jahaaji Blues" brought GB first place in the Young Kings competition and secured him a spot in the prestigious national Calypso Monarch finals, it was never as popular as "Jahaaji Bhai", whose musicality made it a favourite of the 1996 season. GB himself praised the song for its incredibly beautiful melody: "Ah must salute Bro Marvin for melody first / 'cause Ah nearly get diabetes from listening two verse / That magic song is a montage of sweet melodies".[31] Sadly, "Jahaajhi Blues" had the same effect as the retractions which sought to correct the damage wrought by a sensational and inaccurate story. Marvin, who had defined himself as African in "Miss Bhaggan" (1993), defended himself against all attacks by affirming that he was "no Congo man" ("Sing 'bout Dat", 1997). This is a clear reference to the Sparrow classic already mentioned in this chapter.[32]

In 1998 the lessons of the NJAC programme were also invoked by Delamo, who, in "Respect the Little Black Boy", was contesting what he saw as a general attack on African pride delivered by Gypsy's prize-winning "Little Black Boy" (1997). Gypsy had earlier appropriated for himself the label of Black-Conscious on the strength of songs such as "I Am a Warrior" (1979), "Bangala Africa" (1981), "Negro Man" (*ca.* 1992) and "Black as Me" (1996), and he had reinforced this claim with a visit to Ghana, whence he returned with a wardrobe of splendid African garments. His "Little Black Boy" may have been an exhortation to his two eldest sons, who had sought and found the company of maxi-taxi touts and similar marginal characters.[33]

Ignoring all this public knowledge, Delamo lashed out at Gypsy for destroying the self-esteem of little black boys everywhere and demanded that Gypsy include in his lyrics statements which could give a positive example for them to follow. One must point out that Delamo would have seen nothing inconsistent in ridiculing A.N.R. Robinson, prime minister of Trinidad and Tobago between 1986 and 1991, for his identification with Africa ("The Argument", 1992) and later championing Africa in the face of the Gypsy assault. Among his recommendations in "Respect the Little Black Boy" was another look at black history:

> A little Black boy give the world Mathematics
> Put these facts in your lyrics
> So little black boys could be proud of their heritage
> A little Black boy build the first university
> At Timbuktu and from that everybody copy

> Today any Jane and John could get a degree
> That's why Gypsy song is a sacrilege
> To be a little Black boy is a privilege.[34]

Fairness demands that we consider Delamo's "The Argument", which, read against "Respect the Little Black Boy", provides a measure of the ambivalence about Africa which is ever-present in both the calypso and the society in general. "The Argument" is one of the many vitriolic calypsos which contributed to the derogation of Robinson. Within months of assuming office, A.N.R. Robinson had become tremendously unpopular because the austerity policies forced on him by world lending agencies generated great pressures on the working classes. A high point of his brief stint as prime minister was the highly publicized state visit of the Ooni of Ife, the spiritual leader of the Yorubas. Two years after this, when Robinson returned home after attending the Commonwealth heads of government conference in Nigeria, he was accused of having gone to Africa to seek obeah for re-election purposes. The ceremonial walking stick and hat with which he was presented in Nigeria were represented in and out of song as further evidence, as Sugar Aloes put it, that he was "pushing a demon head" ("The Argument", 1989). He had already been indicted in the court of popular fantasy/folly on charges of removing a cock from the Red House and installing a dragon, an act which supposedly resulted in mysterious fires and drownings.[35]

Robinson's electoral defeat in 1991 inspired Delamo to compose "The Argument" (1992), in which a young man is reviewing career choices by examining the success of public personalities:

> He want to be like Chief Olokun Igbaro
> To go back to Nigeria and sue
> The obeah man who take all mih dam' money
> And let them beat mih like Good Friday *bobolee*
> December 16th for mih birthday
> Ah get endless *bois* and *lati mangay*[36]
> In the Red House I did say with full force attack
> But when they attack Ah barely beat NJAC.[37]

Pink Panther's "Why Ah Change" (1992) also made bitter humour of Robinson's defeat:

> And when Ah hear that Chief Olokun Igbaro

> Won a seat over in Tobago
> I felt so good, ladies and gents
> Ah say well at last NJAC reach in Parliament
> But is Bill Trotman who make me to know
> Is really Robinson who they calling so
> But Sprangalang say "Panther doh let Bill fool you
> The man real name is Kunumunu."[38]

NJAC had been the leading organization identified in the 1970 Black Power uprising, and after its withdrawal from conventional politics in the 1970s, it had remained irrelevant to mainstream politics. Entry into mainstream politics in 1980 resulted in a gross take of 2.8 per cent of the national vote; by the 1990s, NJAC's dreams of attaining power via the ballot had been cruelly dashed in several humiliating electoral debacles. In the minds of some people, Robinson's African safari reduced him to the level of the ineffectual NJAC candidates and "legitimized" the derogatory nickname given him by Basdeo Panday, a political associate with whom he had broken in 1988. By ridiculing the honorific title awarded to Robinson in Nigeria and by equating him with the politically inept NJAC, calypsonians and others were signalling that one aspect of identification with Africa had been reduced to *mamaguy*. The irony here is that while this derogation was being articulated in song, celebrations marking the anniversary of emancipation were gaining momentum. Clearly, in the minds of some Afro-Trinidadians there was no real connection between dressing up for the emancipation parade and cultivating a mindset that promoted a responsible evaluation of Africa. "Since 1970," Singing Sandra mourns in "True Colours" (2000), "we come up empty."

Conclusion

The calypso has etched on the public consciousness negative images – or re-inscribed pre-existing impressions – about religious and tribal primitivism as well as of racialized sexual stereotypes. If one accepts that the calypso affords a window into popular attitudes, one cannot help concluding from a survey of calypso on Africa that Trinidad and Tobago locates Africa within the ontology of images mediated by Eurocentric agencies of communication, entertainment and education.

This study shows up several important features of the calypso. First among these is that the text is but one element in the popularity of a particular song. One has to consider as well the musicality of the piece, its time of release, the quality of its performance, and the receptivity of a public which is at best highly unpredictable and unstable. Musicality and rhythm may be just as important and sometimes even more so when one considers that most songs are presented at carnival time, when they have to compete in the cheerful and sometimes acrimonious anarchy of the calypso tent. Also, our most unpredictable and contrary public demands its meed/mead of recognizable and familiar elements. Cypher's "Rhodesia Crisis" may have had more impact than Zebra's "Rhodesia: Calypso Commentary" because it employed *picong*. Although the calypso itself is for public appeal and approbation, message alone cannot generate and/or sustain popularity.

Second, there is no accounting for the workings of the creative soul. Personal contact with Africa and with Africans has produced quite different results. When one considers Kitchener's affirmations, Brynner's mystical experience, Valentino's vision, Merchant's dreams, Sparrow's celebration of sexuality, and the silence of Gypsy, Lady Wonder and Chalkdust, one is awed by Rudder's phenomenal leap of imagination into the agony of South Africa.

Third, one has to factor the larger social context into any examination of the calypso of a particular period. Public feeling ran high in the 1960s, late 1970s and early 1980s, and this may have inspired and contributed to the success of Cypher's "Rhodesia Crisis", Valentino's "Stay Up Zimbabwe", Duke's "How Many More Must Die" and Stalin's "More Come", although one has to bear in mind that other good songs were not similarly acclaimed. A more conscious public will inspire more and more progressive songs on Africa. Although many, including calypsonians, think that the limited gains of 1970 were speedily reversed, the growing importance of Emancipation Day celebrations, public acknowledgement of the Baptist and Orisa faiths, and other indicators signal that Africa may be slowly acquiring a visibility which is voiced by Rudder, Ella Andall and others.

For Ella, this revival is predicated upon public acceptance of ancestral religion; to this end she published the CD titled *Oriki Ogun*, which is, as indicated in the subtitle, a suite of eighteen chants to Ogun. The publication of this CD indicates that Ella is aware of some measure of interest in Orisa on the part of the public, a fact highlighted in an irresponsible and cynical manner by the piracy of the CD. Calypso and society have come a long way from the 1930s, when the stock response to Orisa (and the Spiritual Baptists) was criticism or condemnation. Ella's co-religionist Rawle Gibbons, director of the Centre for Creative and Festival Arts at the University of the West Indies, St Augustine, has supported Ella's project, highlighting the importance of institutions in developing alternatives to Western ontology.

Afro-Trinidadian calypsonians have persisted in a vision of Africa that is partly coloured by their own romantic imagination, which has been conditioned by Hollywood-promoted stereotypes. It would require dramatic and decisive events and another surge of consciousness like that of 1970 to counter the centuries of Western conditioning which have been responsible for the persistence of uninformed images of Africa in the calypso. Although the mass movement has died away, leaving the nation an American satellite with even stronger cable links to the metropole, the continuous marronage of spirit manifests itself in a new and seemingly more viable consciousness. This happened in 1970 and can be credited to the teachings of Chalkdust, Duke and others, as well as the invocations of Ella and Rudder; however, the task of reconstructing Africa in the minds of Afro-Caribbeans or of facing up directly to the realities of the continent remains an uphill task.

When NJAC's education drive was presented through calypso, it achieved a harmonization of two seemingly antagonistic perceptions: that of the ordinary man (the street) and that of the elites (the school). Interestingly, this harmonization had been achieved in calypso and in the person of calypsonians like Chalkdust. Africa of the street is experienced through religion, song-and-dance complexes, cuisine and language, as celebrated in Chalkdust's "They Ent African at All" (1984). Africa of the school is apprehended, in the words of internationally acclaimed novelist Earl Lovelace, "in celebratory mode as the Africa of the elite, of the Pharaohs and the Nile",[39] as celebrated in Chalkdust's "Black Child's Prayer" (1983) and "White Man's Plan" (1985). Lovelace, who appreciates the street/school dichotomy while privileging the ongoing contribution of the street, recognizes that in our need to invoke Africa "we have been left with Africa as distortion, as fantasy, as dream, depending upon our individual need".[40] When, however, we see NJAC cultivating glorious Africa for ideological purposes while dancing to the music of Merchant's darkest-Africa "Umba Yao" for psychological release, we can appreciate the potential of calypso music for uniting our divided halves of self.

Notes

1. Carol Boyce-Davies, "The African Theme in Trinidad Calypso", *Caribbean Quarterly* 31, no. 2 (1985): 67–86 initiates this discourse, but where she accepts nineteenth-century African songs as calypsos, I understand calypso to be a form emerging sometime in the last decade of the nineteenth century. Like her I appreciate the difficulty of accessing calypsos from earlier periods, but I hesitate to conclude as she does that "[b]ecause of the intensity of Garveyism, many African-identified calypsoes should have survived" (70). I am not sure that Garveyism necessarily inspired *many* African-identified calypsos; calypso production responds to many stimuli, of which ideology is just one.
2. Studies which have demonstrated this include Richard Waterman, "African Patterns in Trinidad Negro Music" (PhD diss., Northwestern University, 1943); Charles Espinet and Harry Pitts, *Land of the Calypso: The Origin and Development of Trinidad's Folksong* (Port of Spain, 1944); J.D. Elder, "Evolution of the Traditional Calypso: A Socio-Historical Analysis of Song Change" (PhD diss., University of Pennsylvania, 1967); J.D. Elder, "Towards a History of the Traditional Calypso: A Suggestive" (paper presented at Seminar on the Calypso, ISER, University of the West Indies, St Augustine, 1986); Maureen Warner-Lewis, "The Influence of Yoruba Music on the Minor Key Calypso" (paper presented at Seminar on the Calypso, ISER, University of the West Indies, St Augustine, 1986); Gordon Rohlehr, *Calypso and Society in Pre-independence Trinidad* (Tunapuna, Trinidad and Tobago: Gordon Rohlehr, 1990), 1–42.
3. Many calypsonians of African descent perceive and declare themselves in song to be African biologically and spiritually; Louis Regis, "Ethnicity and Nationalism in the Post-1970 Calypso of Trinidad and Tobago" (PhD diss., University of the West Indies, St Augustine, 2002), 77–151.
4. These three were recorded by Melodisc but do not appear on Melodisc's compilations of Kitch's greatest hits. This has been the lamentable fate of many songs cited in this chapter, and many others were never recorded in the first instance.
5. Josef ben Jochanan, *The Saga of the "Black Marxists" Versus the "Black Nationalists": A Debate Resurrected*, vols. 1–3 (New York: ben Jochanan, 1976), x.
6. Lord Brynner [Cade Simon], "Uhuru Harambee", 1969.
7. After attending a conference in Dakar, Chalkdust confessed that militants in southern Africa were not aware that the calypso addressed their cause. See "Chalkie: I'll Smuggle Protest Tunes to South Africa", *Sunday Punch*, 7 January 1990, 8.

8. Rudder performed the title track during the 1990 tent season.
9. When Rudder remarketed the album, he named it *New Day Dawning*. This probably reflects his new attitude to this work, but "1990" appears twice on this CD: *New Day Dawning* also differs from *1990* in that it includes Tony Wilson's "Africa" (Tony Wilson is a Trinidad-born composer).
10. David Rudder, "New Day Dawning", Lypsoland CR 021, 1990.
11. David Rudder, "Heaven", *Lyrics Man*, Lypsoland CR 023, 1996.
12. Eric Roach, "Hard Drought", in *The Flowering Rock: Collected Poems 1938–1974* (Leeds: Peepal Tree, 1992), 166.
13. Kevin Yelvington, "The War in Ethiopia and Trinidad 1935–1936", in *The Colonial Caribbean in Transition: Essays on Postemancipation Social and Cultural History*, ed. Bridget Brereton and Kevin Yelvington (Barbados: University of the West Indies Press, 1999), 189–225. Yelvington praises Brian Friday's "The Impact of the Italo-Ethiopian Crisis on Trinidad, 1934–1937" (MA thesis, Dalhousie University, 1986), which he had discovered only after he was well advanced in his own project. Friday, who died in a vehicle accident in 1986, discussed his work with me, but I have never seen the thesis.
14 Growling Tiger [Neville Marcano], "The Gold in Africa" (1936), *Calypsos from Trinidad: Politics, Intrigue and Violence in the 30s, including the Butler Calypsos*, Arholie CD 7004, 1991.
15. Cypher [Dillary Scott], "Rhodesia Crisis", 1966.
16. Bally [Errol Ballantyne], "Shaka Shaka" (1988), *Ah Cyah Wait for Carnival plus The Best of Bally*, 2004.
17. The National Joint Action Committee, formed in 1969, was the standard-bearer in the Black Power unrest of 1970. See Selwyn Ryan and Taimoon Stewart, eds., *The Black Power Revolution 1970: A Retrospective* (St Augustine: ISER, 1995).
18. Bro Valentino [Emrold Phillip], "Third World" (1972), *Calypso Antiques*, ca. 2001.
19. The Merchant [Dennis Franklin Williams], "Umba Yao", Kalinda KD-562, 1978.
20. "Congo Man" is one of Sparrow's favourites. Thus far it has appeared on *Congo Man* (1965), *Sparrow's Carnival* (1965), *Spicy Sparrow* (1966), *Sparrow's Greatest Hits* (1969), *The Trinidad Heat Wave* (1981), *Party Classics: Part 2* (1988) and *The Mighty Sparrow Explodes into Calypso Time* (BLS CD 1024, 1999).
21. Boyce-Davies cites Gordon Rohlehr, "Sparrow and the Language of Calypso", *Savacou* 2 (1970), which offers that "Sparrow's use of the white man's stereotype reveals his divorce from the African but in so doing reveals a deep psychic need within the West Indian to prove his manhood through a fulfilled phallic vengeance for ancestral rage" ("The African Theme", 73). But Boyce-Davies, while acknowledging that "Congo Man" is a "glorification of primitivism and barbarism", accepts that "in its irony is communicated a new image of black power in the Congo Man's control after years of powerlessness" ("The African Theme", 74).

22. Mighty Chalkdust [Hollis Liverpool], "We Is We" (1972), *First Time Around*, Straker's GS 7784, 1973.
23. Mighty Chalkdust, "Black Child's Prayer", *With a Bang*, Straker's GS 2246, 1983.
24. Johnny King [Johnson King], "Nature's Plan" (1984), *The Best of Johnny King*, King Charles Productions, n.d.
25. Mighty Chalkdust, "White Man's Plan", *On a Blackboard of Truth*, Straker's GS 2263, 1985.
26. Ibid.
27. Bro Marvin [Selwyn Demming], "Jahaajhi Bhai", 1996.
28. Pearl Eintou Springer, "Some Balance Please, Brother Marvin", *Trinidad Guardian*, 8 February 1996, 8.
29. Keith Smith, "A Tale of Two Songs, Two Singers", *Express*, 27 February 1996, 9.
30. GB [Gregory Ballantyne], "Jahaaji Blues", 1997.
31. Ibid.
32. A short three years before this Marvin had declared himself African ("Miss Bhaggan", 1994) when he was upbraiding Chaguanas parliamentarian Hulsie Bhaggan, who had accused African-Trinidadians of raping Muslim virgins in her constituency.
33. Gypsy's sons contrived many ways to embarrass themselves and their father. His status as junior minister of culture could not prevent them from being arrested on charges of possession of marijuana in 2001; out of government, he was powerless to prevent their being arrested in 2003 on charges of possession of arms and ammunition. Gypsy, who had been elected as a member of the largely Indo-Trinidadian United National Congress, still feels bitterness towards African calypsonians for not supporting him in his short political career.
34. Delamo [Franz Lambkin], "Respect the Little Black Boy", 1998.
35. On the night of the People's National Movement's election victory in 1991, a mob tried unsuccessfully to pull down the dragon. When workmen eventually removed the offending creature, it turned out to be a sea serpent. A new weather vane was installed, depicting an unlikely creature described by a leading zoologist as a defecating dove.
36. *Bois* is the weapon used in stick-fighting, while *lati* is an Indian term meaning "whip". By this Delamo means that Robinson had received blows from the African and Indian voters who deserted his party in favour of their traditional electoral allegiances.
37. Delamo, "The Argument", 1992.
38. Pink Panther [Eric Taylor], "Why Ah Change", 1992.
39. Earl Lovelace, *Earl Lovelace: Growing in the Dark (Selected Essays)*, ed. Funso Aiyejina (San Juan, Trinidad and Tobago: Lexicon, 2002), 107.
40. Ibid., 206.

CHAPTER 9

Bordering on the Transgressive
(Re)constructing Cultural Identities in Indo-Caribbean Fictions

▶ PAULA MORGAN

The formation of modern Caribbean societies, a legacy of early capital- and technology-driven experiments in the transglobal flows of ethnicities and ideologies, has crafted diverse and fascinating manifestations of cultural identity politics – inscribed on bodies, played out in public and private spaces with intense energy, vociferous declarations, subterranean yearnings and ancestral loyalties. The stakes have always been high and passions deep. Fictional reconstructions of Indo-Caribbean identity are continually being invented to serve a complex range of both articulated and suppressed ideological objectives. Drawing from the constructionist as opposed to primordial models of ethnicity,[1] I argue that ethnic constructions vary depending upon the writer's gender and ethno-religious alignment, the period of writing and the ongoing imperative to write back to popular, nationalistic and global discourses. Indeed, Caribbean literature provides rich examples of culture as a "heuristic" device which enables us to talk about differences that set the groundwork for the "mobilization of group identities".[2]

The largest Indo-Caribbean populations exist today in Trinidad, Guyana and Surinam. The Indian immigrants to Trinidad, who are the primary focus of this chapter, belonged primarily to the peasantry of the Gangetic plain, and according to Naipaul transported ancestral customs from the preclassical world: "This peasantry . . . had not been touched by the great Indian reform movements of the nineteenth century."[3] This, and the hostile sociocultural scenario which greeted the indentees in the Caribbean, led the majority of Indians who crossed the *kala pani* to initially reconfigure themselves as rooted in primordialism – that is, identity and kinship based on biologism and genealogy. Yet in spite of pervasive assumptions of a uniform rootedness in the ancestral culture, the reality is that some embraced more flexible identity constructions. In both eventualities, it became necessary to erase, elide, evade and rename several salient dimensions of their lived experience. This chapter reads fictional reconstructions of Indianness as (b)ordering on the transgressive, elements of which are apparent even in conservative fictional subject reconstructions. To delimit the study, the focus here will be primarily on Trinidadian authors writing out of and about the Hindu and Presbyterian experiences. This includes V.S. Naipaul,[4] Lakshmi Persaud, the first Indo-Caribbean female novelist who emerged out of a traditional Hindu background, and Shani Mootoo. The chapter will focus on gendered ethnic identity (re)formation in fictional evocations of the period between indentureship and independence.

Several issues emerge. Assuming that the imperative to reconfigure viable identities is heightened at times of migration, what is Indianness? Can one identify a single or even an overarching, quintessential Indian identity in the fictional scenarios? What is the impact of ancestral religion on the identity formation of migrants? Are Indo-Caribbeans who have converted to Christianity more inclined to embrace nationalistic as opposed to ethnic self-identification? How does the fictional construction of Indianness vary over time and space; for example, what is the impact of evolving nationalist and global discourses? Is there any correlation between the fictional identity reconstruction and the secondary migration of personae/writers?

The crafting of Trinidad's complex social weave is instructive. In Trinidad alone, indentees and their descendants who stayed after their obligatory five-year period numbered over a quarter million. Upon arrival, Indian indentees encountered an extremely complex, highly stratified social scenario. For example, the upper tier of post-emancipation society comprised the planter class, which controlled the lion's share of the colony's resources. This group was itself stratified into expatriates and residents. The residents, the majority of whom were Creoles – a term used in this case to mean descendants of Europeans born on the islands – were further stratified into the English (descended from English and Scottish migrants) and the French, who saw themselves as a superior culture, in short, the island's true aristocracy.[5] By the 1930s this group had been joined by post-slavery immigrants from Portugal, China, Syria and Lebanon who came penniless but, trading on mobility afforded by ethnicity, soon became prosperous via astute dealings in wholesaling and retailing businesses.[6] The middle tier of Trinidadian society originated in the free coloured/black segment of slave society and received a steady influx from the black labouring class, with access afforded though education, land ownership, professional employment and strategic marital alliances. And of course there was the stratified labouring population (predominantly African descended), which formed the third tier.

Even more complex levels of stratification based on religion, class, colour and caste attended Indian settlement into the complex social milieu. Historian Kusha Harracksingh, in "Indenture and Self Emancipation", debunks the notion that the population of indentees was a homogeneous group drawn from among the dispossessed, the exploited and the downtrodden. With reference to administrative manuals prepared by British officials in India, he pinpoints the impact of broad diversities of space, customs and time on the migrant labour pool, ranging from "the wide expanse of the recruiting ground" to the "widely differing ways of naming and doing things, from food and dress to the work of the field, from village beliefs to perceptions both of the outside world and of each other".[7] Moreover he argues that, given the extensive three-quarter-century span of indentured immigration, the cultural baggage of the people who came would have evolved substantially within that period.

Anthropologist Aisha Khan poses a similar argument in relation to the heterogeneity of indentured immigrants to the Caribbean, citing differences in region, language, religion, caste, occupation and cultural history. All migrated in response to diverse forces of "political and social disruption, starvation and to a lesser extent, disease". Pointing to disjuncture between historical determinants of cultural practices and contemporary perceptions, Khan concludes: "The quintessential Indian cultural signature, working of one's land, was recounted to me by many Indo-Trinidadians as being brought from the subcontinent to the Caribbean untrammeled and undisrupted, a dignified if humble pursuit

... this heritage was far more complex and far less idyllic than later visions would encourage it to seem."[8]

In the post-indentureship reconstruction of the Indian village in then rural Trinidad, homogeneity is more apparent than real. Lakshmi Persaud writes in her fictional account of a reconstructed Indian village:

> Some may think that because the Pasea villagers were East Indian, there was amongst them a uniformity of colour and culture. What we had in reality is a mosaic of peoples: Moslems who would not eat pork but would eat beef and who distrusted Hindus, and we, Hindus who ate neither and distrusted the Moslems. There were also the short dark Madrassis and the ivory-coloured Brahmins from Northern India, tall, well proportioned people with features like those of the gods and goddesses hanging on our walls.[9]

This simple passage demonstrates the complex components of cultural identity formation. By the same token, any discussion of Indo-Caribbean cultural identity is fraught with pitfalls – the primary one being the risk of oversimplification. Descriptors defining culture are used adjectivally to identify differences, comparisons, contrasts capable of infinite variation, as opposed to descriptors based on inherent qualities bequeathed by biology and genealogy. The passage also indicates the inclusive and dissociative "us and them" nature of cultural identification based on the shifting subject position of the speakers: *us* East Indians as opposed to *them* West Indians (implied); *us* vegetarian Hindus as opposed to *them* beef-eating Muslims, the former dividing again into *us* tall, fair Brahmins as opposed to *them* short, dark Madrassis.

The opening phrase points to the danger of mistaking shared ethnic positioning and geographical location as proof of shared culture. Additionally, it points to the impact of translocal hegemonies, especially those rooted "up north". It demonstrates the privilege conferred on those empowered with voice to articulate the "truth" about cultural "reality". The passage also shows how material markers become the property of groups and, by extension, become naturalized as essential to group identity and privileged as markers of inherent superiority. Finally, these external markers are anthropomorphically projected into the supernatural domain, to become gods made in the image of "superior" man and then transmuted into religious iconography to hang on living-room walls.

Despite the keen perception of internal differences reflected in Persaud's narrative, the external projection of a coherent homogeneous face proved increasingly significant for Indian survival and mobility within the chaotic anomie of the burgeoning post-emancipation culture. From inception, the issue of "who am I?" was problematic for Indian immigrants to the West Indies. They confronted major challenges in terms of conceiving of themselves as West Indian. The contributing factors included their strong ancestral roots and the promise of return on completion of their five-year contracts, combined with a hostile reception from the post-emancipation society, in which they were perceived as scab labour willing to work for minimal pay on the estates the ex-slaves had deserted.

Significantly, the indentees had to choose whether they would remain or return. Lamming, in his presentation "Politics and the Language of Ethnicity", argues that for Indian indentees the decision to stay was predicated on rootedness in the land which was the legitimate entitlement of their indenture. This was in turn supported by a commitment to generate income through feeding the emerging nation. Harracksingh terms the decision to stay as connected to the social "leavening" which attended the jostling for "status and preeminence". The enclosed island space and the diasporic condition afforded release from disempowering ascriptive tenets of class and caste. Moreover, the decision to stay was based on a definition of homeland as the location of family: "they had no one 'there' in India, . . . their family was 'here' in Trinidad".[10]

Paradoxically though, despite the choice to remain, V.S. Naipaul's fictional evocation of pre-independent Trinidad indicates that the process of settling into Caribbean society and the gradual acculturation may have developed for many by virtue of length of tenure rather than conscious embrace: "Despite the solidity of their establishment the Tulsis had never considered themselves settled in Arwacas or even Trinidad. It was no more than a stage in the journey that had begun when Pundit Tulsi left India."[11] Predictably, in relation to the broader Trinidadian political framework, Indians until fairly recently were perceived (as branded in 1958 by then prime minister Eric Williams) as a "recalcitrant and hostile minority" who were resistant to an inevitable creolization process.[12] Brinsley Samaroo attributes this perception in part to a lack of understanding of the philosophical underpinnings of traditional Hindu society, which placed emphasis on communalism.[13] Group mind, along with vestiges of caste sensibility, contributed to a collective resistance to the notion of creolization, on the one hand, and, on the other, affirmation of a unique East Indian cultural identity.

This coincided with the Indians' inevitable progression along diverse pathways of acculturation and assimilation. The paradoxical location was a source of contention with the Afro-Creole society that would relegate Indianness to an exotic element in a Caribbean rainbow coalition.

The shifting nature of these identity politics is captured in the fluid naming of the then ethnic minority. In the topsy-turvy world in which Columbus sailed west to reach east and his partners in imperial enterprise subsequently transported indentees from the East Indies to the West Indies, Samuel Selvon describes the evolving process of naming the immigrants. They were known initially as East Indians to differentiate them from American Indians and West Indians, then later as West Indian East Indians when they assumed settler status, and finally as East Indian West Indians in response to the impulse towards integration.[14] At each stage the dissociative nature of ethnic labelling worked to give meaning to these names, and to assiduously prop up stereotypical assumptions of Indo-Caribbean cultural continuity and preservation as opposed to Afro-Caribbean cultural fragmentation and loss. There are divergent perspectives among historians on how to interpret the evolving process of post-indentureship cultural identity formation. Is it as Harracksingh argues, that change was constant to the diasporic experience: "whole new constructs appeared out of fragmentation and remnants" but these were not "appreciated as a new creation"?[15] Or is it as Samaroo argues: "culture becomes a tool of survival, where people hold on to what they have and are reluctant to adapt to the new norms which must, inexorably, be the bases for our West Indian nationhood"?[16] Samaroo warns that Indian cultural revitalism is not going to blow away, so the issue must be resolved.

The permutations continue in infinite variety, as fictional representations testify. Autobiography is the ground on which testimony on the making of the private self fuses with communal cultural projection and representation of the making of worlds. In the celebratory *My Mother's Daughter: The Autobiography of Anna Mahase Senior*, which covers the period 1899–1967, Mahase, a first-generation descendant of Hindu indentures who converts to Presbyterianism, valorizes liberation from the traumas of family breakup, drudgery, homelessness and poverty. Her salvation comes in the form of a Presbyterian mission orphanage in which religious conversion and Western acculturation go hand in hand, despite a shallow genuflection to Hindu language and culture. Defining a world which excises both the broader creolized social order and the submerged Hindu order, Mahase's triumphant narrative declares her outstanding achievements as the trailblazing first of a cadre of female Indian professionals within an acculturated Presbyterian Indo-Trinidadian framework. She writes: "My teaching career began on May 1, 1917, I being the first East Indian Assistant Teacher to be employed in an Assisted Primary School in Northern Trinidad and later on, in 1919, the first East Indian qualified female teacher in the Island."[17] Negotiating cultural pitfalls and pathways with consummate skill, Mahase variously benefits from and resists both Hindu and Presbyterian paternalistic structures. Her first suitor is discouraged and subsequently rejected outright; she is unwilling to give up her education and enter the traditional extended family network in favour of a potentially more egalitarian, Western-style nuclear family. On the other hand, she also subsequently evades a Presbyterian arranged marriage and independently forges a love match with Mahase.

In this woman's version, she foregrounds, through both title and ongoing juxtapositions, the parallel journey of her mother – the bold, independent, fiery indentee Rookabai, who at age twelve stole money and fled an arranged marriage in India to an aged husband. Rookabai, "a born leader of women and children" who, we are told obliquely, is unable to lead her husband, chooses personal freedom over marriage and maternity. She opts instead for return migration to India with only one of her five children. This autobiographical narrative supports the findings of Rhoda Reddock. Within a socio-economic scenario in which women came not as wives but as independent, wage-earning indentees, Reddock has delineated the manner in which Indian males colluded with colonial authorities to reconstruct women as unpaid housewives, thereby reinterpreting their substantial labour in domestic and commercial food production as domestic work rendered gratuitously for the benefit of the home.[18]

Anna Mahase honours but surpasses her mother as conqueror of all her worlds. The order of her achievements is significant. She emerges first as a successful educator and self-taught musician, then as wife and mother, religious instructor and philanthropist, and then ultimately in the other primary traditional role of domestic food producer – providing for the family table through vegetable and poultry production. Mahase conquers all worlds. Pouchet Paquet argues: "Anna Mahase allies herself with a transnational metropolitan-based religious organization that is both liberating and alienating in the new forms of

consciousness and the feminist activism that it brings to these island dwellers
. . . identity is linked incontrovertibly to transforming transnational and transcultural influences and alliances with people, lands and cultures beyond their Caribbean homeland."[19]

She deploys a peculiar discursive mix of revelation and repression: she erases the grim passage and labours of the indentees, the details of her parents' marital discord and loss of ancestral religion – only vestiges remain. Note the oblique mention of her mother's Brahmin caste, the erasure of her father's presumably lower caste and the acknowledgement of her mother's religious syncretism, as reflected in her creative homemade Divali ritual. Liberatory transcendence and assimilation into a separate, though happy and fulfilling, Indo-Trinidadian world are foregrounded, pressing loss and alienation, personal and ancestral griefs into a shadowy, unarticulated background. Mootoo's revision of the post-indentureship Indian/Presbyterian cultural interface tells a radically different tale. Mahase's first-generation Indo-Trinidadian narrative of self-reconstruction speaks of successful negotiations, creative hybridity and productive assimilation within a Caribbean adopted homeland, effected largely through a major global force of sustained cultural interaction through a religion of conversion.

What of the narratives rooted in closed rural Hindu communities? Culturally rooted reconstructions of India do seem possible, especially in rural, close-knit Indian communities, but again in terms which speak reams about the erasures involved. Lashkmi Persaud in *Butterfly in the Wind*, whose narrative spans the 1890s to the 1930s – the period of "unbridled British apartheid" – speaks to the possibility of reconstruction. As is the case for Walcott's "Saddhu of Couva" and Naipaul's old men, who in a ganja-induced haze dream of their ancestral home at dusk,[20] twilight creates a special frame for imaginary homelands. Persaud's narrator lyrically testifies:

> At dusk it was easy to believe you were in India: shadows and sounds of bullock carts, the aromas of rotis and chulas; fresh water in buckets and cut grass in bales; off-white houses with thatched roofs and glowing wood fires in the yards; the soft gentle sounds of Hindi in the night carried by warm winds along earth red tracks. Even as late as the 1930s it was easy to believe.[21]

Common ancestry and ancient caste certainties were the tools which the former indentees used to craft ethnic solidarity and cohesion in the face of a hostile, unknown environment. The child narrator, whose father came off the ship as a babe in the arms of an indentee, speaks of the necessity to shroud in silence the traumatic crossing and resettlement, to erase the long, humiliating period of contract labour. Persaud portrays instead a people with backs resolutely turned to hardship and humiliation, with unbounded hope in their progeny and eyes resolutely set on tomorrow. The framework Persaud evokes fits the constructs of an ancient rural culture untouched by time, a simple, idyllic, rural, pre-industrial past – rich, earthy and rooted in evocative visual, aural and kinetic images. Predictably, the reconstructed India of the imaginary cannot withstand the moment when the "sun visits the moon" – the advent of electricity. This stasis is fundamentally at odds with the hurly-burly of modern Trinidad, reflected in the encroachment of hostile peoples and more so in kinetic images which create a counterpoint to a romanticized stasis: trains rushing by carrying American soldiers;[22] a threatening, aggressive encroaching African population embodied in husky girls, jealous of economic privilege, who bully and rob Kamla of her bounty.[23]

The dilemma faced by the progeny of indentees was this: What did Trinidadian nationality and nation building require of them? On what terms were they to interweave the legacy of an island birthplace with the legacy of an ancestral culture? The process of change for which I have deployed the contested term *creolization* was inevitable. The issue is what they would be required to give up in the process and how much agency and voice Indo-Trinidadians would have in the naming-which-calls-into-being and the prescriptive configuration of the new indigenous creation, which the group was inevitably becoming. Persaud's fictional account shadows the scenario of the Indian village of Felicity, as explored by Morton Klass in 1957. He recorded then the persistence of ethnic exclusiveness which had disappeared by 1985, by which time "East Indians had become West Indians". He measured adoption of the Trinbagonian way of life in terms of shared "language, social and economic patterns", "material goods and aspirations", shared "commitment to Western education and egalitarian values" and awareness of "economic and other links to North America and the British Commonwealth".[24]

The reconstruction of India in the Caribbean remained a possibility into the mid twentieth century. Among believers in the ancestral faith such as Persaud, it was viewed more positively than by V.S. Naipaul, for example. Yet even this statement stands in need of qualification. Naipaul demonstrates how caste, the lynchpin of the Hindu self-construct, was eroded during indentureship and selectively reconstructed thereafter. The caste system, the steel frame of Hinduism, is held to have been divinely ordained; it is connected with the law of karma, according to which a man's status in life is determined by his actions in former lives. The family system has religious significance, one of its essential purposes is to secure salvation of the spirits of past members by the offering of oblations. Caste differentiation was doomed by the journey, which necessitated shared food and sanitation of ship and barrack-yard. In the process, a new, ascriptive kinship system emerged – a brotherhood of the boat, generated by the common adversity of the crossing. Yet spatial disjuncture brought transgressive potentialities which would never have been possible within the old geocultural space, including the opportunity to escape inherited caste disability.[25] This possibility is subtly attached even to the sacred Pundit Tulsi:

> The Tulsis has some reputation among Hindus as a pious, conservative, landowning family . . . Among Hindus there were other rumours about Pundit Tulsi, some romantic, some scurrilous. The fortune he had made in Trinidad had not come from labouring and it remained a mystery why he had emigrated as a labourer. One or two emigrants from criminal clans had come to escape those consequences of their families' participation in the Mutiny. Pundit Tulsi belonged to neither class. His family still flourished in India . . . and it was known that he had been of higher standing than most of the Indians who . . . had lost touch with their families and wouldn't have known in what province to find them.[26]

In focusing on the Tulsi domain, Naipaul is referring to the Indian who has retained contact, tenuous though it may be, and for this reason is held in high regard. Mr Biswas is thrown into this vanguard of culture, and through his perspective its spiritual paucity and irrationality are unveiled.

Naipaul's evocation of the reconstructed Hindu household is decidedly ungenerous. Transgressive elements are not veiled here; rather, they are exposed to Biswas's satirical eye and tongue as he relentlessly reveals the reconstructed Brahminal clan for the anomaly that it is. Yet caste survives as an important factor in the decision to remain in Trinidad after the five-year tenure, since anyone travelling from "overseas" had to take the *prayaschita*, perform the purification *yagnya*, before he could rejoin his caste as a regular participating member. This constraint forms the basis of one of Naipaul's humorous barbs. Upon Mrs

Tulsi's decision to send her son abroad to study, several of her retainers, "forgetting that they were in Trinidad, and that they have crossed the black water from India and had thereby lost all caste . . . said they could have nothing more to do with the woman who was planning to send her son across the black water".[27] Arguably, despite numerous and subtle reductive ironies, the implied author remains both contemptuous of and nostalgic for old potentialities. Persaud's Kamla (in *Butterfly in the Wind*) can lovingly valorize the industry and expertise of the village commune, cooperative ventures in simple, effective construction and orderly, ecologically sound agricultural practices demonstrated in intercropped gardens which produce food and curative herbs in abundance. On the other hand, Biswas can only grudgingly acknowledge the shelter and provision afforded by the Hanuman House superstructure, while fleeing its engulfing potential. The implied author's hankering for order, purity, greatness, and conversely his obsession with filth and scatological imagery, which persists from text to text, speaks to a Brahminical sensibility bereft of the philosophical accommodation that would tolerate the outworkings of hierarchical social ordering.

Whereas Naipaul revels in the transgressive, for Persaud a different dynamic occurs. The transgressive element in *Butterfly in the Wind* is veiled. Subtle disharmonies are introduced by the intrusion of Western ways and worldviews. Despite the constant affirmation of ancestral faith and culture, the narrative is simultaneously about the initiation of a young Hindu girl into Western epistemologies. Initially Kamla measures Western modes of knowing against the informal familial ways of knowing. She learns from the temple, but primarily her mode of instruction originates from a warm, nurturing female network where she learns the mysteries of faith and the stresses of male/female interaction, with fidelities and commitments which extend beyond rationality. She constantly tests the new knowledge systems against domestic impartations. Kamla can believe in the four and twenty blackbirds baked in a pie because this lines up with mythic tales told by female relatives of cat and kittens who after prayer emerge unsinged from a fired urn.[28] The supernatural, miraculous and fantastic line up with the fantasy world of childhood.

It is in the underlying motifs and imagery that an alternative narrative takes shape. The protagonist is symbolized by a delicate, fragile butterfly buffeted by wind, seeking to escape over high walls. Escape from the closed Hindu village environment is facilitated by mass access to the first major Presbyterian school. Disjuncture surfaces in the sharply contrasting tactile imagery. The traditional village conservatism is portrayed as both warm and nurturing and as cold and alien as a glacier: "And so it was that this gigantic glacier of traditional conservatism began to thaw. I saw ten year olds move easily from one culture to another, from rolling out *roties* in the morning, cooked on a *chulha* with wood from the forests, to making careful written observations through a microscope an hour later."[29]

Spatial imagery points to similar fissures. The idealized, restricted rural space is conveyed in images of limitation and entrapment. Education into Western worldviews opens up realms of infinite possibility. It is the difference between swimming near the seashore as opposed to exploring the ocean's deep canyons. In the subconscious realm, Kamla's dream of being chased by a bull conflates sexual imagery of ambivalent desire and fear of penetration. To escape the bull, Kamla, in an expansion of the butterfly imagery, takes flight, soaring into wide open space only to fly again to the safety of home. The alternative to the mobility and wide open space is oppression – being pressed to the ground by the house, which represents the great weight of expectation and tradition: "I begin to feel claustrophobic. I try to shout, to scream, but my mouth is squashed into the earth. I am crying but my sounds are too muffled, too feeble. I can hear noises from outside. They drown me, they suffocate me. I am like the frog."[30]

Escape materializes by the end of the novel, when the young scholar is poised to migrate to a Scottish university, which gives her a passport into the emerging professional, urban social grouping. It is an excellent individual and family accomplishment, but even more important is what it signifies to the group. Only at this point of an affirming journey are the erasures of the indentees' crossing dissipated. The tongues of the aged ones are loosened in the face of this ultimate triumph: "Do you know what my grandmother said? . . . turn this way, turn that way, nothing else but water for six slow months. And how do you think they were treated? What do you think they were given to eat? . . . Others talked about . . . how bad it had been in the old ships and how many had died."[31] The protagonist is now fully acculturated, and moreover her "arrival" validates the suffering and sacrifice of the entire community. Her dress reflects her in-betweenity: a cocktail dress with patterned sequined stockings, court shoes and a firm, steady classical Indian hairstyle.

In Persaud's second text, *Sastra*, a very different dynamic emerges. *Sastra* is a fictional evocation of process which Stuart Hall terms a reach for "ancestral groundings",[32] or what Simbonath Singh terms a process of ethnic renewal: "ethnic renewal is a process by which existing ethnic identity can be reconstructed either by reclaiming a discarded identity or by amending or replacing an identity or by simply filling a personal ethnic void.[33] She also engages in a far more overtly politicized discourse with the Trinidad national community and Afrocentric creolizing forces. What can one learn from this fictional account of an emerging ethnic consciousness, and how does it link with the modern nation-state and the incipient violence which shadows this narrative? *Sastra* demonstrates the operations and limitations of primordialism, that is, notions of group identities based on blood, soil, language, religion and memory. Appardurai argues that these concepts are commonly linked to two poles of collective behaviour – the pole of group violence, ethnocide and terror and the pole of an assumed anti-modernity manifested in elements such as sluggish recalcitrance in relation to participation in the state apparatus.[34]

In the reconfigured space described in *Sastra*, all ignorance of the significance of Hindu ritual reflected in *Butterfly in the Wind* is replaced by keen knowledge. The narrator says of a venerable elder woman and role model: "Her religious values and her cultural values were one. Her culture was her way of life, it was all encompassing. Dharma was to her the path of righteousness, the way of life handed down, by teaching and example".[35] Persaud is constantly pushing back the boundaries of the natural world in an attempt to capture, through evocation of simple domestic acts, the essence of life. And it is the women who embody the spiritual essence of the space – simple village women who, in the act of kneading flour and preparing traditional dishes, infuse the air, "evoking a near spiritual warmth, entrancing the imagination, lifting it higher than soaring kites . . . . But it is their fingers which attract: stretching, opening, filling, closing. The mystery is locked within the dough. But unlike bees buzzing into the sweet floral vortex of nectar, these fingers are not programmed by a common genetic code, but by the powerful order of tradition."[36] Predictably, it is the women and not the men who are figured as the embodiment of the tradition. The primary platform for the outworking of this model is the domestic sphere, in which the women function as the quintessential preservers of the domestic culture, the picture of grace and subservience. Their ritual acts of obeisance create within the home an enchanted nurturing retreat in which their men can recover from the despoliation of the broader society.

Yet perhaps because these lofty positions, though philosophically ennobling, are in reality restrictive for women, Persaud is careful to identify that these roles are prescribed not by genetic code or by the transcendent primordial elements of blood and relation, but by tradition. And gender modelling has always played a special function in this regard. Patricia Mohammed identifies a disjuncture between the traditional notions of maleness and femaleness which were an integral part of the baggage of Indian migrants and the actual gender characteristics which they exhibited in their daily lives: "Such gender images drew heavily upon the sexual imagery conveyed through myths, cultural symbols, artifacts, religious rituals and festivals which made concrete their ideas about what constituted male and female characteristics and behavior."[37] Ultimately though, in terms of gender identification, Persaud's text negotiates an ambiguous space between loyalty to the traditional mores and breaking free of their constraints. *Sastra* manages to valorize arranged marriages while the protagonist negotiates to marry the lover of her own choice.

In terms of ethnic identification, both the positive and negative elements of primordial construction of ethnic identity are in evidence. The sense of "we-ness" created by ethnic identification can generate the positive manifestation of pride in self and ancestry, as well as dignity and self-assertiveness, or it can generate exclusiveness, hatred, an impulse towards domination of the Other and affirmation of supremacy as demonstrated by the right of rulership. In *Sastra*, emerging Creole nationalism becomes a troubled social framework for besieged Indians, who in their assessment carry the national economy and feed the nation, yet are disallowed (arguably by their own sense of contradictory difference) access to political power. They complain, ". . . and we have no one, we are on our own here . . . but we are a hard working people",[38] "we pay taxes . . . to keep them in cushy government jobs".[39] This sense of being besieged is manifested very powerfully in the account of the brutal murder of a moneylender and his family, which is interpreted, in the absence of any evidence, as racist in its motivation – *their* crime against *us*. The crime is thereby vaguely related to the definitive elements commonly labelled as the stereotypical ethnic characteristics: the Indian's economic wealth, and the criminal waste of the African seeking money for carnival frivolity. Within the text, the psychic laceration created by this crime is borne by the entire Indian community, as a personal act of violence perpetrated by the entire African community.

Finally, whereas *My Mother's Daughter* and *Butterfly in the Wind* and even *A House for Mr Biswas* are all firmly rooted in place and test the potential for reconstruction of an Indian community within multicultural Trinidad, *Sastra* extends the issue of "who am I?" into the metropolitan terrain. We see here a fictional evocation of translocal ethnic renewal which opens the door to a whole new mosaic of identity politics. The protagonist negotiates secondary migration to Canada in quest of a larger space in which to flourish. Drawing reference to *Sastra*, I have argued elsewhere:

> Published two years before the 150th anniversary of the arrival of Indians in Trinidad and Tobago, in the very year that the nation welcomed its first Indian Prime Minister, it is remarkable that Persaud's protagonist locates herself, at the end of the narrative, outside of the framework of Caribbean society. In the faceless anonymity of the metropolis, she defines a new pathway: "Across the city, other communities from all parts of the world were establishing and making lives for themselves: Chinese, Jamaicans, Trinidadians, Italians, Greeks, Indians from the sub continent and *Indians like herself from the Caribbean*" (p. 272) [my emphasis]. As an educated, wealthy, Brahmin burdened/empowered by caste sensibilities, the thorny issues involved in crafting a space within the Trinidad nation state are irrelevant – not when she can opt for a space within a Canadian bourgeoisie . . . . She chooses a unique discursive space – an Indian from the Caribbean: "Maybe they were all becoming Canadians" (p. 272).[40]

The text demonstrates the impact of global resurgence of religio-ethnic identity formation and its provision of a counter-discourse to Trinidadian nationalism.

As third-generation descendants of indentees take up their leg of what promises to be an endless cycle of transmigrations, new identity politics emerge. Of primary interest to this essay is Mootoo's revisioning of the post-indentureship period, with its focus on gender and familial relations. In this evocation, the transgressive is not on the border; rather, I argue that it is the central focus of the literary representation.[41]

This reformulated narrative of origin constructs mindscapes of home within transmigratory frameworks. It plays with the powerful impact of global flows in ideology on continuities and disjunctures in identity formation. Mootoo returns to the past as it might have been, to create space for a future emergent self to flourish. This text goes beyond the paradoxes of primordialism in the interest of inscribing instead fluidity in gender and ethnic formation. The primary objective is to destabilize normative heterosexual identities in keeping with the post-modern ethos. The construction can be aligned with the contention of gender theorist Judith Butler: "No longer understood as a product of cultural and psychic relations long past, gender is a contemporary way of organizing past and future cultural norms, a way of situating oneself in and through those norms, an active style of living one's body in the world".[42] Fluid gender formation is represented in the narrative as a natural extension of the broader post-colonial agenda – to rescue/recoup the stability of the individual subject from colonial displacement and abuse.

In this novel, set in an imaginary Caribbean island and a retelling of the past, the text reframes the issue of "who am I?" into "who and how and what am I becoming?" In the process, Mootoo formulates representational strategies to rescue queer post-colonial subjectivities from narrative erasure. She unearths/articulates subject positions of her silenced characters and roots them in a rearticulated version of the Caribbean physical and sociocultural landscape. Her fictional enquiry raises salient issues about the correlation between narrative and heterosexual ideology; how this in turn connects with post-colonial narrative reinscriptions; and the potential for literary representation to project liberatory paradigms. Mootoo's narrative eschews fixed identities, opting rather to interpolate complex subjects in process.

In a skilful deployment of post-modern play, she engages the grand meta-narratives of Christianity and colonialism, particularly as they inscribe gender and ethnic identity formation. Post-modern engagement can be traced in the destabilization of gender and sexual orientation; rejection of a homosexual/heterosexual binary in favour of a fluid play of queer identities; representation of traditional gender roles as unnatural performances/constructs designed to maintain patriarchal privilege and female subordination; construction of the nuclear family as a site of incipient and manifest violence as opposed to nurturance and protection; undermining of the possibility of unified coherent subjectivity; undermining of social, cultural, political, religious and domestic authority structures. I read *Cereus Blooms at Night* as a provocative subaltern articulation employed in favour of indeterminate and transgressive subjects in formation.

A central theme is the epistemic violence practised by the Presbyterian mission in the process of imposing a brand of Christianity which bears the imprint of the Shivering Northern Wetlands. The impact works itself out on several predictable levels. The primary target of the civilizing Christianizing process, Chandin Ramchadin, is adopted by the missionaries to better facilitate the process of coercion, erasure and imprinting. The result is displacement, dispossession and internalization of the alienating colonizing gaze. Chandin thereafter lives with deep-rooted self-revulsion and a sense of non-belonging, his subjectivity distorted by ambivalence of desire, a site of profound splitting and doubling. One consequence of the inscription of subordination and self-loathing on Chandin's dark body is transformation of the white woman into the embodiment of all that is good and fair, the epitome of all he has been constrained to love, the focal point of his desire. Union with his adopted sister comes to represent the ultimate affirmation that he is not an imitator or a besmirched inferior. Interracial sexual attraction and the threat of miscegenation come to focus on Lavinia Throughly, daughter of the missionaries. Absorption into the beloved Other represents for him the potential for transformation – for possessing and becoming one with the whiteness which he craves.

The colonial meta-narrative is etched most deeply on his body. In the family tableau, Chandin's place is the straight-backed chair. This comes to represent the harsh cultural strictures which he must embrace to be at home in the new environment, as opposed to the pliable hammock of his parental home. Indeed, the text implies that male identity constructed as fixed, strong and coherent, with a stiff backbone, is itself a colonial import epitomized by the imperial spiritual overlord. Race is such a powerful determinant of placement in the hierarchical order that its implicature overflows to encompass yet another key marker of social positioning: gender. Chandin's natural father is feminized by his weak spine and supine postures.

The racialized (read contaminated) body in the Manichean social order synecdochically represents the whole man. And in the hegemonic narrative it is only the heavy hand of Europe's civilizing order which can lighten the dark soul and thereby create a disjuncture between the outer black skin and the inner enlightened man. The colonizing meta-narrative inscribed upon the body and the mind of the subject race creates an impulse towards transformation which is forever doomed to failure. Mimicry at its very best can produce only a poor reflection and can result only in an enduring sense of inferiority. When his idolized love object seduces and runs away with his wife, Chandin reacts in his anger and rage by embracing inner blackness. In response to Sarah and Lavinia's flight he demolishes the contents of his house, as surely as he demolished the inner constructs carefully erected by the missionaries. He takes instead to alcoholism and incest.

Mootoo engages these spatial, ontological and epistemological dichotomies in order to break down the privileging of civilization over savagery, white over black, culture over nature, male over female, good over evil. In most cases the dualisms appear to be dialectically broken down to introduce shades of grey into an apparently crisp black-and-white scenario. Arguably Mootoo, in her correlation of these modes of ontology and epistemology, is investigating the potential of an oppressed people to recover more authentic modes of being and ways of knowing. In the process she valorizes rootedness to the earth, to nature and simple lifestyles of minimal consumption, all of which are alien to postcolonial and neocolonial hierarchies. In other words, in the exploration of the potential for psychic recovery, Mootoo affirms characters and characteristics which are located outside of the endorsed meaning-frames of colonial and postcolonial society. Rootedness is essential, but paradoxically, as I argue subsequently, so is a season of exile.

Chandin's incestous relationship with his daughters is related to his epistemic rape by an alienating order. Released by rejection and betrayal from the lofty colonizing intent and moral constraints of Presbyterianism, he also loses hold of cultural anxieties in relation to incest. Having lost the highest place in the hierarchical order, he shamelessly sinks to the lowest. The narrative raises and does not necessarily resolve a range of issues. Given the trauma which Chandin suffers, we are encouraged to understand, though not to endorse, his "unspeakable act". Chandin's incestuous penetrations of "*my* Pohpoh" are fed by the broader cultural assumption of the female as non-person bound by patriarchal ownership. The text holds the mirror to a social order which gazes with mild disapproval at a long-term incestuous liaison but pounces fiercely on the mentally unhinged old "victim" as a criminal. In the figural play of the narrative, the gross inappropriacy of the social response is shrouded in deliberate understatement. Its clearest signifier is the thick cloud that breaks up when Mala's childhood persecutor-turned-supporter, Walter Bissey, turns the Janus-faced legal machinery to a compassionate visage.

Tyler, the homosexual narrator and central interpreter of the reality, is a mystery to himself. As a result of his sexually transgressive identity, Tyler is initially located outside of socially acceptable ontology as a liminal being. He opts for a foreign land in which he would be marked as a threshold person based on culture, skin colour and language rather than gender. At the beginning of the narrative, Tyler (the authorial mouthpiece) is seeking a basis for reintegration into his natal society. In the process of finding Mala and through the agency of narrative, Tyler finds the missing person that is himself. Empathy between the two is based on shared outsider status: "She and I shared a common reception from the rest of the world".[43] Instructed by the silent Mala, he embraces the concept that fluid gender identities are natural and spontaneous and therefore should not be manacled. Mala creates an enabling environment for Tyler's acceptance and expression of his sexual identity.

Clearly Mootoo sets out to undermine what Judith Butler terms the culturally determined grid of heterosexuality. The gender identities which she presents may be transgressive, but they also remain polarized, recreating a reversal of the terms of discourse, structural inequities, poses and the patterns of oppressive gender interaction. Mootoo returns to the past, in this case to the inception of the emergent nation, to inscribe a narrative of origin on the spatial reality, which can in turn contextualize and undergird the self, which the implied author becomes in a nurturing landscape of the imaginary. In the process, the implied author plays with the perfomative, giving fictional expression to Appadurai's contention that "the past is now not a land to return to in a simple politics of memory. It has become a synchronous warehouse of cultural scenarios to which recourse can be had as appropriate depending on the movie to be made, the scene to be enacted, and the hostages to be rescued."[44]

In conclusion, let us return to the questions posed at the beginning of this chapter. What is Indianess? Despite the pervasive assumptions of cultural rootedness and the persistence of the ancient traditions transported by the indentees, the writers explored here demonstrate the fluidity of Indian cultural identity. In other words, the relevant question emerges as "How and why am I becoming?" Even apparently highly individualist writers demonstrate loyalty to this common representational cause. The most recent exploration/affirmation of boundarylessness in relation to geography, gender and nationally bound categories of belonging reflects the propensity of Caribbean people to hold steadfastly to hospitable imaginary homelands. Writers explored here demonstrate the absolute inevitability of the creolization process, with its attendant fluidity, interculturation, mimicry and indeterminancy. This coexists with a simultaneous resistance to creolization as a paradigm which can adequately accommodate Indo-Trinidadian location within the broader social scenario. The historian Harracksingh puts it simply: "within and beyond the plantation setting the essence of the overseas Indian experience can be viewed as a crisis of being and belonging; of being oneself, however defined, and at the same time of belonging and being regarded as belonging to the land of one's chosen domicile or nativity".[45]

Notes

1. Werner Sollers, *The Invention of Ethnicity* (Oxford: Oxford University Press, 1989); Stuart Hall, "Cultural Identity and the Diaspora", in *Colonial Discourse and Post-Colonial Theory*, ed. Patrick Williams and Laura Chrisman (London: Harvester, 1994), 145–59; Arjun Appadurai, *Modernity at Large: Cultural Dimensions of Globalization* (Minneapolis: Minnesota University Press, 1996).
2. Appadurai, *Modernity*, 13.
3. V.S. Naipaul, foreword to Seepersad Naipaul, *The Adventure of Gurudeva and Other Stories* (London: Deutsch, 1976), 13.
4. Remarkable similarities turn up in the backgrounds of the writers. Naipaul writes of his grandfather being brought to Trinidad as a baby from eastern Uttar Pradesh sometime in the 1880s. After the early death of this father and supporter, the children, rendered destitute, were scattered among various relatives. This shadows the background of the paternal indentured migrants whose children were scattered after the separation of the parents in Mahase's narrative.
5. The personal narrative of my own adoptive mother is telling. The child of a washerwoman and her French Creole estate-owning master, Leain was sent regularly to the paternal household to be taught manners. She carried throughout her life a legacy of "excellent" manners and deep contempt for the social group, which she would manifest by scoffing, "Aristocrats turned rusty rats."
6. By the 1920s many representatives of the Portuguese and Chinese communities had joined the upper tier, while the Syrian Lebanese by 1930 had become prosperous in the retail cloth business and a closed, empowered group. Close on the

heels were the free coloured, who tended to be of French Creole extraction and nurtured ongoing nostalgia for family tradition. They were what Bolland calls Euro-Creole in their orientation.

7. Kusha Harracksingh, "Indenture and Self Emancipation", in *Enterprise of the Indies*, ed. George Lamming (Port of Spain: Trinidad and Tobago Institute of the West Indies, 1999), 39.
8. Aisha Khan, "Purity, Piety and Power: Culture and Identity among Hindus and Muslims in Trinidad" (PhD diss., New York University, 1995), 92–93.
9. Lakshmi Persaud, *Butterfly in the Wind* (Leeds: Peepal Tree, 1990), 90.
10. Harracksingh, "Indenture", 40.
11. V.S. Naipaul, *A House for Mr Biswas* (Harmondsworth: Penguin, 1961), 390.
12. Colin A. Palmer, *Eric Williams and the Making of the Modern Caribbean* (Chapel Hill: North Carolina University Press, 2006), 266. In 1958 the Indian-dominated Democratic Labour Party, under the leadership of Badase Sagan Maharaj, led a coalition to victory in the federal elections against the PNM-led team. The racially charged campaign did much to entrench race-based politics in the nation. The defeat of the PNM was seen as a repudiation of the party and its leadership and a hemorrhaging of the nation's spirit, soon after it had attained independence in 1956. On 1 April 1958, Prime Minister Williams delivered a stinging address titled "The Danger Facing Trinidad and Tobago and the West Indian Nation", in which he castigated the winning team for fighting an election to bring into being a West Indian nation on the issue of "our Indian nation". Williams accused Hindus of being "the recalcitrant and hostile minority of the West Indian nation masquerading as 'the Indian nation' and prostituting the name of India for its selfish, reactionary political ends".
13. Brinsley Samaroo, "Asian Identity and Culture in the Caribbean", in *The Enterprise of the Indies*, ed. George Lamming (San Juan: Trinidad and Tobago Institute of the West Indies and Trinidad and Tobago Review, 1999), 42–45.
14. Samuel Selvon, "Three into One Can't Go: East Indian, Trinidadian, West Indian" (opening address to the Conference on East Indians in the Caribbean, University of the West Indies, St Augustine, 1979), in *India in the Caribbean*, ed. David Dabydeen and Brinsley Samaroo (London: Hansib, 1987), 13–24.
15. Harracksingh, "Indenture", 41.
16. Samaroo, "Asian Identity", 45.
17. Anna Mahase Sr, *My Mother's Daughter: The Autobiography of Anna Mahase Snr 1899–1978* (Trinidad: Royards, 1998), 38.
18. Rhonda Reddock, "Indian Women and Indentureship in Trinidad and Tobago, 1845–1917: Freedom Denied" (paper presented at the Conference on East Indians in the Caribbean, University of the West Indies, St Augustine, 1984).

19. Sandra Pouchet Paquet, *Caribbean Autobiography: Cultural Identity and Self-Representation* (Madison: Wisconsin University Press, 2002), 213.
20. Naipaul, *Mr Biswas*, 192–93.
21. Persaud, *Butterfly*, 81.
22. Ibid., 55.
23. Ibid., 67–68.
24. Morton Klass, *East Indians in Trinidad: A Study in Cultural Persistence* (New York: Columbia University Press, 1991), 59.
25. This was one of the motives for indentureship offered by recruiters, which Mootoo ascribes to her fictional character the old man Ramchandin.
26. Naipaul, *Mr Biswas*, 81.
27. Ibid., 349. Harracksingh, in "Indenture", 40, speaks of a sense of disorientation and spatial dislocation of the indentee: "Sometimes, in the literature, this is coupled with the supposed ritual dangers for Indians in particular of crossing the oceans, but there is little direct evidence that the indentured themselves agonized over this matter."
28. Persaud, *Butterfly*, 18.
29. Ibid., 162.
30. Ibid., 171.
31. Ibid., 194.
32. Hall, "Cultural Identity", 393.
33. Simbonath Singh, "The Invention of Ethnicity: Creating a Second Diasporic Indo-Caribbean Identity", in *Identity, Ethnicity and Culture in the Caribbean*, ed. Ralph Premdass (St Augustine: School of Continuing Studies, University of the West Indies, 1999), 526.
34. Appadurai, *Modernity*, 140.
35. Lakshmi Persaud, *Sastra* (Leeds: Peepal Tree, 1990), 37.
36. Ibid., 59.
37. Patricia Mohammed, "From Myth to Symbolism: The Construction of Indian Femininity and Masculinity in Post-Indentured Trinidad", in *Matikor: The Politics of Identity for Indo-Caribbean Women*, ed. Rosanne Kanhai (St Augustine: School of Continuing Studies, University of the West Indies, 1999), 62.
38. Persaud, *Sastra*, 73.
39. Ibid., 71.
40. Paula Morgan, "East/West/Indian/Woman/Other at the Cross Roads of Gender and Ethnicity", *Ma Comere* 3 (2000): 121.
41. Elements of this discussion are drawn from a more comprehensive analysis of *Cereus Blooms at Night* in a chapter I authored titled "From a Distance: Territory, Subjectivity and Identity Constructs in Mootoo's *Cereus Blooms at Night*", in *Caribbean Literature in a Global Context*, ed. Funso Aiyejina and Paula Morgan (San

Juan: Lexicon Publishers, 2006). This paper expands on some ideas in Persaud's narratives which were initially explored in my essay "East/West".
42. Judith Butler, "The Subject", in *Modern Literary Theory*, ed. Philip Rice and Patricia Waugh (London: Arnold, 1997), 148.
43. Shani Mootoo, *Cereus Blooms at Night* (London: Granta, 1996), 20.
44. Appadurai, *Modernity*, 327.
45. Harracksingh, "Indenture", 38.

Part 4

The Way Forward

CHAPTER 10

Issues in Caribbean Cultural Studies
The Case of Jamaica

▶ JOSEPH PEREIRA

If cultural studies is the study of the often concealed relationships of power within the multiple cultural elements of a society, then the Caribbean offers a rich resource for the application of the discipline. The dialectics of difference and the bondings of affinities are reflected throughout our history and within the ever-shifting realities of our present, providing a narrative of tension and power plays, integration and resistance. We read these cultural texts from our varying mental and social locations, and in our discourses question and deconstruct the old hegemonies even as we reconstruct self-definitions.

Perhaps the most persistent issue in Caribbean cultural concerns has been identity. This is neither surprising nor straightforward, given the major racial and cultural differences that shaped the post-Columbus Caribbean. The military supremacy of the European colonizing powers facilitated the hegemonic rise of European culture in the region, so that the colonial arena rapidly got constituted as a place of "Othering". The Amerindian and then the African, the Indian and other Asians were subordinated as less than human. The hegemonic dominance of a European normative in order to ensure and entrench its own position required negation of the values, validity and contributions of the Othered groups. Language, religion, artistic expression, architecture, food, dress and other material expressions of culture were all engaged in the project of subordination, which was buttressed by the economic controls of the plantation and colonial systems. And part of that process included the agency of the Other – sometimes acculturated and co-opted into the cultural model in a complex web of ambiguities and ironies. Yet we are here today as we are because there was also a culture of resistance and contestation, in which certain of the Others refused to accept subordination and definition of self by someone else – the European Other.

In that context, the issues of identity in the past century are heightened by the imperatives of resistance and affirmation, which see their larger political expression in the growth of nationalism. But even the notion of nationalism requires the question "Whose nationalism?" Which social classes were the main proponents of the nationalist movement? What was their relationship, for example, to the pan-Africanist trends and movements of others, most notably Garvey and Garveyism? Was there a politics of exclusion behind the apparent inclusivity of the notion of a creole society? Is there even a façade of homogeneity in the construction of such identity?

English-, French- and Spanish-speaking Caribbean intellectuals have all pointed to a "difference" that marks Caribbean cultural identity. *Creole*, *créolité* and *mestizaje* are terms that have evolved in meaning to signify this "new creation" that is no longer the original cultures (European, African, Indian or Amerindian) but a new synthesis. To what extent, though, is this thesis a genuine reflection of Caribbean identity? In Brazil it has been argued that this notion of a "mestizo society" was a paradigm developed to maintain the hegemony of a particular group that assumed power in the post-colonial period, concealing inequalities and masking exploitations.[1] The creole narrative has equally been challenged in the Caribbean as suppressing reclamation of an African identity (and, in certain territories, an East Indian identity) while facilitating the dominance of those whose cultural practice does in fact reflect a higher degree of "mixing".

Where, for example, is the Jamaican speaker of Jamaican, the adherent of the Revivalist religion, to be placed in this definition of *creole*? Why is the model not projected as a continuation and evolution of an African-based culture? Is this to ignore the fact that in many respects the cultural practice of that Jamaican is no longer the same as his or her West African relative's in, say, Ghana? Proponents of an African model would argue not, reading this reality as part of the extension of Africa into its diaspora. As Garvey said, "Africa for the Africans, at home and abroad."

It has always been an instructive marker that at the height of the independence fervour in Jamaica in 1962, ordinary Jamaicans could say that their concern was not with independence but with repatriation. And if this chapter gives prominence to Jamaican realities because that is the scope of my work, it is a pattern that can extend to other territories. These include those where East Indian descendants have wrestled with the hyphenated life of the Indo-Caribbean, reaching back to the motherland and yet evolving as a different shoot, interfacing and engaging with various sets of Others.

Representation also encodes the concealed power plays of this mestizo/creole society. Perhaps the most dramatic, and some would say outrageous, representation is the signification given by the dominating culture to the national flag of Jamaica; even forty years beyond independence, the black in the flag officially stands for hardships. It is not surprising that a new flag has emerged that is almost as prevalent: the red, green and gold Ethiopian-derived flag of Rastafari. Ownership of cultural representations is crucial to any sense of belonging, and there is still a problematic encapsulated in these alienating or marginalizing representations. The national motto of Jamaica (and here it should be noted that the mimicry found in the very notion of a national motto extends to imitative translation, with minor adjustment, of the United States motto E *pluribus unum*) indicates the level of political positioning for cultural power. "Out of many, one people" belies the reality of the overwhelmingly African origin of Jamaican society, even as it gives apparent legitimacy to the myth of a "plural society".

Debates over artistic representation of significant "national" icons or moments provide an excellent set of case studies of contestations for space. Edna Manley's representation of the declared national hero Paul Bogle met with significant opposition in its time to the "ugliness" of the face the artist portrayed. Similarly, but with a different set of values contending, Alvin Marriott's project of a national monument – representing independence via intertwined naked bodies capped by a naked couple – set off another round of debates regarding sexual representation. None of these, however, reached the levels of controversy created by Laura Facey's monument to emancipation in 2003. The issues largely involved the appropriateness of the larger-than-life figures in depicting/representing the notion of emancipation, but also, once again but in greater proportions, the issue of sexual representation. While both male and female bodies were naked, it was the naked male that became the focus of attention. In deconstructing these responses, there is the tension over gender: the general acceptance (by silence) of the female body on display but outcry over male genitalia in larger-than-life projection. There is, however, also the issue of race: could a "high-brown" Jamaican sculptor really grasp and interpret the significance of the experience of emancipation? Yet each of these debates opens new ways of reading the texts of our reality and helps re-shape and re-member the cultural landscape.

If such situations give opportunity for contestation of models that serve the old hegemonies, adjusted to reflect the post-colonial emerging elite, then at the level of the grassroots, Rastafari has been the single most important catalyst for deconstruction, reclamation and self-creation in the colonial and post-colonial reality. The boldest formulation of Rastafari is in the assertion of a black God. Bold because religion has been an underpinning and a pervasive force in the shaping of consciousness and practice in most societies. Bold because the Eurocentric hegemony appropriated the Christian god as a white and European representation. It is a reflection of the inroads into the colonized mind that the ancient and authentic Christianity of its Ethiopian Orthodox branch has been so successfully excluded from the religious culture and Christian traditions of the Caribbean; even now, where it exists, it runs the risk of being read as a Rastafarian religious space. Indeed, Rastafarian rejection of the linguistic centre of the Christianity shaped by Europe has led to the practice of "burning" Jesus (the Jesus appropriated by European Christianity in its colonizing enterprise), so much so that in some orthodox churches in Jamaica, Rasta-based elements in the congregation make it difficult for the priests to use the words *Jesus Christ*; hence they opt for the more acceptable Ethiopic term *Yesus Cristos* to signify Christ.

This example of language as a site of contestation extends to various other Rastafarian deconstructions of Standard speech, ranging from concepts such as *Carried-us-beyond* for *Caribbean* to *downpressor* for *oppressor*, through the "Dread Talk" described by Velma Pollard.[2] The practice affords a new way of looking at familiar things, words and the ideas they contain, the contaminations they conceal and the liberating possibilities of creative alteration in a process of reconceptualizing.

Such practice is of course a conscious engagement with language, but in a very organic way language has been a site of identity formation and contestation for centuries. The emergence of a "nation language" or Creole adaptation of lexicon and syntax from original languages is not without great debate; the ability to speak near-standard English is often used as an indicator of superiority that is challenged and undermined by the everyday communicative practice of Creole. Radio, for example, has been a tool of both the oppressive and the liberatory use of language. While the "official" voice of radio news readers and announcers has for the most part been Standard English, the voice of the talk shows that has emerged since the seventies, and now has so much air time, has facilitated the articulation and validation of the nation language. Forays of this contestation have now penetrated university levels with the landmark delivery in the Jamaican language of Carolyn Cooper's inaugural professorial lecture in 2003.

As in so many other areas of cultural contestation, what is regarded as rupturing and subversive often becomes, fairly soon, an alternative that raises less and less controversy as space is made to accommodate it. In some other societies this would fit within theories and practice of post-modernism, attaching validity to the differing cultural practices that coexist and undermining notions of superiority and inferiority or centre and periphery. For us it is the liberatory process of our anti-colonial/post-colonial engagement, where different political and social forces take positions – not always along similar lines, but always opening up both fissures and potentialities for changing the readings of our reality and the realignment of power, as well as altering of practice.

In the arena of popular culture, it is music that has most played a role in dismantling the old cultural hegemonies and constituting a new cultural order. The origins of most successful Jamaican popular music have been the working classes in the inner-city communities of Kingston and a few rural areas. The vibrancy and creativity of both the music and the many dances that are constantly being invented to accompany it have made an impact in a multiplicity of ways. They have shifted the location of recognized creativity and value to the classes and communities that create them. Sometimes a not too subtle form of class struggle, the music has overwhelmed the old hegemonic controls of traditional Eurocentric music culture, and of the owners and controllers of radio that have been one of the controlling mediations. It has appropriated technology with great rapidity, from sound systems to the local recording industry, local cable TV channels and the Internet, to expand its influence and redefine the culture of the society. Reggae and Bob Marley have become global brandings for Jamaica. By its very success, the music has empowered and given assurance to ordinary Jamaicans. With its widely dispersed and received lyrical messages, especially those of Rastafari and other "conscious" artistes, it has deliberately engaged and contested ideological and cultural forms and notions of control.

But Jamaican popular music continues to be a site of contestation, as the events and analyses surrounding Sting 2003 highlighted. Here the violence that is traditionally and authentically contained in the lyrical clash of artistes overflowed into a physical clash between two of the DJ performers and their fans. This unleashed not only a litany of blame but also (and of interest to cultural studies) a counter-attack on the cultural expression by elements long hostile to what they saw as the violence and slackness/lewdness of the dancehall scene. This reflects a long-standing conflict over dancehall which sometimes masks an effort by old ruling-class elements and allied sections of the middle class to regain control over the values and behaviour of those from the majority classes in the society. I imagine that much the same type of dispute would be familiar to Trinidadians of an earlier era, regarding calypso. "Decency" becomes the fat to fry other, hidden issues surrounding dominance.

Fortunately, dancehall self-corrects its own excesses when it determines them to be excesses. In fact, with credit to Benítez Rojo, behind the apparent chaos of the cultural practice is its own peculiar order, "a certain way"[3] of functioning on the brink of transgression. It was the refusal of the once-marginalized to conform to ground rules of behaviour and practice set by others that allowed for dismantling of the old controlling cultural system in the first place. Nor is this "playing outside the rules" confined to artistic expression. The majority of informal commercial importers and traders – local and internationalized higglers – have broken out of the economic confines of old money relations to create their own space, despite the laws, values and practices that serve the formalized socio-economic order and cultural hegemony. The same may be said of the widespread practice of squatting as a form of land access.

One of the few sites where playing within the rules of the game has actually assisted in demarginalizing working people has been sports. Both cricket and football provide rich ground for studies of sport as a contestation of old models and a re-presentation of identity. Cricket, as studies by a range of cultural analysts have shown, has been an arena for debunking the notion of Eurocentric supremacy.[4] The victories of West Indian teams over England in particular in the late colonial period went way beyond the boundaries of the sport – into psychological self-affirmation and self-worth. The ability of the Jamaican football team to reach the 1998 World Cup – the road to France – engaged the emotional identity of Jamaicans as never before, unifying for a brief moment the disparate and frequently conflicting elements in society to identify as a nation under the Jamaican flag and anthem. It was a unity not achieved (or achievable) by political parties or economic or social forces, but attained by and large by working-class communities; for that very reason their successes in a world arena became the successes of the nation, in all its constituent parts.

If culture is located in the mind, valorizing of the hitherto Othered and marginalized self is an important – some would say critical – part of the process of emancipation from mental subordination or enslavement that is an inexorable pressure in Caribbean society. It is an emancipation of the whole society, and sectors within the society, from its colonial subordination, from the various types of oppression that seek to contain and maintain power, even if it is the power to mediate and articulate for others without allowing the Other to speak for his or her self.

One of the interesting features of many of those battle sites of culture is that they are largely urban, based in the general Kingston/St Andrew area. Yet there is a long tradition of rural contestation that has fed this urban space through migration. The "little traditions" of daily life among country people also constitute an important arena of reclamation. One early and excellent fictional exploration of this is Claude McKay's *Banana Bottom*, while the novels *Jane and Louisa Will Soon Come Home* and *Myal* by Erna Brodber continue to reflect those contributions to cultural definition embedded in rural Jamaica. They recognize the humanist traditions and self-assurance inherent in the practices that struggle daily with the "great house"–derived pressures.

In each of the sites of cultural tension, closer analysis beyond the scope of this chapter can flesh out the complex, sometimes ambivalent and even contradictory forces at work within individuals, groups or sectors and so on that are participants and agents in this process of cultural development and transformation.[5] There are the intersections of ideological, political, religious, economic, geographic, racial, class, gender, age and similar factors that contribute to where each individual, group or sector stands and how they read the many texts that their daily lives and exposures constitute. Engagement of these elements provides possibilities for reclamation of a denied or diminished human self in all its fullness. The specific Jamaican examples repeat in their essentials throughout the region. Caribbean identity, or collisions and fusions of identities, will continue to be problematic despite the several myths that are thrown up to give cohesion, direction and a sense of belonging that constantly negotiates between inclusivities and exclusivities.

Notes

1. For example, in Martin Leinhard, "Of Mestizajes, Heterogeneities, Hybridisms and Other Chimeras: On the Macroprocesses of Cultural Interaction in Latin America", *Journal of Latin American Cultural Studies* 6, no. 2 (August 1997): 183–200.
2. Velma Pollard, *Dread Talk: The Language of Rastafari* (Kingston: Canoe Press, 1994), 3.
3. Antonio Benítez Rojo, *The Repeating Island: The Caribbean and the Post-Modern Perspective*, trans. James E. Maraniss (Durham, NC: Duke University Press, 1996), 4–5.
4. See, for example, articles such as Orlando Patterson, "The Ritual of Cricket", *Liberation Cricket: West Indies Cricket Culture,* ed. Hilary Beckles and Brian Stoddart (Kingston: Ian Randle, 1995).
5. Several studies have emerged in recent years which explore and enrich our understanding of the cultural issues engaged by multiple facets of Jamaican society. These include publications such as the following: Mervyn C. Alleyne, *Roots of Jamaican Culture* (London: Karia Press and Pluto Press, 1988); Donna P. Hope, *Inna Di Dancehall: Popular Culture and the Politics of Identity in Jamaica* (Kingston: University of the West Indies Press, 2006); Nathaniel Samuel Murrell, William David Spencer and Adrian Anthony McFarlane, *Chanting Down Babylon: The Rastafari Reader* (Kingston: Ian Randle, 1988); Rex Nettleford, *Inward Stretch, Outward Reach* (London: Macmillan, 1993); Verene A. Shepherd and Glen Richards, eds., *Questioning Creole: Creolization Discourses in Caribbean Culture* (Kingston: Ian Randle, 2002); Imani M. Tafari-Ama, *Blood, Bullets and Bodies: Sexual Politics below Jamaica's Poverty Line* (Kingston: Multimedia Communications, 2006); *Caribbean Quarterly* 43, nos. 1–4.

CHAPTER 11

The School as a Forum for Cross-Culturalism
The Curriculum as an Intervention Strategy

▸ SANDRA INGRID GIFT

Introduction

The school in Trinidad and Tobago is, of necessity, a forum for cross-culturalism, given the encounter of diverse cultures in that space. The classroom consequently reflects this cultural diversity, one that may not always be fully understood or appreciated by either students or their parents, and perhaps not even by teachers at times. The potential for misunderstanding, conflict and general devaluing of cultural differences can be mediated through a curriculum designed to access modes of knowing and based on integration of cultural life into the life of the classroom, as well as on inculcation of respect for difference rooted in an appreciation of self and the Other, as enshrined in universal human rights principles. This deeper integration of the cultural dimension into the classroom can contribute to enhancement of the quality of the learning experience.

Methodological Issues

This chapter focuses on the use of an experimental curriculum designed to address students' knowledge and attitudes relating, inter alia, to cultural and human rights issues. The curriculum was developed with a team of five secondary school teachers in collaboration with the writer over the period 1990 to 1992. The teachers represented a mixture of government and denominational single-sex and coeducational secondary schools in north and south Trinidad. The experimental curriculum document was field-tested in 1994 for seven and a half weeks, at the levels of forms 1 to 4, by teachers in the social studies department of an urban coeducational secondary school in Trinidad. The head of department identified the teachers who would participate in the field test of the curriculum. She was satisfied that the content of the experimental curriculum was relevant to the scheme of work which was to be covered in these classes for the term. A case-study approach was employed with a view to gaining insights into the impact that exposure to the curriculum would have on students' knowledge and attitudes regarding cultural and human rights issues.

Data-Gathering Techniques

Data were gathered from structured and unstructured classroom observation and interviews with teachers. Data-gathering instruments included a Likert scale administered to students as a pre-test and post-test to assess values, beliefs and opinions (a sample of which is provided in appendix 11.1); a questionnaire administered to students to find out what they thought about the parts of the curriculum to which they were exposed; a questionnaire administered to teachers; and field notes. Each Likert scale used was pilot-tested among students in the classes participating in the inquiry. The Likert technique presents a set of attitude statements; students were asked to express agreement or disagreement on a five-point scale. A high score on the scale was interpreted as a favourable attitude, with favourable statements being scored 5 for "strongly agree" and 1 for "strongly disagree". Unfavourable statements were scored 1 for "strongly agree", going up to 5 for "strongly disagree". A total score was arrived at for each student by totalling the scores for each individual statement on the scale. These strategies served to establish trustworthiness of the findings. The concern was to have more than one source of findings and therefore more than one slice of the reality, so as to better understand the social context which was involved in the inquiry.

The School Context

Teachers

Five teachers, all university graduates, participated in the field-testing of the curriculum. They were holders of first degrees in areas which included history, sociology, economics and English literature. Two were trained teachers, one was enrolled in the Diploma in Education programme at the University of the West Indies, and two were untrained. The duration of their teaching experience ranged from two to fifteen years. Teachers participating in the inquiry were very cooperative and the principal was very supportive of the exercise.

Student Population

The teachers explained that in recent times the school had been receiving more students from central Trinidad, an area with a high concentration of Indo-Trinidadians, and that consequently there were more Indo-Trinidadian students in the school than before. Prior to this, the school population had been predominantly Afro-Trinidadian. Though present in the school in larger numbers than previously, Indo-Trinidadian students were still a minority in terms of their numbers. Nonetheless, the principal found it necessary to organize staff training programmes on multiculturalism to enable staff members to deal successfully with this change in the composition of the student population.

Theoretical Concepts

Human Rights

The concepts of cultural relativism versus universalism have generated considerable debate among human rights scholars. At the centre of this debate are practices which do not conform to universal human rights and which are justified on grounds of moral or cultural relativism. Cultural relativism is often invoked against the universality of human rights. Jerome J. Shestack opposes the conceptual stance of cultural relativists that there are no human rights absolutes. He disagrees with the idea that "the principles which we may use for judging behaviour are relative to the society in which we are raised, that there is infinite cultural variability and that all cultures are morally equal or valid".[1]

The basic tenet of cultural relativism, as described by Shestack, is that the diversity and wide range of preferences, motivations and evaluations of cultures mean that it is not possible to recognize human rights principles at all times and in all places. He offers counter-arguments to this conceptual stance, one being that all cultures are not equally valid; some cultures are imbued with evil elements and lack "any rational, intuitive or empirical claim to moral equivalence with non-abusive cultures".[2] For the purpose of this discussion set in the Trinidad and Tobago context, this writer considers all cultures in Trinidad and Tobago to be equally valid. At the same time, human rights principles are accepted, particularly for their capacity to create an environment of mutual respect for cultural elements which are different, an environment that is non-abusive and can promote positive identity development.

Identity

Identity is a complex concept. It is shaped by individual characteristics, family dynamics and historical factors, as well as by social, cultural and political contexts. The formation of identity is significantly influenced by the messages communicated by the environment: by parents, peers, teachers, neighbours, the media and cultural images. An individual's omission from cultural images also negatively affects identity formation. Identity is mediated by various factors such as age, class, sexual orientation, religious beliefs and gender. Subordinate groups function within parameters set by dominant groups. The dominant group determines the ways in which power and authority can be acceptably used.[3] This includes determining whose history will be taught in schools and the relationships which society will validate. In a society such as Trinidad and Tobago, where the dominant groups reflect the composition of the majority of the population, one would not expect issues of identity to arise. They do, however, in part because of the traditional impact of North American cultural imperialism and the pervasive inadequacies of the education system in contributing to positive identity formation.

Greater integration of Trinidad and Tobago culture, in all of its manifestations, into the formal learning process can facilitate young people's access to information and affective experiences that can support positive identity formation. However, it is important to avoid the elements of popular culture which perpetuate images and messages of particular ethnic or cultural groups as defective or substandard. The classroom has a role to play in positive identity development, that is, in helping young people to define for themselves what it means personally and socially to belong to a given social or cultural group. This process must be based on knowledge and affective experiences that are empowering.

Concepts of Curriculum

There are various conceptions of curriculum. These include curriculum as a means or end and curriculum as "a plan for or a report of actual educational events".[4] For the purpose of this discussion, the concern is with the operational curriculum, that is, what was actually taught by the teachers using an experimental curriculum document as a guide. There are two aspects to the operational curriculum: (1) the content emphasized by the teacher in class and (2) the learning outcomes. George J. Posner also notes that the "operational curriculum reflects teachers' interpretation of the official curriculum, based on their own knowledge, beliefs and attitudes".[5]

Affective Category

The experimental curriculum under consideration here was designed with a significant affective dimension. Feelings, attitudes and sensitivities constitute the values-oriented components of a culture and make up the affective element of the curriculum. Affective objectives in a curriculum shift emphasis from subject matter to the individual's needs and concerns and the development of values.[6] Each learning activity should be linked to the widest range of cognitive, affective and skill objectives. David Pratt argues that attitudes are concerned with people's feelings, and that it is important to address in the curriculum planning process the feelings of learners that the curriculum will strengthen or engender.[7]

Allan C. Ornstein and Francis P. Hunkins discuss the taxonomy of objectives presented by Krathwol and colleagues, which consists of five principal categories in the affective domain.[8] The five categories are (1) receiving, (2) responding, (3) valuing, (4) organization and (5) characterization. Category 1, receiving, concerns objectives which refer to learners' awareness, willingness to receive and selected attention. Category 2, responding, deals with learners' active attention to stimuli such as feelings of satisfaction. Valuing, category 3, refers to learners' beliefs and attitudes of worth such as acceptance, preference and commitment. Organization, category 4, treats with the internalization of values and beliefs. This involves conceptualization of values and organization of a value system. Category 5, characterization, represents the highest level of internalization; at this level, objectives are related to behaviour which reflects a generalized set of values and a philosophy of life. These considerations relating to the affective domain in the curriculum planning process are pertinent to the discussion of curriculum issues in this chapter.

Hidden Curriculum/Null Curriculum

The hidden curriculum refers to institutional norms and values not openly acknowledged by teachers or school officials. It tends to be unacknowledged by educators and administrators, its profound and sustained impact on students notwithstanding. Issues of gender, class, race and authority are among the messages of the hidden curriculum. There is also the impact of the "null curriculum", or the subject areas that are not taught. Considerations of the null curriculum must focus on the reasons that certain content-knowledge areas are ignored in the school system.

Beliefs, Opinions, Attitudes and Values

The writer employs the concept of attitudes as a general category to understand students' responses to the experimental curriculum. A landscape of beliefs, opinions and values represents varying degrees of intensity of an attitude, on a continuum with opinion at one end and attitude at the other.[9] Opinions are verbal expressions of beliefs, attitudes or values, which they reflect as a matter of inference. Attitudes are seen to be beliefs (information people possess about something) with an evaluative dimension. They are acquired behavioural dispositions representing a person's worldview or knowledge about the world. Attitudes and values both involve expressions of preference or evaluation. However, while attitudes are learned predispositions and are directed at objects, people or ideas, values are directed at principles.

Like beliefs, values may be consciously conceived or unconsciously held, and must be inferred from behaviour and what an individual says. Beliefs, however, are presented as ideas which may be possible explanations for a situation. Beliefs or opinions are interpreted as expressions of attitude. While the cognitive, the affective and the behavioural comprise three dimensions of attitudes, the minimum condition of an attitude is the cognitive. This suggests that inculcation in the minds of young people of positive attitudes towards cross-culturalism can be achieved through the cognitive dimension of the formal and non-formal school curriculum. David Katz argues that it is more difficult to change an attitude that has strong links with a given value system; attitudes are easier to change if they are isolated from a person's value system.[10] One can target either the belief component or the affective, or feeling, component when seeking to change attitudes. Katz supports the assertion that "an effective change in one component will result in changes in the other component".[11]

The curriculum which was the subject of the inquiry reported in this chapter set out to present students with information to increase their knowledge base of the different cultures in Trinidad and Tobago, and thus inform their beliefs so as to impact positively upon their affective learning, and consequently their attitudes towards these cultures.

Findings from Field-Testing the Experimental Curriculum

The parts of the curriculum that were field-tested during the inquiry represented 63 per cent of the experimental curriculum document. This chapter reports on some of the findings for two of the curriculum units: Units B and C

Unit B: Culture

Section 2: Festivals

All of the lessons in Unit B(2) were used in one Form 1 class, as follows:

Lesson 1	Subtopic: Overview of festivals in Trinidad and Tobago
Lesson 2	Subtopic: Carnival
Lesson 3	Subtopic: Eid-ul-Fitr
Lesson 4	Subtopic: Divali

UNIT C: Human Rights/The United Nations

Lesson 1(a)	Subtopic: What is a person? (one Form 4 class)
Lesson 1(b)	Subtopic: Differences among people (one Form 4 class)
Lesson 2(a)	Subtopic: Discrimination (two Form 4 classes)
Lesson 2(b)	Subtopic: Discrimination in the international community (two Form 4 classes)
Lesson 3(a)	Subtopic: Defining rights (two Form 4 classes)
Lesson 3(b)	Subtopic: Human rights issues (two Form 4 classes)

Items relevant to the parts of the curriculum that were not used were retained in the pre-test and post-test. The purpose of this was to determine whether students would nonetheless be influenced in the sense of critically developing a predisposition to view issues and to draw from past experiences to take positions on contemporary matters which should be of concern to them.

Students' General Responses to the Curriculum

The presentation of data will proceed from the general to the specific. The general presentation proceeds with the use of students' open-ended comments to support some of the findings presented. The discussion of students' general reactions to the curriculum includes their degree of interest in and enjoyment of the curriculum; their desire to learn; their willingness or reluctance to share their culture with others; and their appreciation of the opportunity to actively participate in class activities. Some general observations of students' behaviours during class are also discussed.

Students' Sensitivities to Culture

The Form 1 students' comments about the lessons on festivals (Unit B, Section 2) revealed their sensitivities to positive values relating to an appreciation of diverse cultures, as well as an interest in learning about the religion and culture of others. Some indication of this was seen in the following statements about the parts of the curriculum to which they were exposed: "I think it teaches our children today to respect one another's religion et cetera. That is what I called living in harmony"; "I think that teachers should really teach the children about different cultures because if you don't teach them about other cultures other than their own they would not understand other people and they might become racial."

Students' comments also revealed their prior lack of knowledge and awareness about the religion and culture of others: "I did not really know anything about Eid. But this lesson helped me learn a lot. Not only on Eid but also Islam." The following comments also revealed their desire to learn more: "The lesson was too short"; "There should have been more."

Based on the observation of students during the lessons, the writer noted that, in general, students seemed familiar with most of the festivals celebrated in Trinidad and Tobago. That is, they had heard about them but did not know a great deal about the reasons for their celebration. There was, therefore, a need for greater knowledge and understanding about these festivals. Class discussions demonstrated a general appreciation on their part of the concept of culture. Some examples of their definitions of culture were "traditions", "heritage" and "background".

Students were particularly attentive to Teacher C's explanations about the differences between Christianity and Islam, and some interrupted her with questions as she lectured. During Lesson 3 (subtopic: Eid-ul-Fitr), Teacher C gave a lecture on Islam. The writer overheard two female students talking softly. One was saying that God gave Adam one wife, not seven. She concluded her remarks with, "They just like woman!" They appeared to be discussing the question of polygamy, which was not dealt with by Teacher C. This indicated that the lesson in progress had stimulated their interest.

When at the end of this class *sewaian* (a drink served by Muslims for Eid) was served, it was clear that it was unfamiliar to many students. Some smelled it, others laughed, a few tasted it, and some did not take any, while others drank it all. During the lesson on Divali, students' desire to learn more was again exhibited by the questions they asked. For example, one Afro-Trinidadian student wanted to know why Lakshmi had four hands; another asked why money was falling out of her hands.

Willingness or Reluctance to Share Culture

There was evidence of some students' willingness to share their culture. Three Hindu male students sang a Hindu song, which one of them translated into English afterwards, while another said a prayer. The latter tended to laugh as he prayed, perhaps out of embarrassment. A female Muslim student assisted Teacher C by filling in the gaps in her information, and she also gave a demonstration of Muslim prayer positions for the class. It was noticeable, however, that other Hindu students, who appeared to be in the great minority in the class, did not wish to volunteer information about their religion. One Hindu student was invited by Teacher C to say something, but he declined. Others either responded shyly to the teacher's questions about their religion or chose not to respond.

Enrichment of the Quality of Students' Learning Experience

The experimental curriculum included activities which sought to engage students actively in their own learning and to tap their creativity and resourcefulness. Students expressed enjoyment of opportunities for singing, group work, cooperating with other students, engaging in research, debating, dramatization, and creative expression – all of which were facilitated by the design of the curriculum. Form 1 students commented on the lesson on carnival as follows: "I like the way that the children in class were able to participate on a much larger scale"; "I also enjoyed when I singed [sic] Shadow's song."

Many students commented on how much they enjoyed group work and co-operating with other students when the opportunity was provided. The following comments taken from Form 1 students were illustrative of this: "I liked how Miss divided us into groups, it really did work"; "I enjoyed mostly the coming together of all the students and forming groups to study this lesson on carnival"; "I like the way the class was able to use their creativity to make lessons for all to share."

Many students also expressed satisfaction over the opportunity to engage in research work, either individually or in groups. They exhibited by their comments a desire for acquiring new knowledge. Form 1 students expressed these views: "I like to be in groups when we are researching"; "I enjoyed the group research . . . I would like this to happen again"; "I enjoyed finding information which I told my class and they found it very interesting"; "I learned a lot and wish to learn more." One Form 4 student taught by Teacher D commented in writing on the lesson on discrimination: "The lesson was a bit enjoyable due to the fact that a part of the lesson was to do research for yourself to get information on the various discrimination 'fighters'. This I found to be very educative as I learned to cooperate with others as well as get information for myself on certain topics."

Students' Appreciation of Creative Modes of Learning

Enjoyment of dramatization and role play was expressed by students at both the Form 1 and Form 4 levels. Form 1 students wrote: "I also enjoyed the little acts done by the different groups"; "I enjoyed . . . especially the grouping of students to perform in front the class just like the Dimanche Gras Show." A Form 4 student taught by Teacher D said that "[t]he most interesting part of the lesson was when our teacher tests us to see whether or not we would recognize the discrimination which she displayed to a few other students and what we would have done about it".

Students' comments also revealed that they savoured opportunities for use of their creativity, display of talent, self-expression and having fun while learning, as revealed by another Form 4 student taught by Teacher E: "This lesson should have been dramatized. When youths our age actually act out the roles, we are able to come to terms with what is happening. This would have made the subject stick in our heads and assist us in the future to remember our human rights."

The lesson on carnival in Unit B, Section 2, provided much opportunity for students' creative expression and enjoyment, and students articulated their appreciation of this: "I enjoyed talking about J'ouvert. It gave us a chance to express yourself and show our talents"; "I enjoyed the designing and the craft of it"; "We had to do drawings and go up and read. It was a lot of fun." Their comments also revealed an enjoyment of the products of their creative expression: "I enjoyed most when they showed some of the costumes. I found them colourful"; "I enjoyed the pictures drawn up on the Bristol board and the singing of Roman's [a fellow student's] group."

General Observations of Student Behaviours

The Form 1 students who did Unit B, Section 2 (Festivals), responded with great enthusiasm; in one instance, the teacher actually had to ask one student to control his enthusiasm. This teacher, Teacher C, described as an unforeseen outcome the "great enthusiasm" with which students responded to the lessons tried out. Students responded to questions readily and gave numerous examples of festivals or celebrations of all types. When not participating verbally, students were quite attentive and took notes from the blackboard. Participating in group work appeared to have been a big event for this class; Teacher C explained that it was the first time he had given the class group work.

In relation to Unit C (human rights/the United Nations), taught to the Form 4 students by Teacher E, there was generally evidence of selective attention. During a discussion on the rights and responsibilities of parents, one male student – who had said at the start of the class that he had a headache and put his head down on the desk – sat up and started to take part in the discussion. The class came alive during the discussion, whereas before it began some had not been paying attention at all. In this class, while some students tended to be disruptive during a lesson, others sat passively. On one occasion the class came to a complete halt over a student's allegedly missing hat, which he was not supposed to be wearing according to the school's regulations.

In respect of Unit C in the Form 4 class taught by Teacher D, I interpreted as interest in the lesson the fact that one male student read out the homework assignment of another who was absent, but who had asked that his work be read out for the class. Another male student with a speech defect got up to read his contribution but laughed throughout, suggesting either embarrassment or his being unaccustomed to such participation in class. Whenever students spoke softly, others would complain that they could not hear, and Teacher D would urge them to speak up.

Impact of the Curriculum on Students' Attitudes

For each unit of the curriculum, a Likert scale was administered as a pre-test and post-test. The statements included on the tests reflected the content of each unit. Statements were formulated to convey either a negative or positive attitude or uncertainty in relation to a particular issue captured in either positive or negative statements. The statements took for granted some degree of knowledge on the part of students in relation to the specific content areas. Responses solicited were more affective than cognitive. Nonetheless, the students' lack or possession of certain knowledge was noted in some instances. Findings are presented for the individual classes that covered particular units of the curriculum. Students' open-ended responses will be presented, followed by a comparison of their performances on the attitude pre-test and post-test for the units of the curriculum discussed in this chapter. The terms *very positive, positive, fairly positive, poor* and *very poor* will be used to describe students' scores within the different ranges of scores on the attitude pre-test and post-test.

Students' written and oral responses are presented as written and articulated by the students themselves. In order to arrive at an understanding of students' reactions and responses to the curriculum and of its impact on their attitudes, the following guiding research question was addressed: "What was the impact of the parts of the curriculum to which students were exposed, as seen in their performance on the attitude pre-test and post-test?" Evidence of a change in disposition towards an issue or a situation was seen as an attitude existing in some form. However, the inquiry did not seek to measure the intensity or strength of the disposition towards ideas or preferences; rather, it sought indicators of evidence of students' disposition. Based on their utterances, behavioural responses and replies on the attitude test, the writer was looking for an improvement or change in the states of students' dispositions or attitudes.

Impact of Unit B: Culture, Section 2 (Festivals)

Students' Open-Ended Comments

Students' open-ended responses were reflective of positive attitudes both towards the festivals treated in Unit B, Section 2, and the opportunity to learn about them. Students' comments illustrated a strong link between knowledge of a culture and understanding and acceptance of the people associated with that culture. Commenting on the lesson on Divali, a Hindu festival, students wrote:

> Hinduism is a lovely religion and I'd like to learn more about the religion of Hinduism.
>
> It is nice to know that students in schools should participate in these contributions and learn more about the cultures and religions of Trinidad and Tobago.
>
> ... if we continue this lesson we shall surely reach somewhere, where everyone should understand each other.
>
> My grandparents are Hindues [sic] and I hardly knew anything about Divali. I thought it was just a holiday now I know its significance.

Commenting on the lesson on the Muslim festival of Eid-ul-Fitr, students wrote:

> ... although I am a different religion, I was glad to know the history of Eid.
>
> I really enjoyed the part of the lesson when Salisha did the positions for prayer.
>
> Eid-ul-fitr is a very sacred festival celebrated by people in our society. Their festival can teach us a lot of things about them ... I hope to learn more about these festivals celebrated in our country.
>
> I did not really know anything about Eid. But this lesson helped me learn a lot. Not only on Eid but also Islam.

The lesson on carnival also brought out some comments which reveal the importance of knowledge in shaping attitudes and values:

> I found it very interesting how I thought I knew so much about Trinidad's carnival when I found I knew nothing.
>
> I learned a lot about the different aspects of our tropical carnival.

I wish it was a little longer because there are still many things I have to know about carnival.

This lesson taught us about our history, different religions, how we got our economy going and our creativity.

Teacher C, commenting on students' reactions to this part of the curriculum, expressed the view that "[t]he students have become more exposed to other cultural activities; certainly there is more understanding and acceptance".

Results of the Attitude Pre-Test and Post-Test

The results of the post-test in figure 11.1 provide a good indication of a possible change in students' attitudes.

On the post-test there appears to be a slight improvement in students' performance in the range 50 and over ("very positive"). Whereas 13 per cent scored in this range on the pre-test, 24 per cent scored in this range on the post-test. In the range 45–49 ("positive"), performance was also better on the post-test: 38 per cent scored in this range on the pre-test while 45 per cent scored in this range on the post-test. On the post-test, fewer students scored in the range 40–44 ("fairly positive"): 38 per cent on the pre-test and 17 per cent on the post-

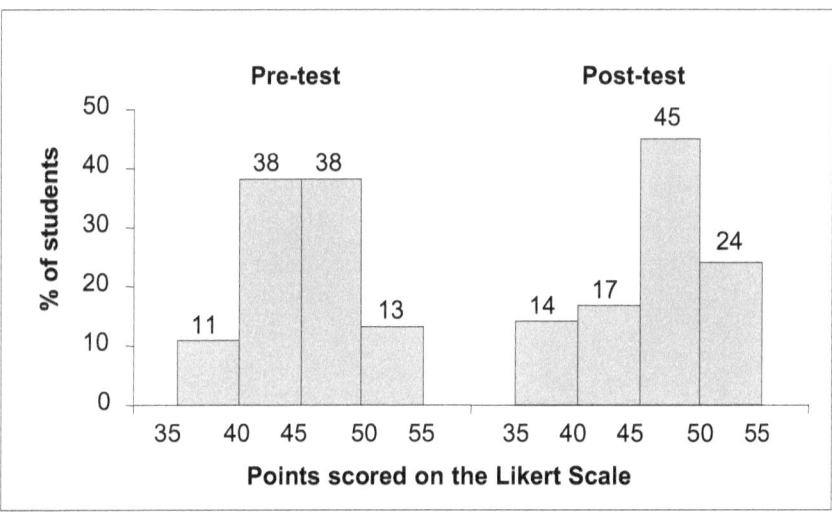

Figure 11.1: Students' performance on the pre-test and post-test, Unit B: Culture, Section 2 (Festivals). Form 1, taught by Teacher C. Number of respondents on the pre-test: 37. Number of respondents on the post-test: 29.

test. However, there was a three-point increase in students scoring in the range 35–39 ("poor"): 11 per cent on the pre-test and 14 per cent on the post-test; this might have been due to some students' failure to complete the entire questionnaire. No student scored in the range 30–34 ("very poor") on either the pre-test or the post-test. Overall, students' average score on the Likert scale improved, indicating a shift from attitudes that were positive or fairly positive to attitudes that were predominantly positive or very positive. One can conclude that the curriculum seemed to have a positive impact on these Form 1 students.

On the post-test, the positive statement most strongly supported by students was "The festivals of Trinidad and Tobago are a valuable part of our cultural heritage" (88 per cent strongly agreed). This reflected a possible positive impact of Lessons 1 to 4 of Unit B(ii). The positive statement most strongly supported on the pre-test was "Human beings should solve differences by discussion and compromise rather than by force" (81 per cent strongly agreed).

Unlike the pre-test, where the negative statement most supported by Form 1 students was "Culture has little to do with a people's way of life" (32 per cent either agreed or strongly agreed), the negative statement most supported on the post-test was "Young people today can do little to contribute to world peace" (33 per cent either agreed or strongly agreed). There was also a shift in students' areas of uncertainty on the post-test, with most students (17 per cent) being uncertain about the statement "It is *not* possible to learn how to prevent conflict among people." On the pre-test, the statement about which there was most uncertainty was "There is no connection between understanding other people's culture and ensuring world peace." On the post-test, the negative statement most supported and the area of greatest uncertainty related to aspects not directly addressed in Unit B(ii) of the curriculum. The shift in responses indicated above seems to testify to a significant positive impact of the parts of the curriculum to which students were exposed.

Impact of Unit C (Human Rights) on Students' Attitudes

Students' Open-Ended Comments and Samples of Written Work

Form 4 students' comments about Unit C (Human Rights) were generally indicative of positive attitudes towards appreciating each person, avoiding discrimination and enjoyment of human rights. They exhibited sensitivity to the need to understand a person through "personality, attitudes and their backgrounds", as one student put it. The mind was also considered by a few as an important dimension of a person. Such appreciation of the characteristics of a person is reflected in one student's statement: "A person that I like as a friend has to have respect, identify . . . their true identity and also their background . . ." One student valued the opportunity to think about himself and to interact with other students: "It was interesting to get to know more about oneself and it was fun talking to one another and getting to know each other better."

Some examples of students' written work on this subject are as follows:

What constitutes a person:

1. personality
2. environment, attitudes, background
3. mind

A person is someone who has a personality which means the way he/she acts or the manner in which they behave. Environment and background also tell how a person may behave or act, and attitudes also. A person has to make decisions on their own. The mind helps that person to make decisions on their own.

Students' open-ended responses also reflected a healthy outlook on the issue of discrimination within the national community and an awareness of issues of discrimination in the international community:

I learned that all people should be treated equal no matter their race, religion or colour. I also learned that people should not be discriminated against because they make you feel less than a person.

Everybody should be treated equally, no matter what colour, race, nationality etc. Also I learned about people who dealt with discrimination in their environment e.g. Martin Luther King, Nelson Mandela and Ghandi [sic].

I think we could have gone into greater detail about discrimination and prejudice.

Several students taught by Teacher E articulated their opinions on discrimination in terms of not judging a person: "I learned that you must not judge a book by its cover . . . . It is just like a person, you must not judge them before you know what is their case"; "I learned that judging a person before things happen is wrong . . ."

Fewer students expressed an opinion that rights must be accompanied by responsibilities or that sometimes we may need to fight for our rights. Those who did came from the Form 4 class taught by Teacher D, who had in fact emphasized this point. Indeed, Teacher D identified the following difficulty: "Many . . . had difficulty in determining the responsibilities which go along with rights." Some students expressed the following views: "When making out your rights you must also know your responsibilities to back it up"; "We should do more about the things people went through, like their suffering, pains and all those things just to stop discrimination and to gain freedom."

Students in the Form 4 class taught by teacher D were asked to indicate responsibilities which accompany certain rights. The following excerpt of a student's written work indicates an appreciation of the dimension of responsibility along with the enjoyment of human rights.

> Human Rights and Fundamental Freedoms
> (a) The right of the individual to equality before the law and protection of the law.
> RESPONSIBILITY: not to commit any racial acts and don't display any sort of racism.

A few students exhibited a poor attitude to the issues dealt with or found the lessons meaningless, as revealed in the following excerpts from their open-ended comments on the student questionnaire: "I rather not comment on this lesson because I consider myself very discriminating to race"; "Nothing I had not known before."

Sample of Students' Verbal Responses

As was also revealed in their written opinions, students' verbal responses at times indicated positive attitudes while the curriculum was being operationalized. In some instances, however, their verbal responses were indicative of poor attitudes. For instance, there was frightening evidence of students' poor attitudes in the Form 4 group taught by Teacher E. During the lesson on discrimination, Teacher E introduced a discussion about the possibility of a well-known female

Indo-Trinidadian politician winning the general election, and asked students for their reactions to this possible development. Students' responses included remarks such as "suicide (ah go kill meh self)"; "blow up parliament"; "negroes would have no say"; "riot, coup"; "she would be assassinated"; "carry her in the canefield".

These comments were made – seemingly in jest – largely by the male Afro-Trinidadian students, while for the most part the Indo-Trinidadian students remained quiet. When discussing approaches to solving the problem of discrimination, one male student responded, "Eliminate the problem" (referring to the female Indo-Trinidadian politician), and laughed. One female student suggested inter-group discussion as a solution for solving discrimination. It was noticeable that the constructive suggestions tended to come from the female students. Another male student suggested, "Embarrass your MP." This latter comment pointed to the impact of the media, for at the time a television advertisement was encouraging citizens to embarrass their members of parliament in order to get some action against crime.

Form 4 Students' Attitudes Towards Discrimination, Rights and Parental Responsibilities

Form 4 class discussions revealed very strong attitudes among the students which deserved some special focus. Students in the Form 4 class taught by Teacher D expressed with considerable passion their feelings about and experiences with discrimination. Female students focused on discrimination in the home. In the Form 4 class taught by Teacher E, the male students were particularly vocal about their parents meeting their responsibilities to their children.

Students' expressions about how they felt when they had been the victims of discrimination included feeling less than a person, embarrassment, nervousness and feeling left out. A few students said they experienced discrimination within their families. One female student complained that her brother was allowed to go out but she was not. Another female student said she had housework to do but her brother did not have any. Reacting to these comments, one male student seated next to the writer mumbled, ". . . you can't expect boys to wash dishes . . ."

For a homework assignment on discrimination given by Teacher D, one male student wrote about the poor treatment he received from a teacher and expressed his concern that he was being deprived of his right to an education. Examples of rights cited by male students included the right to an attorney and the right to one phone call, which conjured up in the writer's mind the world of crime as seen on television. Rights cited by female students included the right to freedom of thought and expression and the right to freedom of religious belief.

Male students expressed particularly strong opinions about their parents' "right" to provide for them, regardless of their parents' circumstances; by *right* I understood them to mean their parents' responsibility. When Teacher E gave as an example a father's right to give his children no more than two dollars per day, this caused an uproar, particularly among the male students. Some of them commented: "I didn't ask him to make me"; "People with too many children are slack. They are not thinking right"; "Protect yourself before you wreck yourself." They clearly felt very strongly about their parents' responsibility towards them and their irresponsibility for having too many children.

Results of the Attitude Pre-Test and Post-Test: Form 4, Taught by Teacher D

The results of Teacher D's Form 4 students' performance on the pre-test and post-test are presented in figure 11.2.

Figure 11.2 illustrates an overall improvement in students' performance on the post-test. In particular there was a significant shift in attitudes from fairly positive to positive. The positive statement most supported by students on the post-test was "Human beings should solve differences by discussion and compromise rather than by force" (81 per cent strongly agreed). On the pre-test the positive statement most supported was "Young people need to inform themselves about world problems such as AIDS, illiteracy and malnutrition" (72 per cent strongly agreed). The negative statement most supported on the post-test was "The United Nations always talks about problems but does little to solve them" (29 per cent either agreed or strongly agreed). It was also the statement about which most students were uncertain on both the post-test (43 per cent)

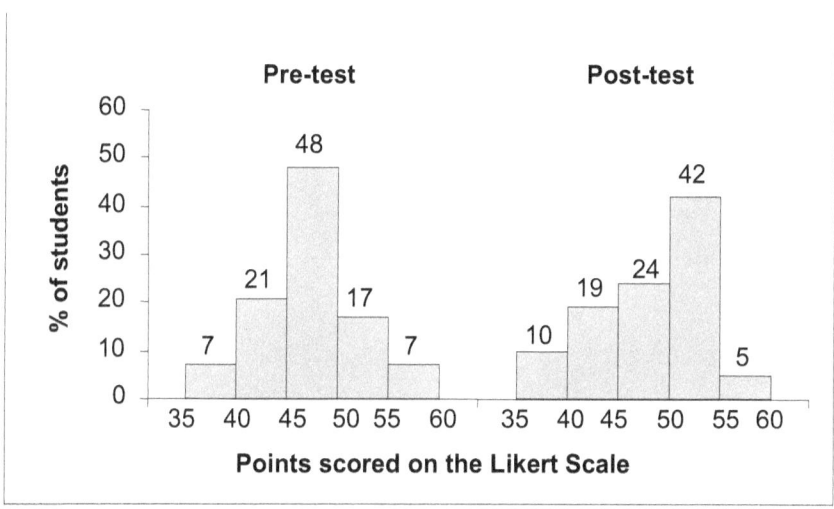

Figure 11.2: Students' performance on the pre-test and post-test, Unit C: Human Rights/ The United Nations. Form 4, taught by Teacher D. Number of respondents on pre-test: 29. Number of respondents on post-test: 21.

and the pre-test (35 per cent). On the pre-test, the negative statement most supported (48 per cent either strongly agreed or agreed) was "People all over the world enjoy human rights." It must be noted that the lessons on the subject of the United Nations were not tried out at all. Given the 25 per cent increase in students scoring in the range 50–54 (positive), as well as a shift in most students' selection of a positive statement to one that directly reflected the objectives of Unit C, the writer concludes that the curriculum that was taught seemed to have some positive impact on attitudes and values. None of the lessons tried out in Unit C, however, dealt directly with the issue of solving differences by discussion and compromise; rather, this came up in the course of general class discussions. The apparent increase in this attitude, therefore, might have been caught indirectly and would have reinforced students' existing predisposition to this attitude. The remaining uncertainty over the effectiveness of the United Nations reflects the fact that students did not have an opportunity to be influenced by the relevant lessons.

Results of the Attitude Pre-Test and Post-Test: Form 4, Taught by Teacher E

The results of Teacher E's Form 4 students in the pre-test and post-test are presented in figure 11.3.

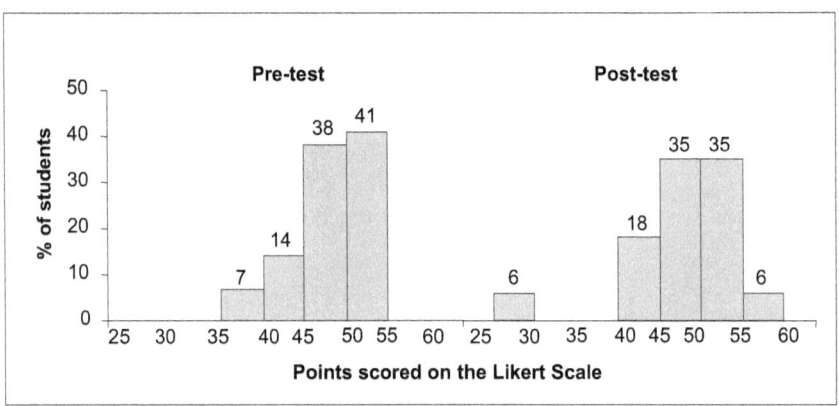

Figure 11.3: Students' performance on the pre-test and post-test, Unit C: Human Rights/The United Nations. Form 4, taught by Teacher E. Number of respondents on pre-test: 29. Number of respondents on post-test: 17.

On the basis of the results of the pre-test and post-test indicated in figure 11.3, the writer cannot claim unreservedly that the curriculum had a positive impact on these students' attitudes and values. This was especially illustrated in the case of one student who scored 29 out of 60, indicative of very poor attitudes.

The positive statement most supported on the post-test was "Human beings should solve differences by discussion and compromise rather than by force" (71 per cent strongly agreed). On the pre-test the positive statement most supported was "Young people need to inform themselves about world problems such as AIDS, illiteracy, malnutrition, and so on" (90 per cent strongly agreed). On the post-test the negative statement most supported was "We should be more concerned about our rights than about our responsibilities" (35 per cent agreed). On the pre-test it was "The United Nations always talks about problems but does little to solve them" (38 per cent either strongly agreed or agreed). Teacher E did not focus a great deal on the question of the responsibilities which go with human rights. The statement about which most students were uncertain

(29 per cent) on the post-test was "It is *not* in the interest of the people of Trinidad and Tobago to learn about the work of the United Nations." On the pre-test the statement about which most students were uncertain (31 per cent) was "The United Nations always talks about problems but does little to solve them." As on the pre-test, the most significant area of uncertainty related to the United Nations, which was not addressed during the curriculum tryout.

It is noteworthy that in the two Form 4 classes the positive statements most supported by students on the pre- and post-tests were the same. As in the case of the class taught by Teacher D, students in the class taught by Teacher E would have been influenced by general classroom discussions in respect of the positive statement most supported. That Teacher E did not focus on responsibilities in the lessons on human rights and that the unit on the United Nations was not taught were also evident in the pattern of students' responses.

The curriculum seemed to have been effective in reinforcing a positive attitude towards the issue of not using force to solve differences. On the post-test there was no disagreement with this statement, whereas on the pre-test there was a strong disagreement in the case of 7 per cent (two students).

Students' Responses to Items on the Unit C Pre-Test and Post-Test

Figures 11.4 to 11.8 represent Form 4 students' responses to individual statements on the Likert Scale used for the attitude pre-test and post-test. A legend is provided within each figure.

In figure 11.4 we see a nineteen-point increase in students in strong agreement with this positive statement, and absolutely no disagreement, both of which speak of a likely positive impact of the curriculum. This outcome was similar to that of the Form 4 class taught by Teacher D.

In figure 11.5 the eleven-point increase in students in strong agreement with the statement, the reduction of uncertainty, and the shift from 7 per cent strong disagreement to 6 per cent disagreement indicate some possible positive impact of the curriculum, though not entirely what was desired.

The increase in figure 11.6 in the percentage of students in strong agreement with this negative (i.e., false) statement is an unexpected outcome. It suggests that either "not all people enjoy human rights" was not sufficiently clear for all

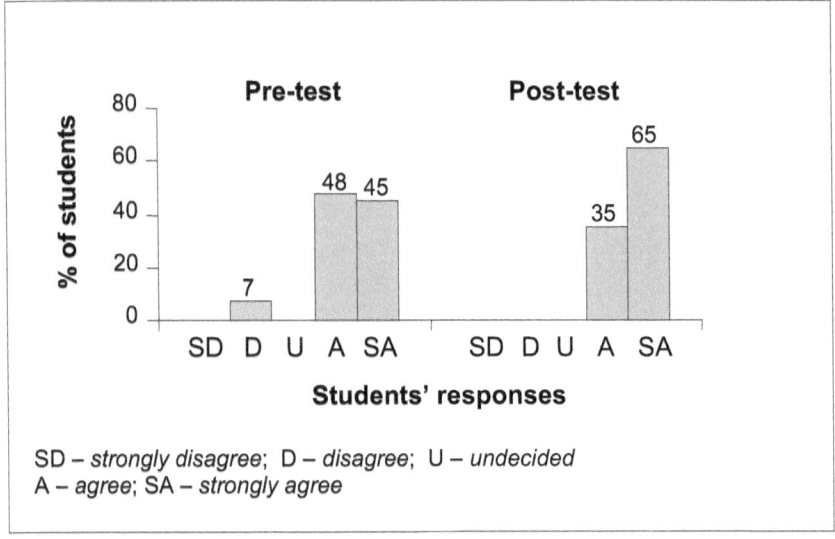

Figure 11.4: Students' responses on the Unit C pre-test and post-test to the item "People may be different but they are equal." Form 4, taught by Teacher E. Number of respondents on pre-test: 29. Number of respondents on post-test: 17.

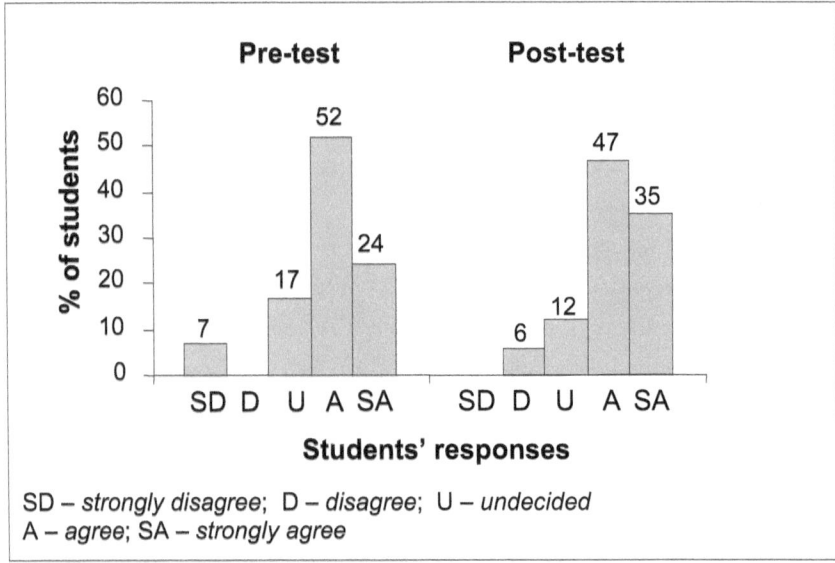

Figure 11.5: Students' responses on the Unit C pre-test and post-test to the item "There is a strong connection between the respect for human rights and the maintenance of peace." Form 4, taught by Teacher E. Number of respondents on pre-test: 29. Number of respondents on post-test: 17.

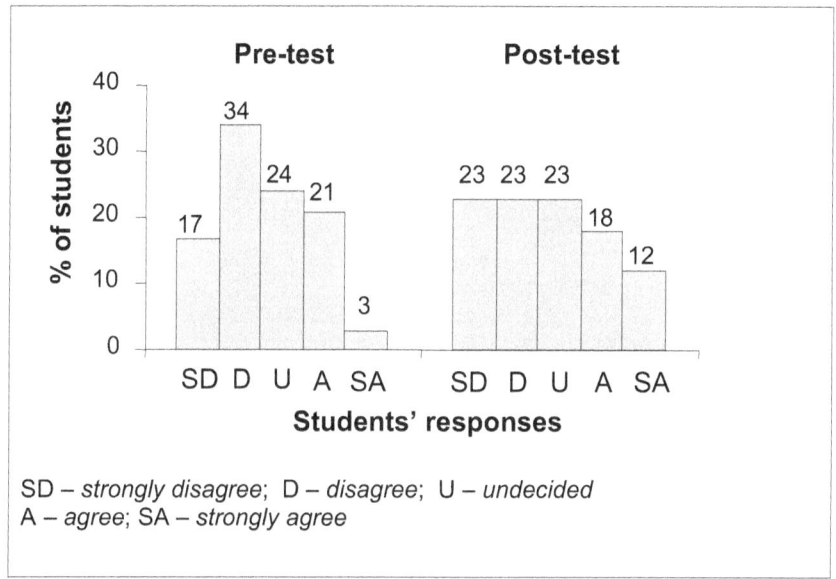

Figure 11.6: Students' responses on the Unit C pre-test and post-test to the item "People all over the world enjoy human rights." Form 4, taught by Teacher E. Number of respondents on pre-test: 29. Number of respondents on post-test: 17.

students, or the statement itself was not clearly understood as a negative statement. However, it is still encouraging to see the six-point increase in students in strong disagreement and the one-point fall in uncertainty. Overall, the curriculum did not seem to have been as effective on this issue with this class as with the Form 4 class taught by Teacher D. In Teacher D's Form 4 class, 62 per cent of the students disagreed with the statement and 6 per cent strongly disagreed with it.

The pattern of responses to this negative statement in both fourth-form classes indicates clearly the value of directly addressing an issue with students; the results of the post-test in figures 11.7 and 11.8 show the difference in outcome. In figure 11.7 the percentage of students in strong disagreement with this negative statement fell by nineteen points on the post-test as compared with the pre-test, while the percentage of students in disagreement rose by four points on the post-test in comparison with the pre-test. Uncertainty fell by six points on the post-test and agreement increased by twenty-eight points on the post-test – an unexpected outcome. In the Form 4 class where Teacher D spent a

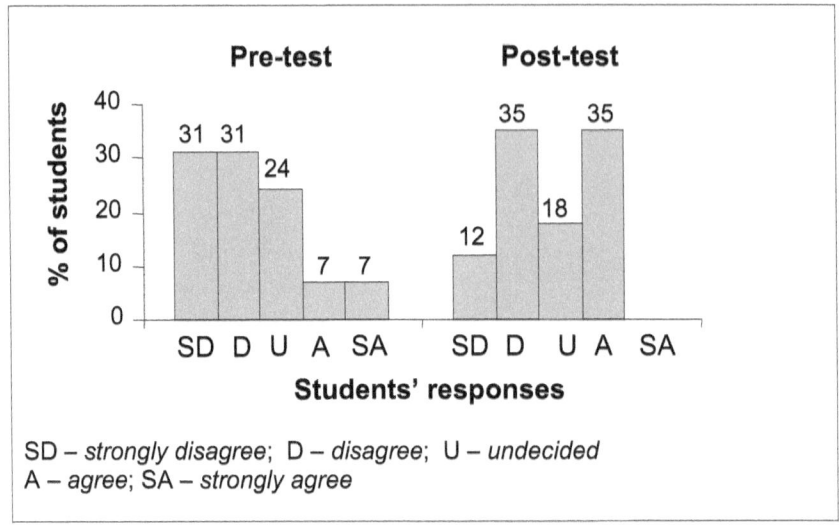

Figure 11.7: Students' responses on the Unit C pre-test and post-test to the item "We should be more concerned about our rights than about our responsibilities." Form 4, taught by Teacher E. Number of respondents on pre-test: 29. Number of respondents on post-test: 17.

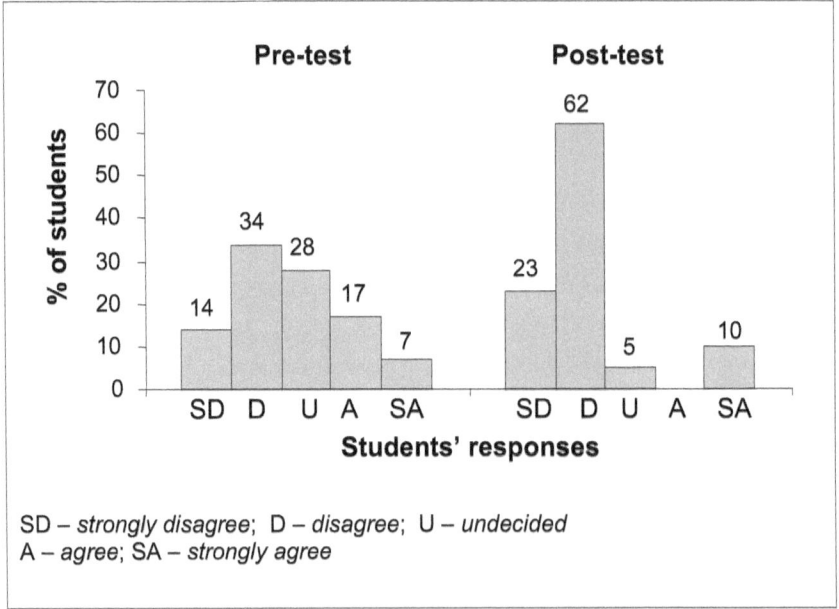

Figure 11.8: Students' responses on the Unit C pre-test and post-test to the item "We should be more concerned about our rights than about our responsibilities." Form 4, taught by Teacher D. Number of respondents on pre-test: 29. Number of respondents on post-test: 21.

great deal of time focusing on the issue of the responsibilities which accompany human rights, student attitudes were more positive on the post-test. This is illustrated in figure 11.8.

In the case of the Form 4 class taught by Teacher E, seen in figure 11.7, overall 47 per cent of the students were either in strong disagreement or disagreement with this negative statement on the post-test, whereas in the Form 4 class taught by Teacher D, the result for the two combined categories of responses on the post-test was 85 per cent, compared with 48 per cent on the pre-test. Also, in the case of the Form 4 taught by Teacher E, while uncertainty fell by 6 per cent on the post-test, it was still 13 per cent higher than in Teacher D's Form 4. There was also a significant difference in the level of agreement with this statement. In the Form 4 taught by Teacher E, 35 per cent of the students were in agreement on the post-test, whereas in Teacher D's Form 4 class the result was 5 per cent. From this result it would seem that where a lesson dealing with an issue was well taught, a positive outcome could be expected. Where an issue appeared not to be addressed or seemed to be addressed inadequately, one could not expect a positive outcome in terms of a change in students' attitudes. What was also significant about the Form 4 class taught by Teacher E was that the students seemed to have more positive attitudes towards rights and their concomitant responsibilities on the pre-test than on the post-test. This negative change in attitude was an unexpected outcome. This probably occurred because of the strong emphasis Teacher E placed on rights, and in particular children's rights, without also discussing their responsibilities.

These findings, while reflective of some slight change in students' opinions or points of view, point to the need for more in-depth orientation for the teachers using a curriculum such as this one. In particular the orientation should focus on appropriate teaching approaches and areas of emphasis. It should also highlight the need to so treat with the content of each curriculum theme that together they may contribute to giving students a clear appreciation of a holistic concept of peace – one that embraces respect for cultural differences, human rights and responsibilities.

Conclusions

In Unit B: Culture, Section 2 (Festivals), Form 1 students' open-ended comments revealed a good appreciation of the link between knowledge of a culture and understanding and acceptance of the people associated with that culture. Their comments also revealed positive opinions not only about the festivals dealt with in this unit but also about the opportunity to learn about the festivals. On the basis of these students' performance on the post-test, the writer concluded that the curriculum might have had a positive influence. Nonetheless, some students seemed to remain uncertain about particular statements and agreed with a negative statement, indicating that there was still work to be done to shape these students' attitudes relating to the content of this unit. In Unit C: Human Rights/The United Nations, Form 4 students' comments were generally indicative of positive opinions concerning appreciation of each person, avoiding discrimination, and enjoyment of human rights. Students' open-ended responses on the student questionnaire also reflected a healthy outlook on the issue of discrimination. Not all students, however, demonstrated an appreciation that the enjoyment of rights must be accompanied by the exercise of responsibilities, yet in one Form 4 class, male students in particular were extremely vocal about their parents' responsibilities towards them. In some instances students' verbal responses during class (and again, more so for male students) were extremely disturbing and indicative of very poor attitudes in relation to the issue of discrimination.

The results of the post-test for both Form 4 classes were an indication that where an issue was well treated by the teacher, the likelihood of positive student outcomes in terms of opinions and beliefs could be expected, and that the reverse was also true: where an issue was not addressed by the teacher, or inadequately so, positive outcomes could not be expected. This notwithstanding, students' responses on the post-test appeared to indicate a shift towards more positive opinions in relation to issues which were not directly addressed in the inquiry, but which might have been influenced by overall exposure to the parts of the curriculum which teachers used.

Overall, the younger students (Form 1) seemed to exhibit more positive attitudes as reflected on the post-test, where comparatively higher percentages of students showed evidence of desirable attitudes. Nonetheless, the findings also point to the likelihood that the attitudes of older students could be positively shaped with effective use of the curriculum by teachers.

Notes

1. Jerome J. Shestack, "The Philosophical Foundations of Human Rights", in *Human Rights: Concept and Standards*, ed. Janusz Symonides (New Delhi: UNESCO, 2000), 56.
2. Ibid., 59.
3. Beverly Daniel Tatum, *Why Are All the Black Kids Sitting Together in the Cafeteria?* (New York: Basic Books, 1999), 23.
4. George G. Posner, *Analyzing the Curriculum* (New York: McGraw Hill, 1995), 5.
5. Ibid., 11.
6. F. Michael Connelly, Albert S. Dukacz and Frank Quinlan, eds., *Curriculum Planning for the Classroom* (Toronto: OISE Press, 1980), 62.
7. David Pratt, *Curriculum Planning: A Handbook for Professionals* (Toronto: Harcourt Brace, 1994), 85.
8. Allan C. Ornstein and Francis P. Hunkins, *Curriculum: Foundations, Principles and Issues* (New York: Pearson, 2004), 286–87.
9. Martin Fishbein, *Readings in Attitude Theory and Measurement* (New York: John Wiley and Sons, 1967); Lynn R. Kahle, "Attitudes and Social Adaptation: A Person–Situation Interaction Approach", *International Series in Experimental Social Psychology* 8 (1984): 1–7; Milton Rokeach, *Beliefs, Attitudes and Value* (San Francisco: Jossey-Bass, 1972); Harry C. Triandis, *Attitudes and Attitude Change* (New York: John Wiley and Sons, 1971).
10. Daniel Katz, "The Functional Approach to the Study of Attitudes", in *Readings in Attitude Theory and Measurement*, ed. Martin Fishbein (New York: John Wiley and Sons, 1967), 457–68.
11. Ibid., 460.

Appendix 11.1: Samples of Likert Scales Used as Pre-Tests and Post-Tests

Unit B – Culture

Please indicate the extent to which you agree or disagree with each of the following statements by circling your response

Strongly agree   Agree   Uncertain   Disagree   Strongly disagree

1. Learning about other people's culture helps us to understand them better.

   SA   A   U   D   SD

2. There is no connection between understanding other people's culture and ensuring world peace.

   SA   A   U   D   SD

3. Some cultures are better than others.

   SA   A   U   D   SD

4. Culture has little to do with a people's way of life.

   SA   A   U   D   SD

5. Human beings should solve differences by discussion and compromise rather than by force.

   SA   A   U   D   SD

Unit B – Culture

Please indicate the extent to which you agree or disagree with each of the following statements by circling your response

Strongly agree   Agree   Uncertain   Disagree   Strongly disagree

1. The future of mankind is dependent on new generations being able to maintain peace on earth.

    SA   A   U   D   SD

2. It is *not* possible to learn how to prevent conflict among people.

    SA   A   U   D   SD

3. Too much importance is given to world peace today.

    SA   A   U   D   SD

4. Young people today can do little to contribute to world peace.

    SA   A   U   D   SD

5. The festivals of Trinidad and Tobago are a valuable part of our cultural heritage.

    SA   A   U   D   SD

6. Religion is a part of culture.

    SA   A   U   D   SD

CHAPTER 12

Cultural Studies
The Way Forward

▶ Rex Nettleford

I would be the last person to make exaggerated claims for this new attraction in the academy. I am referring to Cultural Studies – capital C, capital S. As with all supposedly new discoveries/achievements, we need to be reminded that it is only in the Book of Genesis that anything was created from the void. And in any case, it took some six or so days for that world conceived by creationists to take ideal form and purpose. Even the Big Bang theory is predicated on something existing before the noise. So it is with cultural studies! I, for one, was amazed to learn that much of what I had been doing for years in the quest for relevance and for the kind of truth that is rooted in the reality immediately around me could be subsumed under the new mantra of cultural studies. I must not scoff at the belated legitimization that this implies, since the academy, by its very nature, insists on a certain pedigree for any of its members to gain active and meaningful membership in the fellowship. I acknowledge this without denying that there are some very special advantages such a marginalization can bring to the academic outsider.

Much has changed with the great revolution that has taken place in the knowledge business, not only with respect to the instant transmission which information technology affords the art of communication, but also to the content of what is being transmitted, with its complex textured, kaleidoscopic contours demanding of all of us who engage it layers of insight, comprehension and grasp of the ever-shifting and diverse phenomena being observed. The implications for the whole task of *knowing* – grandly designated epistemology – are indeed far-reaching.

One of the first challenges, then, for the way forward is emancipation of self from the rather tight and obstinately controlling structures of academic disciplines clustered (and cloistered) into academic categories called faculties in the British system of higher education, and protected with arrogant clerical God-is-on-my-side certainty by those whom the American system of higher education refers to as "the faculty". There exists still in many universities, including our own, a somewhat self-serving "purity" of vision about the parameters and perimeters of this or that academic discipline, preventing in too many instances desirable experimentation and the sort of daring exploration which is what a university, as an agent of intellectual discovery, is all about. To get stuck in the received/inherited methodologies that serve investigation into the humanities, the social sciences, the medical and the natural sciences, is a recipe for progression like a cow's tail – that is, growing down.

That such a fate should be ours is, to my mind, highly avoidable. After all, issues of ontology and cosmology, which are both determined and informed by our historical and contemporary realities (taking in both the imperialism of the past and its transmuted latter-day version, now called globalization), challenge us to a quest for what, if not permanently true, is constantly serviceable. The landscape to be reconnoitered is in any case itself so rugged, varied and complexly configured that it needs not only bulldozer but also pickaxe and hoe – even fingernails and bare hands – to get to the nuggets of gold the academy likes to call truth.

The idea of culture, with its all-embracing and overarching paradigmatic peculiarity, has been found by a great many people to be a useful vantage point from which to strategize the reconnoitering. It is not by accident, then, that many a multilateral development agency has been turning to cultural analysis to help in achieving what economic determinism alone has not been able to achieve. Even when filtered through the prism of such development imperatives as health care, environmental protection, food policy and agricultural development, science and technology, education and social development, it is cultural phenomena that have been seen as the light to be refracted. For isn't this the overarching *thing* that embraces all that eventually defines the human being as agent of his or her own destiny in fundamental acts of creating, reproducing and ratiocinating?

Whether it be the art of communicating (language) or the positioning of a Maker (from God or Shiva through Allah to Jah and the numerous divinities in our myriad Caribbean creole religious persuasions); whether it be the matter of ethnic certitude or the design of valid kinship patterns; whether it be the unique products from exercise of the creative imagination (individual and collective, and manifested in music, literature, art, dance, drama and so on) or the specific designs for social living; or whether it is the patterns of law and order *in praxis* embracing attitudes to authority that are not likely to be disintegrative or methods of production and exchange of goods and services, as well as preservation of the natural environment that can sustain life and living – none of these fall outside the ambit of *culture*, which is the human glue of intellect and imagination that makes it possible for us to be engaged in discourses like this, and is manifested in all thought and all action.

The way forward must therefore be on this same journey of greater delineation of methodologies to get to the truth about human society, and specifically Caribbean society, which is still to secure a knowledge base underpinning its integrated and interconnected existence, and to explain to us all the inner logic and consistency that keep us alive and kicking – and I mean kicking, that is, jumping from one foot to the other, knowing that one can stand on neither. So, as the institution with major responsibility for development of the human resources of the Commonwealth Caribbean, the University of the West Indies recognizes that it must take the lead in developing a cadre of persons grounded in a sensitive understanding of their own history and cultural heritage, who can articulate and infuse this understanding into the society at every level. Their research should form the basis of a new approach to education, with changes in the curriculum which can create building blocks for a just and more humane Caribbean society.

Some of the fields being researched under the Cultural Studies Initiative are and should continue to be Caribbean Creole, global ethics, governance for the twenty-first century, creativity and empowerment, the media and cultural expressions, heritage tourism, cultural policy, culture and health, cultural and social capital, and Caribbean attitudes to authority, justice, citizenship, work and so on. Hopefully the findings will be able to provide governments of the region and civil society with research data which can inform decisions being made on matters of social and economic development, and to ensure that the policymakers of the region are aware of that interlocking which exists between an understanding of one's culture and the possibilities for social wellness and economic growth.

The way forward assumes that the findings will also lay a foundation in the University of the West Indies for an ongoing multidisciplinary programme of cultural studies which will underscore, through strategies to be developed in all the faculties and through a study of the curricula, the fundamental importance of a sensitive understanding of our culture to enhancement of the quality of life and the dignity of the human being. The ultimate goal must be to empower every citizen and to ensure a clear understanding of the real purpose of a university, which is to empower, enliven, enrich and generally make the community in which it exists a better place by allowing the society to which it relates to see with new eyes and new minds.

The threatened destruction of the fabric of Caribbean society, which is still in formation, presents a major challenge to the university. Development in all its forms is the goal of all Caribbean leaders, but this can only be accomplished in an atmosphere of safety and with a population grounded in respect for itself and for humankind. It is becoming more and more evident that no lasting development can be guaranteed in a society where a large percentage of the population feels undervalued and has little sense of self-worth.

The Cultural Studies Initiative is still intended to address the underlying problem through a diagnosis of the root causes, an analysis of these causes, and recommendations for a new dimension to the education process, both in the schools and through public education for the wider society, so that every member of the society can feel valued and capable of making a contribution. This is meant to relate to current urgent social problems of drug trafficking, violence and urban criminality as well as the chronic/endemic ones of underproductivity, unemployment and the lack of will for self-reliance.

The way forward must embrace this mission on the journey. Strategic alliances are here critical for that journey. Education is a mandatory ally, and culture-in-education is critical to shaping curricula in all the planned educational reform strategies. To this we can add *literary arts* (some scholars of literatures in English have regarded cultural studies as integral to, if not synonymous with, literary criticism, though lack of expertise in the social sciences or history sometimes renders such exclusively literary-based cultural studies limited); the *social sciences*, including such cross-over disciplines as socio-linguistics, as well as established social and cultural anthropology, sociology and politics; the *medical sciences*, especially social and preventive medicine, now challenged by the AIDS pandemic and other lifestyle diseases, as well as nutrition and alternative medicine, itself challenged by ancestral myths and lasting legends; the *natural sciences*, for example, natural products and medicinal chemistry; *environmental sciences* (here human action is a vital consideration, as in the treatment of forests and the cause or prevention of erosion related to the need and procurement of firewood); and even *engineering*, especially civil engineering, which is directly related to transportation and housing for human use. In addition, there are such seemingly natural and obvious allies as *history, literature, archaeology, creative arts* (covering a large range of artistic manifestations) and *theology* (both traditional and native-bred belief systems).

Such are the critical strategic allies of cultural studies programmes offered in the academy. Entrapping the fledgling discipline called cultural studies within closed and hermetically sealed borders should be avoided in the way forward, since this may well turn out to be detrimental to the activity's core rationale: a multidisciplinary approach to the generation and transmission of critical knowledge.

Two areas that suggest themselves in implementing the Cultural Studies Initiative here in the University of the West Indies are research and a programme for artists-in-residence. The University of the West Indies must continue trying to identify funding for postgraduate research fellowships in culture and entrepreneurship, culture and work attitudes, culture and community development, culture and education, ethnicity and identity, and gender issues. The International Development Research Centre of Canada and the Ford and Rockefeller foundations in the United States have responded positively so far. Private-sector groups in the region now need to be sensitized to this, beyond the sort of project done recently by CLICO in Trinidad in mounting a competition among painters for some twelve art works for its 2004 calendar. The US$300,000 spent on this is, after all, a tidy sum. Hopefully the findings that emerge from similarly funded research will provide critical information for future planning in all aspects of national life in the region.

A programme of artists-in-residence, be it in the fields of dance, music, drama, cinema, literature, architecture, painting, sculpture or festival arts, should attract individuals with the kind of intellectual rigour and vigour that can act as a source of energy, both on the campuses and in the non-campus countries (later morphed into the University of the West Indies Open Campus) – an energy that will spark enthusiasm for creative thinking to generate new ideas in young scholars and challenge them to venture along new paths. The combination of research findings and one-on-one contact with creative minds that have established themselves over time through the integrity of their own unique artistic talents could bring a new dimension to the academic life of the university, a dimension that will contribute to the concept of education informed by the arts of the imagination as against mere certification, which too often narrowly characterizes institutions of higher learning.

The University of the West Indies has a unique role in the Caribbean, with a clearly defined mandate to act as a catalyst for regional development. The region comprises some fifteen territories served by the university, with close association with such neighbours as Suriname, Cuba, Santo Domingo, Haiti, Colombia, Venezuela, Mexico and Central America, and the French and Dutch Antilles, as well as Puerto Rico and the American Virgin Islands. We remain a wellspring of the cultural diversity that is a global phenomenon, of which the Caribbean is a microcosm.

Since the introduction of the Cultural Studies Initiative, applications have been invited from suitable candidates for a number of research fellowships working towards M.Phil. or Ph.D. degrees in cultural studies. The way forward must see to the acquisition of a greater number of such fellowships. These research fellowships are for programmes of research into the ways in which people connect economic activity and informed public policy to aspects of life and culture covering different localities and groups in the Commonwealth Caribbean. Under this programme, successful candidates should be required to formulate and execute specific research projects on the culturally embedded constructs of the various cultural groups and social strata of the societies of the Commonwealth Caribbean. The programme should involve at least two years of study and research, covering fieldwork and publication of theses on completion of the work. And theses should be judged on the basis of possibilities for practical implementation of the recommendations.

The objective should still be to seek to develop a cadre of persons grounded in a sensitive understanding of their own history (including the many narratives of our multilayered past) and cultural heritage, and who can articulate and infuse these understandings and research findings into social and economic policymaking at every level. The specific areas that have been considered and should continue so to be are as follows:

- information on the ways in which people connect economic activity to other aspects of their life and culture, their normative, ethical and spiritual beliefs and their aspirations for themselves and their fellow citizens;
- studies in the role of gender relations in Caribbean social and cultural transformation, much of this relating to child rearing and socialization of males and females, family patterns and gender roles within them;
- studies of local and regional networks for the purpose of developing mechanisms for regional and local decision-making in the development of cultural industries and other productive sectors – for example, the economic scope and potential of popular music, cultural tourism (though not touristic culture) in the African diaspora, dance, literature, carnival and other festival arts – and analysis of the economics of the international entertainment industry and the scope for increasing Caribbean participation in the value chain;
- culture and entrepreneurship: attitudes and behaviours of different sections of the Caribbean population to business as an occupation, savings and investment versus consumption, long-term versus short-term investment, capital accumulation, risk-taking, innovation, science and technology, and different kinds of economic activities;
- strategies and mechanisms for designing more efficacious systems of economic and social management, especially at local and regional levels, as well as the economic potential of the Caribbean diaspora as a source of capital, entrepreneurship and technology, taking into consideration cultural factors likely to impact on the design, formulation and operation of such strategies and mechanisms. There is a huge market for yam and ackee in the Caribbean diaspora, for example, not to speak of jerk this, that and the other;
- encouragement of the creativity of ordinary people and specification of methods of realizing this creativity for social/cultural/economic development;
- culture and work: attitudes and behaviours related to the world of work,

employment, self-employment, work-related discipline, types of work (for example, manual, clerical, intellectual), labour relations, cooperation, teamwork, flexible production, employer attitudes and values regarding training and skill upgrading, and psycho-cultural factors impacting on workplace relations;
- development of planning methods which return humankind to the centre of all planning activity;
- protection of intellectual property, copyright and the legal provisions related to this; and
- everyday understanding of economic concepts such as savings, whether cultural activists are to run cultural institutions, investment, unemployment, wages and salaries, prices, economic development, inflation, the market and how it functions, and devaluation, and their relationships to Caribbean cultural phenomena.

The way forward shall require a deepening and heightening of efforts to address all the above, with the university's Cultural Studies Initiative being a driving force, but with the good sense to get added fuel through strategic alliances in synergistic collaboration. Such is the path originally designed to be travelled. And such is the path to be traversed further on. The way forward should be one that hopefully will help bring into the mainstream of research and teaching in the academy a greater appreciation of the centrality of cultural variables in the development equation, and the paramount importance of the human being to the development process everywhere, as well as the validity of the arts of the imagination on the route to cognition.

Contributors

Jennifer Rahim is Senior Lecturer and Co-ordinator of Literatures in English, Department of Liberal Arts, University of the West Indies, St Augustine, Trinidad and Tobago. She is the author of many articles on Caribbean literature, three collections of poems, *Mothers Are Not the Only Linguists; Between the Fence and the Forest and Approaching Sabbaths;* and one collection of short stories, *Songster and Other Stories.*

Barbara Lalla is Professor of Language and Literature, Department of Liberal Arts, University of the West Indies, St Augustine, Trinidad and Tobago. Her publications include *Postcolonialisms: Caribbean Rereadings of Medieval English Discourse; Defining Jamaican Fiction; English for Academic Purposes; Language in Exile* and *Voices in Exile* (both co-authored/co-edited with Jean D'Costa); and the novel, *Arch of Fire.*

Jeannette Allsopp is Director of the Centre for Caribbean Lexicography and teaches Linguistics in the Department of Language, Linguistics and Literatures, University of the West Indies, Cave Hill, Barbados. She is the author of the *Caribbean Multilingual Dictionary of Flora, Fauna and Foods, in English, French, French Creole and Spanish.*

Sandra Ingrid Gift is Senior Programme Officer, Quality Assurance Unit, Office of the Board for Undergraduate Studies, University of the West Indies, St Augustine, Trinidad and Tobago. She is the author of *Maroon Teachers: Teaching the Transatlantic Trade in Enslaved Africans.*

George Lamming has held numerous visiting professorships in the United States, the Caribbean, the United Kingdom and Europe. He is the author of *In the Castle of My Skin; The Emigrants; Of Age and Innocence; Season of Adventure; Water with Berries; Natives of My Person;* and *Coming, Coming Home.*

Paula Morgan is Senior Lecturer and Head of the Department of Liberal Arts, and Co-ordinator of the Cultural Studies Graduate Programme, University of the West Indies, St Augustine, Trinidad and Tobago. She is co-author of *Language Proficiency for Tertiary Level and Writing about Literature* (with Barbara Lalla) and *Writing Rage: Violence in Caribbean Discourse* (with Valerie Youssef); and co-editor of *Caribbean Literature in a Global Context* (with Funso Aiyejina).

Rex Nettleford is Vice-Chancellor Emeritus, University of the West Indies; founder of the Trade Union Education Institute; former Professor of Continuing Studies and Director of the Department of Extra-Mural Studies; and the primary architect of the Cultural Studies Initiative at the University of the West Indies. He is co-founder of the National Dance Theatre Company of Jamaica, and the author of numerous publications, including *Mirror Mirror: Identity, Race and Protest in Jamaica; Manley and the New Jamaica: Collected Speeches and Writings, 1938–1868; Caribbean Cultural Identity: The Case of Jamaica; Dance Jamaica: Cultural Definition and Artistic Discovery; Inward Stretch, Outward Reach: A Voice from the Caribbean; The University of the West Indies: A Caribbean Response to the Challenge of Change* (with Philip Sherlock); and editor of *Caribbean Quarterly*.

Joseph Pereira is Senior Lecturer in Spanish and Deputy Principal, University of the West Indies, Mona, Jamaica. He has published in the areas of Cuban literature, Afro-Mexican studies and Jamaican popular music, and has translated various Cuban poets, including Roberto Fernandez Retamar, Nancy Morejón, Georgina Herrera and Marino Wilson Jay.

Sandra Pouchet Paquet is Professor of English and Director of Caribbean Literary Studies, University of Miami. She is the author of *Caribbean Autobiography: Cultural Identity and Self-Representation* and *The Novels of George Lamming*; and coeditor of *Music, Memory, Resistance: Calypso and the Caribbean Literary Imagination* (with Patricia Saunders and Stephen Stuempfle); and editor of *Anthurium: A Caribbean Studies Journal*.

Louis Regis is Lecturer, Department of Liberal Arts, University of the West Indies, St Augustine, Trinidad and Tobago. He is the author of *The Political Calypso: True Opposition in Trinidad and Tobago, 1962–1987; Maestro: The True Master;* and *Black Stalin: The Caribbean Man*.

Brinsley Samaroo is retired Professor of the Department of History, University of the West Indies, St Augustine, Trinidad and Tobago. His publications include *The Construction of an Indo-Caribbean Diaspora* (with A. Bissessar); *The Art of Garnet Ifill: Glimpses of the Sugar Industry*; *Pioneer Presbyterians: Origins of Presbyterian Work in Trinidad*; and *Across the Dark Waters: Ethnicity and Indian Identity in the Caribbean* and *India in the Caribbean* (both with David Dabydeen).

Patricia Saunders is Associate Professor of English, University of Miami. She is the author of *Alien/Nation and Repatriation: Caribbean Literature and the Task of Translating Identity*; co-editor of *Music, Memory, Resistance: Calypso and the Caribbean Literary Imagination* (with Sandra Pouchet Paquet and Stephen Stuempfle); and assistant editor of *Anthurium: A Caribbean Studies Journal*.

Leon Wainwright is Lecturer in History of Art and Design, Manchester Metropolitan University. He is the author of numerous articles, works of art criticism and exhibition essays and reviews and a member of the editorial board of *Third Text: Critical Perspectives on Contemporary Art and Culture*.

Valerie Youssef is Professor of Linguistics, University of the West Indies, St Augustine, Trinidad and Tobago. She is co-author of *The Languages of Tobago: Genesis, Structure and Perspectives* (with Winford James) and *Writing Rage: Unmasking Violence through Caribbean Discourse* (with Paula Morgan).

www.ingramcontent.com/pod-product-compliance
Lightning Source LLC
Chambersburg PA
CBHW021822300426
44114CB00009BA/277